Learning Language and Loving It

Learning Language and Loving It

A Guide to Promoting Children's
Social, Language, and Literacy Development
in Early Childhood Settings

Second Edition

**Elaine Weitzman and
Janice Greenberg**

A Hanen Centre Publication

Learning Language and Loving It™

By Elaine Weitzman and Janice Greenberg

A Hanen Centre Publication

© Hanen Early Language Program, 2002.
Second Edition

Library and Archives Canada
ISBN 0-921145-18-7

Copies of this book may be ordered from the publisher:

THE HANEN CENTRE
1075 Bay Street, Suite 515
Toronto, Ontario
Canada M5S 2B1

Telephone: (416) 921-1073
Fax: (416) 921-1225
E-mail: info@hanen.org
Web: www.hanen.org

Parts of this book were adapted from It Takes Two To Talk® by Ayala Manolson (1992) and *More Than Words*®: *Helping Parents Promote Communication and Social Skills in Children with Autism Spectrum Disorder* by Fern Sussman (1999), both Hanen Centre publications.

Illustrations: Ruth Ohi and Christine Tripp; colouring by Kathryn Adams
Design: Counterpunch / Linda Gustafson
Editor: Susan Goldberg
Proofreader: Matthew Sussman

The first edition of Learning Language and Loving It™ was supported by funding from the Department of Health and Welfare Canada through the Child Care Initiatives Fund. All views expressed herein are those of the author and do not necessarily reflect the views of Health Canada, formerly the Department of Health and Welfare Canada.

Printed in Canada by Transcontinental Interglobe Inc.

Table of Contents

Acknowledgements from the authors

In the ten years that have passed since the first edition of this book, many things have changed, but many things have stayed the same.

What has remained unchanged is our good fortune in working with colleagues who have contributed so much to *Learning Language and Loving It* – The Hanen Program® for Early Childhood Educators and to this guidebook. We are particularly grateful to Fern Sussman, who made such a valuable contribution to the early development of the *Learning Language and Loving It* Program for her ongoing valuable input. Thanks also goes to the other Program Managers – Cindy Earle, Jan Pepper, and Barb Wylde for their interest and input. We would also like to thank Luigi Girolametto, associate professor in the department of Speech Pathology at University of Toronto, who partnered with us to do research on the *Learning Language and Loving It* Program. This research produced interesting outcomes, which stimulated much discussion and helped us to further refine the program.

The Hanen office staff, particularly Vilia Cox, Tom Khan, Kamila Lear, and Penny Tantakis, did whatever it took to help us get the project completed. Each one plays an important role in helping us disseminate this new resource. We could not ask to work with a more enthusiastic, committed team.

The Hanen Centre Board of Directors has been extremely supportive of our efforts to continually develop new and updated resources. We truly appreciate the ongoing commitment of all our board members: Edmund Clarke, Frank Copping, Elizabeth Milne, Juli Morrow, Derek Nelson, and Enid Varga. We would especially like to thank Jim Wooder, chairman of The Hanen Centre Board of Directors, for his unfailing interest in, and support of, our new projects. His leadership has guided the centre through a period of exceptional growth and change.

The production team of professionals who helped us make the book as readable, user-friendly and attractive as it is, has been exceptional. Linda Gustafson, our designer from Counterpunch, knows how to stay calm under duress and has a flair for taking ordinary words and making them come alive on the page. Susan Goldberg, our excellent editor, and Matthew Sussman, our diligent proofreader, both worked hard to make the text readable and to keep our inconsistent use of punctuation somewhat consistent. Our illustrators, Ruth Ohi and Christine Tripp, have brought the early childhood setting to life with their beautiful illustrations, which were given added colour and dimension by Kathryn Adams.

This book has been enriched from its inception by the input of many inspiring and committed early childhood educators, especially Elaine Everett, Shanley Pierce, and Joan Arruda. While we have not maintained contact over the years, their insights and approach to early childhood education continue to be reflected throughout this book.

Finally, we would like to thank Ayala Manolson, founder of The Hanen Centre. Her vision of helping children learn to communicate by training and educating their caregivers is reflected in our approach to this book.

Elaine Weitzman would like to say . . .

They say you can't choose your relatives, but I would have chosen mine anyway. I am fortunate to have two wonderful sisters, Margie and Adele, who provide both support and comic relief whenever I need it. My sister-in-law, Sheila, as close to a sister as anyone can be, can always be relied upon to help out, even though she is the busiest person I know. My mother, Annette Schneider, is a constant source of love, support, and encouragement.

To my wonderful children, Joanne and Kevin – who were always at home when the first edition of this book was written, but who now seldom are – your love, companionship, and humour make being your mother one of life's greatest gifts. And to my husband, Irvine, who makes everything possible and who keeps life so interesting, "thank you" can't capture what I want to say – and I have no way of saying it all. So I'll take a page from your book and leave it at that.

Janice Greenberg would like to say . . .

I would like to thank my husband, David, and my daughters, Laura and Carly, for their endless love and support during the many hours I spent at the computer writing this book. I would also like to thank my parents, Rose and Jack Rosen, for always encouraging me to do my best.

A note on the use of "he" and "she"

Use of "he" and "she" is alternated in the chapters of this book. For simplicity's sake, the teacher is almost always referred to as "she." However, in recognition of the male teachers in the field of Early Childhood Education, the reader will notice that some of the illustrations and examples are of male teachers.

Introduction

The Connection between Early Childhood Experiences and Academic Success

A director of a preschool in Toronto recently said:

> *As early childhood educators, it is our responsibility to give each child the best experiences, knowledge, and growth in all areas of development so we can put that child into a success mode for the rest of his life.*

It is now widely recognized that the early years of a child's life are the most critical for brain development. This means that the quality of a child's experiences in early childhood settings will contribute significantly to that child's ultimate success in life. As a teacher of young children, what you do and how you do it will have an impact on any child in your classroom. Now that children with special needs are being included in typical early childhood settings, your challenge is even more daunting.

In the few short years that children are in early childhood settings, they need to develop a strong foundation in two vital areas of development:

- **social skills** – so they can establish and maintain effective relationships, and
- **language skills** – so they can communicate effectively and succeed in all areas of academic learning.

If you take a look at any of today's elementary school academic curricula in countries like Canada, the United States, and the United Kingdom, you will find that they are based on the expectation that children entering school at age five or six will:

- be able to use language for a variety of purposes, such as asking and answering questions, sharing ideas and information, hypothesizing, and imagining
- use appropriate communication and conversational skills with peers and adults, and
- have a growing vocabulary and use sentences of increasing length and complexity.

These are just a few of the requirements for success in the early years of school and for the development of literacy, which is so strongly linked to language development.

This guidebook contains the tools for setting up children for lifelong success as friends, communicators, readers, writers, and learners. Read on – and you'll learn both how to encourage children to be active conversational partners and how you can engineer the kinds of interactions and conversations that promote their language skills and enrich their understanding of the world. Read about how to help children develop peer relationships, essential both for mental health and for learning. Discover ways to encourage children to use language to imagine, negotiate, plan, and problem-solve. Building on these essential language skills, you will see how closely language and literacy are interrelated and how you can prepare children for literacy, starting in infancy.

This child-centred approach to facilitating children's social, language, and literacy development is drawn from *Learning Language and Loving It* – The Hanen Program₍®₎ for Early Childhood Educators and Preschool Teachers, an intensive training program offered on-site by Hanen certified speech-language pathologists to teachers in early childhood settings. This book provides a user-friendly guide to integrating this approach into everyday interactions and activities so that children can go to school equipped for lifelong learning.

Introduction to Observation Guides

There are four Observation Guides in this book: at the ends of Chapter 1, Chapter 2, Chapter 6, and Chapter 9. Each Observation Guide is designed to help you use the information in the chapter to become more aware of individual children's abilities and needs.

The Observation Guide in Chapter 1 ("The Child's Interactions with Teachers and Peers," page 26) helps you to identify a child's conversational style and the situations in which he or she is most and least interactive.

The Observation Guide in Chapter 2 ("The Child's Stage of Language Development," page 54) helps you to identify a child's stage of language development and his or her ability to engage in social interactions. If the child is verbal, the guide will direct your observations of her or his expressive and receptive language skills.

The Observation Guide in Chapter 6 ("The Child's Interactions with Peers," page 218) helps you to identify a child's ability to interact with peers.

The Observation Guide in Chapter 9 ("The Stages of Development of Pretend Play," page 317) helps you to identify a child's level of pretend play.

If you are concerned about a child's ability to communicate, we strongly recommend that you complete these Observation Guides. In the chapters that follow, much of the information has been divided into sections that address the needs of children according to their stages of language development and their conversational styles. By completing the Observation Guides in Chapters 1 and 2, you will know which sections of the book are most relevant for individual children in your classroom.

Please note: All Observation Guide pages may be photocopied.

Take a Closer Look
at Communication

Part 1 of this book is about taking a closer look at communication.

In Chapter 1, we take "An Inside Look at Interaction in Early Childhood Settings" and examine children's conversational styles and the roles teachers play during their interactions with the children. We see how teachers and children affect each other's interactive behaviour, and what happens to children who can't or don't participate fully in those critical everyday interactions.

In Chapter 2, "The Stages of Language Development: Talking Takes Time," we look at the stages of communication and language development so that you know what to expect from children at different ages and stages. As you read Parts 2, 3, and 4 of this book, the information on the stages of language development will help you apply the information to the children you work with.

So read on. In taking a closer look at communication, you are taking an important first step in helping children become accomplished communicators.

Learning Language and Loving It

Chapter 1

An Inside Look at Interaction in Early Childhood Settings

There's so much a child can learn about communication from a caring teacher.

A. Building relationships that build trust and communication

André, aged 19 months, is new to Sunshine Child Care Centre. On this, his first day, his mother is about to leave – and he knows it! He clings to her, and kicks and screams when she leaves. Maria, André's teacher, picks him up and tries to comfort him, getting kicked in the process!

What should Maria do next? What is the best way to handle a child who is new to the centre, very frightened, and unsure of his surroundings?

It's worth thinking about, because what Maria does next will make an enormous difference to André – to how he will feel about the child-care centre, how he will feel about himself, and how he will grow and develop in this new environment.

Maria could comfort André for a while and then leave him alone to see what he will do.

Or she could spend some time playing with him so they can begin to develop a relationship and André can learn to trust her.

Maria decides on the play.

A new child comes to the centre – and he is scared and upset.

Maria takes André over to the sand table. After a while, he calms down and starts to dump sand, using a small bucket.

"Oh," says Maria, "You're dumping the sand!"

She follows suit, and then stops to watch him.

He points to her bucket, as if to tell her, do it again!

"My turn to dump the sand?" she asks. "Okay!"

And Maria dumps sand out of her bucket. This turns into a game, with Maria and André taking turns dumping sand out of their buckets. As they play together, smiling and laughing, André looks quite different from the distressed child whose mother left 20 minutes earlier. Even when Maria leaves him to attend to some other children, he continues to play contentedly.

Over the next few days, Maria and André play the sand dumping game again a few times. As André becomes more comfortable in his new surroundings, he begins to communicate with the other teachers as well as with the other children. He now says "Sa!" (for "sand") when he wants Maria to play with him!

Does Maria realize how much André has gained from his interactions with her? Maybe she hasn't given it much thought – she's just relieved that he's so much happier! If we take a closer look at how much André has gained, however, we can begin to appreciate just how important these kinds of day-to-day interactions are, not only to children's social and language development, but to their feelings about themselves and about being in an early childhood environment. Maria followed her instincts in how she handled André, but in fact she fulfilled the two conditions that fuel the development of communication and language learning:

- **interaction** and
- **information.**

There's so much a child can learn about communication from a caring teacher!

Interaction

Communication and language learning take place within the everyday interactions children have with their caregivers and, in time, with their peers. These interactions must be enjoyable and frequent and should continue over an extended period of time (the longer, the better). Most important, the child should participate actively in these conversations – only by communicating with experienced conversationalists can he learn to become a conversationalist himself. Language learning can take place only if interaction comes first – as it did for André, whose interaction with Maria during the sand dumping game was fun and long-lasting.

Information

During interactions, children need their conversation partners to provide them with information that relates to the topic of conversation. This information must be relevant and appropriate to the child's language level so he can use it to build upon what he already knows. Maria kept saying the word "sand" when she and André were dumping the sand. She said it again and again, simply and clearly. André heard it so many times when he was doing something with the sand that he was able to figure out that this was the name of the stuff he was putting into his bucket and dumping out.

Simply knowing a word, however, isn't enough motivation for a child to use it. He has to have a *reason* for using it. In this case, André said "sand" because he really wanted Maria to play with him. André's use of the word "sand" is an excellent example of the fact that the desire to interact with others is the most powerful motivation for communicating.

This is how language learning works. First there must be positive interaction between child and adult. Then, the child can use the information provided by the adult to expand his language skills within the ongoing interaction.

Maria created an ideal language-learning environment for André. As well, her warmth and responsiveness gave him the motivation and confidence he needed to communicate both with her and with others in his strange new environment.

This is the kind of environment all children in early childhood settings need – an environment where they are nurtured and provided with opportunities for positive, enjoyable interactions throughout the day.

Children with language delays need even more of these opportunities.

These are the challenges facing you as an early childhood educator.

B. The challenge of including children with special needs

The challenge of providing children with a nurturing, interactive environment is even greater when a child has a special need, such as a language or a developmental delay. Parents of children with special needs are often advised to send their children to an inclusive preschool or child-care centre so they can be with typically developing children. It is a common assumption that a child with delayed development will develop better social and language skills just by being in the same environment as their typically developing peers. However, teachers in early childhood settings know that this is not necessarily the case.

 Justin, who is three years old, has been in Sheila's preschool classroom for just one month. Unlike the other children in the classroom, who can speak in sentences, Justin communicates mostly by pointing, using gestures, and making sounds. He can say a few words, like "more," "gone," and "car," but he seldom uses them. Justin's parents are hoping that his language will improve now that he is with other children on a daily basis.

Although Justin seems to have settled into this new preschool, he still spends most of his time playing alone. He seldom approaches the other children and they tend to ignore him. He does go to Sheila when he wants something or needs help, but she often has difficulty understanding what his sounds and gestures mean. When she sits and plays with him, he becomes very animated, especially at the water table. He enjoys giving her a cup of water, which she pretends to drink. He even says "more" and "dink" (for "drink") during this game. Justin will sit briefly with the other children during music and story times, but he doesn't participate in the activities and his attention fades within a few minutes.

Sheila now has personal experience with a common myth about inclusion – that once a child with a delay is placed in a typical setting, he will learn new skills just by being with children his age. Her observations have been borne out by research, which has shown that:

- children who can't communicate easily with their peers often become isolated or rejected, especially if the delay is more severe
- typically developing peers are less likely to select a child with a language delay as a playmate
- children with special needs are more likely to interact with their teachers than with other children when in a group, and
- if the child with special needs is included by the other children, it is often only in a passive or inappropriate role. For example, a child with special needs may be included in the "house" centre, but always as the baby with few opportunities for communication.

A child's ability to be included comes down to his social and communication skills. Without good communication skills, children like Justin cannot effectively negotiate for favourite toys or for turns in an activity. They may resort to simpler means, like grabbing, pulling, or pushing – behaviours that do not win them many friends! Even when a child with a delay does attempt to interact with his peers, he is often ignored by them. And unlike children with more developed communication skills, a child with communication difficulties may not persist in his efforts to join a group of children if his first attempt is not successful. After all, why risk repeated rejection? For these reasons, a child with a delay is much more likely to gravitate to the more patient, accommodating adults in the room, like Justin did.

Research also shows that children don't outgrow these difficulties as they get older. If they aren't helped to develop social relationships in preschool, they are more likely to continue to have trouble getting along with their peers when they start school.

A child with special needs requires very specific and consistent support to become an active and participating member of the classroom. Successfully including a child with special needs in a typical setting depends very much on how you, the early childhood educator, support his development and interactions with others.

> You take care of your brother while I go to work.

Justin is a three-year-old Communicator with a language delay. Sara and Julie are happy to include him in their play, but they always give him the role of the baby, with few opportunities to communicate.

C. Take a closer look at children's conversational styles

To provide children with an environment that promotes self-esteem and language learning, we need to tune in to their individual differences. We can learn a great deal about children's ability to interact with others by observing them more closely during their everyday interactions.

Picture yourself in an imaginary preschool classroom during free play and take a closer look at the children's communication – with you and with each other.

Patrice, who is always smiling and full of energy, runs up to you and shows you her new shoes. She says they are special because they glow in the dark. Then she calls to her friend and runs off to play with her.

Carlos, who is busy building a tower in the block centre, is playing alongside three other children. They are all engrossed in their constructions. Every now and then they comment to each other about some aspect of their creations.

In the dramatic play centre, a group of four children is playing "Doctor." They are having a heated discussion about what kind of treatment the "patient" needs. After much arguing and negotiation, they all agree that the patient needs both medicine and a needle.

Erin, a quiet, solitary child, is watching the group playing "Doctor" from a distance. After a while, she comes to sit beside you and shows you her doll.

Michael, who is developmentally delayed, stares into space, taking no notice of the other children. He doesn't respond when you greet him, but then he seldom responds when anyone talks to him.

Without realizing it, you are likely to interact differently with each of these children because of their different **conversational styles,** which have evolved from the time they were born. Each child is born with his or her own personality, and each parent or caregiver has his or her own way of relating to a child based on that unique personality. In time, child and caregiver develop a way of interacting with each other, like two dance partners coordinating their moves. Within these interactions, caregivers become the child's mirror, reflecting back their impressions of his ability to communicate. They give feedback on how well the child sent a message (When a parent says, "Oh, you want your bottle!" the crying baby knows that his message was picked up loud and clear) and on whether the message was well received (When a parent says, "What a big smile! You're so happy!" the baby knows that his smiles get smiles in return, as well as lots of animated noises!).

Children's conversational styles evolve as they see themselves through other people's eyes and – in later childhood – as they compare themselves to others. From the thousands of interactions children have with their caregivers, siblings, and peers, they gather internal pictures of themselves, which they paste in an imaginary photo album in their heads. From these pictures, they form their own views of themselves as communicators.

Patrice and the group playing "Doctor" look like confident communicators and seem to have positive internal pictures of themselves. And while Carlos isn't interactive when he's engrossed in his construction, in general he seems to be a sociable, confident child.

However, Erin's style may be telling you that her internal picture is of someone who doesn't expect to get a positive response from others. And Michael's style seems to tell you that he hardly pictures himself as a communicator at all.

Understanding children's conversational styles gives us a better appreciation of why some children communicate so naturally and why others find it so difficult.

Identifying the four conversational styles

When identifying a child's conversational style, consider two important aspects of his interactions with others:

- Does he spontaneously approach others and **initiate** interactions?
- Does he **respond** when others initiate interactions with him?

In general, you will notice that:

- Some children **initiate** interactions with ease – others don't.
- Some children **respond** readily during interactions – others don't.

By looking at how frequently children initiate and respond during interactions, we can identify four different conversational styles, each of which describes the way a child interacts most of the time. It is important to remember, however, that a child's conversational style may vary depending on the situation and with whom he interacts.

Conversational styles are described below in terms of a child's intentional, purposeful communication with others. However, typically developing, very young infants and some older children with severe delays in development have not yet learned to initiate or respond to others intentionally. In these cases, we can still get a sense of their future conversational styles by looking at how often they show interest in others or seem to try to get attention by making sounds, changing facial expressions, or performing actions. Although these sounds and actions are not performed with a clear purpose, they are still signs of the child's awareness of and desire to interact with others, and they give us some clear insights into what the child's conversational style is likely to become.

The Four Conversational Styles

1. The Sociable Child

2. The Reluctant Child

3. The Child with His Own Agenda

4. The Passive Child

1. The Sociable Child

The sociable child initiates interactions constantly and is very responsive to others' initiations. Even in early infancy, sociable children initiate interactions to draw attention to themselves. Some sociable children interact freely in any situation, but others are more sociable with their peers than they are with their teachers, or vice versa.

If language delayed, the sociable child may be slow to talk or difficult to understand, but this doesn't deter him from interacting with others. However, he may be less socially mature than his peers.

2. The Reluctant Child

The reluctant child seldom initiates and is often on the outside of group activities and interactions. He may take a long time to "warm up" and respond to you when you approach him. Given time and opportunities, he will interact with you and other teachers, but peer interactions may be more difficult for him.

If language delayed, this child's reluctance to initiate may be related to his language difficulty. He may be reluctant to interact with others because he can't make himself understood or he may not yet have learned to communicate appropriately in social situations. However, a reluctant child usually responds when others make an effort to interact with him.

3. The Child with His Own Agenda

The child with his own agenda spends a lot of time playing alone, appearing uninterested in interaction with adults and peers. He may initiate when he needs something, but he frequently rejects or ignores your efforts to engage him. Typically developing children may go through this independent phase when they want to "do their own thing." However, they still enjoy interacting with others in some social situations.

4. The Passive Child

The passive child seldom responds or initiates, demonstrating little interest in the objects or people around him. It can be very hard to elicit a smile from him or to engage him in any sort of playful interaction. If this is the child's consistent style of interaction, it reflects a developmental delay.

Teachers can't help but be affected by children's conversational styles

If you take the time to think about the different children in your classroom, you will realize that you don't interact the same way with each of them.

How do children's conversational styles affect you? To find out, ask yourself the following questions:

- Which children do I interact with the most?
- Which children do I most enjoy interacting with?
- What are their conversational styles?
- Which children do I interact with the least?
- What are their conversational styles?

You may or may not be surprised to discover that the children who get the most attention from you are the **sociable** children. It's important to understand why.

They get attention from you because they demand it (in a very nice way, of course!). They initiate interactions with you all the time – and naturally, you respond. They make you feel good because they are interesting and entertaining, and it's human nature to respond positively to people who make us feel good.

But what about the children who don't demand attention or who demand it in negative ways? Because these children are difficult to interact with, once again human nature comes into play – they don't engage you, so you are less likely to engage them, and you end up having fewer interactions with them. What's more, when you do interact with them, the interaction may be limited to talking about necessities, like whether they need to go to the toilet or whether they want more juice. This limited interaction can occur with children who are language delayed or with those who simply lack the confidence to communicate freely. As a result, these children miss out on the wonderful conversations you have with their sociable peers about their families, friends, opinions, and experiences – conversations that build confidence and language learning.

> For children who are not involved in frequent, social interactions, the consequences are obvious – they have fewer opportunities than their sociable peers to develop social and language skills.

For children who are not involved in frequent interactions, the consequences are obvious – they have fewer opportunities than their sociable peers to develop social and language skills. Also, their negative perceptions of themselves as communicators are confirmed. "I'm no good at communicating. That's why I can't get them to pay attention to me," they might think. What devastating consequences this can have!

Children who are reluctant or passive, or who have their own agenda, need help to become more active conversation partners. That's not an easy task. In many cases, it involves helping the children change their view of themselves as communicators.

That's where the teacher's role comes in . . .

D. Teachers play many roles during interactions with children

The way you interact with individual children is likely to vary, depending on each child and situation. You will find that you adopt different "teacher roles" throughout the day. Take a moment to think about which of the following teacher roles you play when you interact with children, because your role can make or break an interaction.

1. The Director role

In this role, the teacher maintains tight control over the children and their activities. She spends much of her time making suggestions, giving directions, and asking questions. Her behaviour tells children that they are not expected to initiate, just to respond as directed. While a teacher needs to direct children some of the time, if this is her predominant role, it makes it very difficult for children to be spontaneous and to play an active role in interactions.

Teachers frequently take on the Director role with children who have language delays, especially when they focus on teaching new skills and "getting the child to talk."

Put the green block on top of the red one...

2. The Entertainer role

Hello Mr. Puppet! Say hello to my puppet! He's come to see you....

In this role, the teacher is playful and lots of fun, but she does most of the talking and playing, giving children few opportunities to get actively involved in the interaction.

Teachers often play the Entertainer role with a child who is language delayed or with children who have passive or reluctant conversational styles. If a child rarely initiates or reacts during activities, it's natural for a teacher to try whatever it takes to get a reaction!

3. The Timekeeper role

In this role, the teacher rushes through activities and routines in order to stay on schedule. Busy schedules are a fact of life in busy preschool classrooms and in child care, but the Timekeeper role can and does result in very limited interactions.

Teachers may end up playing the Timekeeper with children who have special needs and who may have difficulty keeping up with the other children.

4. The Too-quiet Teacher role

In this role, the teacher sits with the children, but hardly interacts with them, even when they initiate.

Teachers frequently take on the Too-quiet role with children who have their own agendas, since these children often prefer to play alone.

5. The Helper role

In this role, the teacher thinks that a child won't be able to express himself so she talks for him or offers help before he has shown any need for it. This may reflect a teacher's desire to help a child or to reduce his frustration, but the end result is that the child learns not to expect much of himself.

Teachers often adopt the Helper role with children who have language delays because these children have such difficulty getting their messages across.

6. The Cheerleader role

In this role, the teacher gives the child lots of praise and gets very excited when a child accomplishes a task, large or small. She often says the word "Good": "Good job!" "Good sitting!" "Good talking!" She is a strong believer in positive reinforcement. Children seem to get pleasure from her praise. She uses praise with all of the children in her classroom, but particularly with those who are reluctant communicators or who are developmentally delayed.

The disadvantage of praise is that children can become too dependent on it and may not develop their own motivation to learn new skills or take on new challenges. In addition, Cheerleaders usually end the conversation with their praise – the interaction seldom continues after the child is told how well he has done.

7. The Responsive Partner role

In this role, the teacher is tuned in to the children's abilities, needs, and interests. She responds with warmth and interest to each child, which encourages them to take an active part in interactions, both with her and with their peers.

At different times, you'll find yourself playing different roles – depending, for example, on the type of child you're interacting with, on how many children are with you, on their general behaviour, on the time you have available, and on your mood!

Which role do you play *most* of the time?

Teachers' roles and children's styles don't always match

When the teacher's role and the child's conversational style don't match, the teacher and child never really connect. Not only do they both feel frustrated, but the child's potential for language learning is not fulfilled.

It's important to realize that children's conversational styles significantly affect the roles teachers play. When children aren't responsive and don't communicate spontaneously, it's natural to direct, question, entertain, and help them in an effort to get an interaction going. But these tactics seldom work! In fact, they can have the opposite effect – very often, the child communicates even less!

Let's look at the thought processes of teachers and "hard-to-reach" children as the teachers try to connect:

The director teacher and the passive child

The helper teacher and the reluctant child

The entertainer and the child with his own agenda

The only role that consistently provides children with the encouragement and support they need to learn to communicate is the *responsive* role.

In later chapters we'll discuss how to adopt this role with all children, regardless of their conversational styles.

Summary

In early childhood settings, teachers are responsible for creating environments that build strong relationships and promote language learning. Interactions between teachers and children can be varied and complex. Interactions depend on children's conversational styles, on the role the teacher plays, and on children's ability to play with peers. By being aware of how partners in an interaction affect each other, teachers can observe the interactions in their classrooms to see whether each child's need for frequent, enjoyable interactions is being met. The knowledge gained from these observations helps teachers ensure that every child becomes a fully participating member of the group.

Observation Guide 1:
The child's interactions with teachers and peers

Let's assume that a child in your classroom has language and social skills that seem immature for his age. You might have noticed that he's very quiet and doesn't interact much with you or with his peers. But perhaps if you observe him closely, you'll discover that there *are* situations in which he does interact. While you know his weaknesses in terms of his ability to interact with others, can you identify some of his strengths?

This guide is designed to help you take a closer look at a child's interactions in your preschool or early childhood setting. Before you begin your observations, remember to observe the child in many situations over an extended period of time. A child's communication and interaction may vary from day to day, from activity to activity, and from conversation partner to conversation partner. Other factors can influence how much or how little a child interacts: illness, lack of sleep, and problems at home will all affect his desire and ability to communicate. It is wise, therefore, to observe the child in many different situations, both indoors and outdoors, and to spread your observations over a number of days.

Observation Guide 1:
The child's interactions with teachers and peers

Child's name: _____

Age at time of this observation: _____

Child's first language: _____

Child's ability to speak English (if child is verbal): _____

Date: _____

1. Observe the child's conversational style

I think (child's name) _____'s conversational style is (you may want to check off more than one):

- ❏ **Sociable** because s/he initiates and responds frequently to others' initiations
- ❏ **Reluctant** because s/he seldom initiates, but does respond to others' initiations
- ❏ **Own agenda** because she may initiate, but rarely responds to others' initiations and seems to prefer being alone
- ❏ **Passive** because s/he hardly initiates or responds to others' initiations

If the child's conversational style is reluctant, passive, or own agenda, s/he interacts better with:

- ❏ Teachers
- ❏ Peers
- ❏ Neither

2. Observe the child's interactions with teachers

Names of teachers with whom s/he communicates with the most:

The situations in which s/he communicates MOST and interacts willingly with a teacher:

The situations in which s/he communicates and interacts LEAST with a teacher:

Please note: All Observation Guide pages may be photocopied.

3. Observe the child's play interactions with peers

With which children does the child interact most frequently?

During which activities is the child MOST interactive with her/his peers?

During which activities is the child LEAST interactive with her/his peers?

4. Summary of Observations

The following people, activities, and situations seem to make communication and interaction more enjoyable or manageable for _____ (child's name).

If you want to help a child become more interactive with both teachers and peers, read Part 2 (chapters 3, 4, 5, and 6).

Please note: All Observation Guide pages may be photocopied.

References

Asher, S., Oden, S. & Gottman, J. (1977). Children's friendships in school settings. In L. Katz (Ed.), *Current topics in early childhood education.* Norwood, NJ: Ablex.

Barnes, S., Gutfreund, M., Satterly, D. & Wells, G. (1983). Characteristics of adult speech which predict children's language development. *Journal of Child Language, 10,* 65–84.

Bell, R.Q. & Harper, L.V. (1977). *Child effects on adults.* Hillsdale, NJ: Erlbaum.

Briggs, D. C. (1975). *Your child's self-esteem.* New York: Doubleday.

Charlesworth, R. (1983). *Understanding child development.* Albany: Delmar.

Conti-Ramsden, G. (1985). Mothers in dialogue with language-impaired children. *Topics in Language Disorders*, 5(2), 58–68.

Ervin-Tripp, S. (1991). Play in language development. In B. Scales, M. Almy, A. Nicolopoulou & S. Ervin-Tripp (Eds.), *Play and the social context of development in early care and education* (pp. 84–97). New York: Teachers College Press.

Fey, M.E. (1986). *Language intervention with young children.* San Diego, CA: College Hill Press.

Ginsberg, H. & Opper, S. (1969). *Piaget's theory of intellectual development: An introduction.* Englewood Cliffs, NJ: Prentice Hall.

Guralnick, M. (1981). Peer influences on the development of communicative competence. In P. Strain (Ed.), *The utilization of classroom peers as behavior change agents* (pp. 31–68). New York: Plenum.

Guralnick, M. (1990). Peer interactions and the development of handicapped children's social and communicative competence. In H. Foot, M.J. Morgan & R.H. Shute (Eds.) *Children helping children* (pp. 275–305). New York: John Wiley & Sons.

Halliday, M. (1975). *Learning how to mean.* London: Edward Arnold.

Honig, A. (2002). *Secure relationships: Nurturing infant/toddler attachment in early care settings.* Washington, DC: National Association for the Education of Young Children.

Johnson, J.E., Christie, J.F. & Yawkey, T.D. (1987). *Play and early childhood development.* Glenview, IL: Scott, Foresman.

La Greca, A.M. & Stark, P. (1986). Naturalistic observations of children's social behavior. In P.S. Strain, M. Guralnick & H.M. Walker (Eds.), *Children's social behavior: Development, assessment and modification* (pp. 181–217). New York: Academic Press.

Lieven, E.M. (1978). Conversations between mothers and young children: Individual differences and their possible implication for the study of language learning. In N. Waterson & C. Snow (Eds.), *The development of communication* (pp. 173–187). Chichester: John Wiley & Sons.

McLean, J., & Snyder-McLean, L.A. (1978). *A transactional approach to early language training.* Columbus, Ohio: Charles E. Merrill.

Parten, M.B. (1932). Social participation among preschool children. *Journal of Abnormal and Social Psychology,* 27, (pp. 243–269).

Rubin, K.H. & Ross, H.S. (Eds.), (1982). *Peer relationships and social skills in childhood.* New York: Springer-Verlag.

Rubin, K. (1986). Play, peer interaction and social development. In A.W. Gottfried and C. Caldwell Brown (Eds.), *Play interactions: The contribution of play materials and parental involvement to children's development.* Proceedings of the eleventh Johnson and Johnson Pediatric Round Table (pp. 163–174). Lexington, MA: Lexington Books.

Smilansky, S. & Shefatya, L. (1990). *Facilitating play: A medium for promoting cognitive, socio-emotional and academic development in young children.* Gaithersburg, MD: Psychosocial and Educational Publications.

Snow, C.E. (1984). Parent-child interaction and the development communicative ability. In R.L. Schiefelbusch & J. Pickar (Eds.), *The acquisition of communicative competence* (pp. 69–107). Baltimore: University Park Press.

Sponseller, D. & Lowry, M. (1974) Designing a play environment for toddlers. In D. Sponseller (Ed.), *Play as a learning medium* (pp. 81–109). Washington, DC: National Association for the Education of Young Children.

Tiegerman, E. & Siperstein, M. (1984). Individual patterns of interaction in the mother-child dyad: Implications for parent intervention. *Topics in Language* Disorders, 4(4) (pp. 50–61).

Tomlinson-Keasy, C. (1985). *Child development: Psychological, sociocultural and biological factors.* Homewood, IL: The Dorsey Press.

Wetherby, A. (1991). *Profiling communication and symbolic abilities: Assessment and intervention guidelines.* Presentation at Toronto Children's Centre, Toronto, Ontario.

Chapter 2

The Stages of Language Development: Talking Takes Time

In five short years, typically developing children make incredible progress in their ability to use language.

A. An amazing five-year journey: from "waaaaa!" to "when I grow up, I wanna be a pilot."

In five short years, typically developing children make incredible progress in their ability to use language. They progress from using nonverbal communication (sending messages through sounds, actions, eye gaze, facial expression, and gestures) to using verbal communication or spoken language, which is the most complex skill human beings develop.

Although most babies say their first words at about 14 months, they start learning about communication right from birth. The foundations of both communication and turn-taking develop in that critical first year.

Once children begin to talk, they still have a lot to learn about language and how to use it. Comprehension, conversational skills, grammar, vocabulary, and the ability to use language as a tool for thinking and learning take years to develop and refine.

The task of developing language is much more difficult for children with language delays. Some children with language delays progress through the same stages of language development as typically developing children, but at a slower rate. Other children may get "stuck" at a certain stage and have difficulty moving on to the next one. Some children, however, develop language in very different ways because of their special difficulties. For example, children with Autism Spectrum Disorder may be able to use words, but they use them primarily to make requests. Often, the meanings they attach to certain words are not conventional, resulting in confusion for the listener.

> It is important to be familiar with the stages of language development so you know not only what to expect from children – language delayed or not – at each stage, but also how to help them progress to the next stages.

It is important to be familiar with the stages of language development so you know not only what to expect from children – language delayed or not – at each stage, but also how to help them progress to the next stages.

Before you learn about these stages, however, it's important to understand the "whys" and "hows" of communication. In this chapter, you'll learn about:

- why children communicate
- how children communicate, and
- the various stages of communication and language development.

B. Children, like adults, communicate for many different reasons

When we think about communication, we need to go beyond the "hows" – the gestures, sounds, and words – and analyze the "whys": the reasons those gestures, sounds, and words are used. For example, you may use a word like "peas" for a number of reasons – to ask for peas, to respond to a question about what vegetable you'd like to eat, to express disgust at the thought of eating them, or to express pleasure at finding them on your plate. As you can see, there are many reasons for communicating, and children have to learn all these reasons, at a very young age.

Communication certainly enables us to satisfy our physical needs. The most important reason for communicating, however, is to satisfy our social needs. Human beings have an overwhelming need to connect with others and to share feelings, ideas, and experiences. When we're happy, sad, excited, or frustrated, we often need to talk to someone about it. Once we have done so, we experience an enormous sense of satisfaction.

> When we think about communication, we need to go beyond the "hows" – the gestures, sounds, and words – and analyze the "whys": the reasons those gestures, sounds, and words are used.

In addition to satisfying our need to connect with others, language has another critical function. It is a tool for thinking, learning, and problem-solving. With language, we can consider alternatives, reason, imagine, plan, predict, and find solutions to problems. Every day, we make hundreds of little decisions and solve hundreds of everyday problems using language in our heads.

An easy way to appreciate the many "whys" of communication is to think back to all the telephone calls you have made over the past few days. You probably had a number of different reasons for making those calls, and these are described on the next page. You will see that infants and young children communicate for the same reasons you do. They don't do it as effectively as you do and they may even do it without words, but their purpose in communicating is the same as yours.

Why people communicate

1. To make a request

2. To protest about something (complain, reject)

3. To greet or take leave of someone

4. To respond to another person's communication

5. To ask for information (question)

6. To think, plan, and problem-solve

7. To share feelings, ideas, and interests

Once you become aware of how and why children communicate, you are better able to recognize the kind of support each child needs from you.

For example, a two-and-a-half-year-old who communicates only when she needs help must become involved in playful social interactions if she is to learn to use language as a social tool.

By contrast, a sociable three-year-old who speaks in jumbled sentences and is difficult to understand will need a different kind of support. Since this child readily engages you in social interactions, your focus during these interactions will be on providing her with language models that help her learn more mature ways of expressing herself.

C. Children communicate in many different ways

Children are able to send messages in many ways.

In the early stages of language development, much of their communication is nonverbal and includes:

- sounds
- actions
- eye gaze
- facial expressions, and
- gestures.

As they progress, children learn to use verbal communication, in the form of:

- single words
- combinations of words, and
- sentences.

Most children progress quite smoothly from nonverbal to verbal communication or spoken language. When children first start to talk, they typically use a combination of actions, gestures, and words. Words, however, soon become the preferred (and most effective) way of communicating. However, nonverbal communication is always an important

Juice. You want a drink of **juice.**

Maria finds it hard to say words because of oral motor difficulties. She chooses the picture of the juice and gives it to her teacher, Tanya, to request a drink.

part of communicating. Even as adults, we continue to communicate nonverbally – we would find it impossible to talk to others without gesturing with our hands, using facial expressions, and changing voice tone!

When a child is unable to develop functional speech, possibly because of oral motor difficulties, you should offer an alternative means of communication. This would include hand gestures, signs, or pictures if she is able to understand that a word, sign, or picture has meaning. The better a child's understanding of words, the better will be her ability to use these other forms of communication.

Giving nonverbal children a means of communication through signs or pictures can help ease their frustrations around communication, and help them express needs and desires. A child can use a sign, for example, to ask for "more" or to request a favourite toy or activity. Another child may quickly learn to point to a picture, or to give an adult a picture card, to make a request or answer a question. When children find communication more rewarding and less frustrating, they may be motivated to communicate more, and in a greater variety of ways. Sometimes, for example, children can combine limited use of speech with pictures or signs. (In these cases, the nonverbal form of communication is referred to as augmentative, rather than alternative, since it supplements, rather than replaces, speech. As the child matures and develops speech, she may in time replace augmentative communication with speech.)

D. The six stages of communication and language development

The following pages describe six stages that typically developing children go through as they develop language. An awareness of how and why a child communicates at each stage will give you a good idea of what the next step is and how you can help her get there. The following age ranges represent what can be expected in typically developing children. Children with language delays also follow this sequence of development but can stay longer at individual stages and may not necessarily become Later Sentence Users in the preschool years.

Stage 1: Discoverer (birth to 8 months)

The infant goes from communicating reflexively to becoming really interested in others and wanting attention. She does not yet know how to send messages directly to another person to get what she wants.

> *I cry, I smile, I make sounds, and I look –*
> *Figure out what I mean by hook or by crook!*

Stage 2: Communicator (8 to 13 months)

The infant sends purposeful messages directly to others using a combination of eye gaze, facial expressions, sounds, and gestures. She becomes very sociable.

> *With sounds, looks, and gestures I "talk" to you.*
> *Now, help me learn a word or two.*

Stage 3: First Words User (12 to 18 months)

The infant cracks the language code and begins to use single words.

> *From my mouth the words now pour.*
> *Your job is to give me more.*

Stage 4: Combiner (18 to 24 months)

The child demonstrates a burst in vocabulary and begins to combine words. She also starts to take more turns in a conversation.

> *I put words together and begin to chat –*
> *Converse with me, it's as simple as that!*

Stage 5: Early Sentence User (2 to 3 years)

The child progresses from using two-word combinations to five-word sentences and can now hold short conversations.

> *My words and sentences now have grown –*
> *I can tell little stories on my own.*

Stage 6: Later Sentence User (3 to 5 years)

The child uses long, complex sentences and can hold conversations.

> *I've learned to talk and take my turn.*
> *My job now is to talk to learn.*

I cry, I smile, I make sounds and look
Figure out what I mean by hook or by crook!

Typically developing children are Discoverers until about eight months. Discoverers are interested in others (they look at you, make sounds, and smile at you), but they don't yet send messages directly to their caregivers. This is because they don't yet know that their behaviour can affect others and make them behave in certain ways. You, the caregiver, interpret the infant's behaviour as if she has communicated for a specific reason. For example, if the infant happens to look toward a mobile, you might say, "Oh, you want me to wind up the mobile," and you wind it up. Your responsiveness is what will eventually

lead her to conclude, "Hey! When I behave in certain ways, it makes people do the things I want them to do!"

When Discoverers have a language delay . . .

A child with a significant language delay may be a Discoverer. Children who stay at the Discoverer stage longer than typically developing children usually have associated delays in cognitive and motor development.

Why Discoverers communicate

The Discoverer expresses feelings through behaviours that you interpret as:

- ◆ protests, rejections, signs of distress or displeasure
- ◆ requests for actions or objects, or
- ◆ interest in or awareness of others.

Later on, behaviours are interpreted as:

- ◆ requests for social play routines, like Peek-a-Boo, or
- ◆ calls for attention.

How Discoverers communicate

- At first, the Discoverer produces reflexive responses to physical needs by crying, fussing, looking, moving away, smiling, different facial expressions, vowel-like sounds, body movements, and voice changes (loudness and pitch).
  - Later on, the Discoverer's ability to look at what or whom she wants, to move toward and/or reach for objects, and to produce a variety of sounds make her behaviour much easier for caregivers to interpret.
  - Babbling (long strings of consonants and vowels repeated endlessly – e.g. "dadadadadadada") usually starts at about six or seven months.

How Discoverers interact

- At first, the Discoverer smiles at smiling faces and makes cooing sounds back and forth.
- By four months, she becomes interested in getting and maintaining your attention by looking, smiling, and making sounds in your direction.
- She becomes interested in social turn-taking games like Peek-a-Boo and Row Your Boat, and takes turns by smiling, laughing, making sounds, and moving her body to let you know that she wants the game to continue.
- Gradually she becomes interested in toys and may seem to lose interest in people (although she hasn't!).
- At about six months, her eye contact with you may actually decrease until she learns to coordinate looking back and forth between you and her plaything.

What Discoverers understand

- The Discoverer understands nonverbal cues like gestures, intonation, and the general situation. For example, she gets excited when you ask, "Do you want to go for a walk?" as you pick her up and point towards the stroller.
- She does not yet understand what words mean.

Next steps

A Discoverer becomes a Communicator, who:

- communicates directly to adults with a goal in mind, expecting a response, and
- begins to develop joint attention – that is, the ability to share a focus with a caregiver and to get a caregiver to follow her focus.

Communicator

*With sounds, looks, and gestures I "talk" to you.
Now, help me learn a word or two.*

Typically developing children are Communicators from about eight to 13 months. Communicators send messages to others with a goal in mind – they know what they want to say and that they can get results by sending messages directly to other people. They also become very sociable, communicating with you because it's enjoyable, not just because you get them the things they want. Communicators have developed joint attention, which means that they willingly share their emotions, intentions, and interest in the outside world with you. You can clearly see that they want to share their focus of interest with you from the way they point to things, show and offer you toys and other objects, and look at you, waiting for your response. Not only are they able to share their focus with you, but they are also able to share yours, making it possible for you to help them learn all about the world. The development of joint attention is a critical milestone, opening up endless opportunities for language learning, which takes place through the sharing of information between children and the important people in their lives.

When Communicators have a language delay . . .

An older child with a language delay may be a Communicator. Children who are language delayed and who stay at the Communicator stage longer than typically developing children have difficulty learning to use words. They continue to communicate with sounds, facial expressions, and gestures. Sometimes, their ability to understand language is much more advanced than their ability to express themselves using speech, which makes it easier for you to communicate with them.

Why Communicators communicate

Children at the Communicator stage communicate for a variety of reasons, most of them social. They communicate to:

- direct or control your behaviour by protesting or requesting an action or object
- interact for social reasons (main purpose of communication), by requesting a

social routine (e.g. Peek-a-Boo), calling for attention, asking for comfort, showing off an accomplishment, or greeting, and

♦ establish joint attention by drawing attention to objects, events, or people; labelling; or requesting information through sounds and pointing (this is the beginning of question-asking).

How Communicators communicate

♦ The Communicator uses conventional gestures that are recognizable and easy to understand, like pointing, shaking her head for "no," and waving for "goodbye."

♦ By nine months, a Communicator is able to combine gestures with sounds and eye gaze, which makes it easier for you to understand what she is trying to communicate.

♦ At 11 or 12 months, the child becomes expert at combining various forms of non-verbal communication. If she wants something, she will point and look at the object she wants, make a sound, and look back and forth between you and the object as she repeats the sound.

♦ The child will continue to communicate nonverbally until you respond. If you do not respond, she may add to her message by making a different sound, change the message by repeating it loudly, or throw a tantrum (which usually gets a response!).

♦ Communicators use sounds as if they were words – "guh" may mean "Look at that!"

♦ They may start to use a few single words.

♦ They may produce jargon – long strings of sounds with adult-like intonation, which we can't understand!

How Communicators interact

♦ Children at the Communicator stage communicate mainly for social reasons, like drawing attention to what they're doing or to things of interest around them.

♦ They are able to share your focus – you can look or point at something and they will follow your line of vision or the direction you point.

♦ Communicators can get you to follow their focus by pointing, making sounds, and looking at you to see if you are paying attention! This establishes joint attention, which is critical for language development.

♦ Communicators enjoy games that involve imitating sounds and handing objects back and forth.

♦ They will take turns with eye contact, actions, sounds, and gestures during play with toys and in social routines, like singing "Row, Row, Row Your Boat."

What Communicators understand

- Communicators have not developed a true understanding of words, although they seem to understand much of what is said to them and seem able to follow some directions. However, they rely on clear cues from you in the form of actions, gestures, intonation, and the general situation.
- By 13 months, a Communicator probably understands only a few names of people or objects.

Next steps

Communicators become First Words Users who gradually begin to:

- rely more upon words and less upon sounds and gestures to get their messages across
- communicate with signs or pictures if there are specific difficulties with speech production, and
- participate in brief conversations.

First Words User

From my mouth the words now pour.
Your job is to give me more.

Typically developing children become First Words Users from about 12 to 18 months. First Words Users begin by using only one or two first words, often initially accompanied by gestures, and gradually progress to using about 50 words. First Words Users develop the ability to have very brief conversations with you, although they need your support. You have to simplify your language and ask questions that are easy for these children to answer in order for them to take their conversational turns. That's because First Words Users are in the very early stages of learning how to become conversationalists. Understanding of language (receptive language) really begins to take off at this stage.

When First Words Users have a language delay . . .

Older children with language delays may be First Words Users for a longer period of time than typically developing children. A child may be delayed in the way she expresses herself, but her understanding of language may be appropriate for her age. Or, a child may be equally delayed in both her expressive language and her understanding of language. First Words Users with language delays have difficulty expanding their vocabularies and moving from using single words to word combinations. Instead, they continue to communicate, for an extended period of time, with a small vocabulary of single words accompanied by gestures and facial expressions. Because of their limited verbal skills, they have difficulty participating in conversations. Their use of words may also be inconsistent.

Some children who have severe language delays may have difficulty learning to say words at all. However, if their understanding of language is adequate, they can begin to communicate with pictures and/or signs instead. The degree to which they make progress using pictures or signs is related to their level of understanding.

Why First Words Users communicate

- First Words Users communicate for the same variety of reasons as Communicators.
- They talk mainly about events in the here-and-now.

How First Words Users communicate

- First Words Users use about 10 to 50 single words that refer to people, objects, and events of interest. Some words are simplified versions of adult words (e.g. "baba" means "bottle").
- Particular words may have different meanings in different contexts. For example, "Mama" could be a question ("Is that mama's purse?"), a comment ("There you are, Mama."), or a request ("Pick me up, Mama.").
- A child at this stage may use words too broadly (e.g. "doggie" is used to refer to all animals) or too narrowly (e.g. "baba" is used to refer only to her own bottle).
- She may begin to communicate with signs or pictures if she has specific difficulties with speech production

How First Words Users interact

- Like Communicators, First Words Users communicate mainly for social reasons – but now they use words rather than only sounds and gestures.
- A First Words User will persevere if not responded to by repeating herself, altering the message, or finding another way to get the message across. These strategies for communication are called "repair" strategies.

What First Words Users understand

- First Words Users begin to understand names of familiar people and objects without any cues (like you pointing to the object as you say the word).

Next steps

First Words Users become Combiners who:

- develop a larger number of words within a short period of time
- combine single words into sequences of two words (e.g. "more juice," "big doggie") – a process that begins when the child is using approximately 50 single words
- use combinations of several pictures or signs (if speech is not their main means of communication), and
- take more turns in a conversation, especially around topics they initiate.

Combiner

I put words together and begin to chat –
Converse with me, it's as simple as that!

Typically developing children become Combiners from 18 to 24 months. When children have about 50 single words, their vocabularies undergo a sudden growth spurt, expanding up to about 200 words. Combiners begin to combine single words into two-word sentences, although at first they may still use single words much of the time.

While Combiners start to take more turns in a conversation, they still need lots of support from adults to stay in the conversation.

When Combiners have a language delay . . .

Older children with language delays may also be Combiners. They continue to use mainly single words and simple two-word combinations. These children have difficulty moving on to the production of longer and more complex sentences. Their receptive language skills (language comprehension) may vary a great deal: some children may make considerable progress in their ability to understand language, while other children's receptive skills may be as delayed as their expressive skills.

Depending on how much they understand and on how skilled the adult is as a conversation partner, these children can take part in brief conversations. They can add new information to a topic and may ask questions. However, their limited verbal abilities mean that they still have difficulty answering questions and responding to comments, making it likely that conversations will frequently break down.

A child who uses pictures or signs to communicate due to difficulties with speech production becomes a Combiner when she points to two pictures or produces two signs in sequence to express an idea (e.g., "dog + eat").

Why Combiners communicate

- Combiners communicate for the same variety of reasons as Communicators.
- They talk more about events in the here-and-now than about the past or future.

How Combiners communicate

- Combiners have a "vocabulary growth spurt," increasing from 50 to about 200 words.
- They use two-word sentences (usually beginning when they have about 50 single words) but continue to rely upon single words initially.
- One sentence can have different meanings in different situations (e.g., "Mommy car" can mean "That's Mommy's car," or "Mommy, I want to go in your car," or "I went home in Mommy's car.").
- Combiners express negatives by using the words "no" or "not," usually at the beginning of the sentence (e.g., "no bye bye").
- They ask "yes/no" questions by saying words with a questioning intonation (e.g., "Go bye bye?"), and use "Wh" question words, like "Where?" and "What dat?"
- If a Combiner uses signs or pictures, she points to two pictures or produces two signs in sequence to express an idea (e.g., "dog + eat").

How Combiners interact

- Combiners begin to take part in real (but brief) conversations. They are able to provide new information about a topic you have introduced or will ask a question about what you have said. However, responses to your questions and comments may be inconsistent.

What Combiners understand

- Combiners understand many words out of context (without cues from the situation). For example, a Combiner will understand when you say, "Let's go and wash your hands" when you are not standing near the sink or pointing to her hands.
- Combiners understand simple directions (e.g., "Kiss the baby.").
- They point to pictures in a book (e.g., "Show me the lion.").
- They answer simple questions (e.g., "Where's your blanket?").

Next steps

Combiners become Early Sentence Users who:

- combine more than two words at a time to gradually progress to sentences that are grammatically more complete – a process that begins when approximately half the child's utterances contain two words
- combine more than two pictures or signs at a time (if speech is not the main way of communicating), and
- take even more turns in a conversation, especially around topics they initiate.

Early Sentence User

My words and sentences now have grown –
I can tell little stories on my own.

Typically developing children are Early Sentence Users from two to three years. Early Sentence Users use two- to five-word sentences and can hold short conversations. Conversations with children at this stage are most successful when the child begins them because then the topic is familiar.

Baby dink milk.

When Early Sentence Users have a language delay . . .

Older children with language delays may also be Early Sentence Users. These children do not easily learn the grammatical rules needed to produce longer sentences. They do not use correct verb and pronoun forms (even typically developing children find these confusing at first) and their sentences remain short, simple, and grammatically incomplete. They have difficulty expressing more complex messages and describing events in the past or future. Because of her limited verbal skills, a child with a delay who is an Early Sentence User may also find it challenging to take turns in conversations. Understanding of language may be delayed or age-appropriate. A child's level of understanding will also influence how able she is to engage in conversations.

Why Early Sentence Users communicate

- Early Sentence Users begin to use language to find out meaning and purpose: they start to ask "why?" questions, even though they can't themselves answer "why?" questions.
- They also begin to use language to tell stories, although the stories they tell may be disjointed and hard to follow.
- They begin to use language imaginatively.
- They use language to express feelings.

How Early Sentence Users communicate

- Sentence length continues to increase up to about five words.
- Sentences gradually become more grammatically correct, as the child at this stage begins to use:
    - prepositions (e.g., in and on)
    - pronouns (At first, *me*, and then *he, she, they, we*)
    - verbs (-ing verbs; helping or auxiliary words like *gonna, gotta, wanna, can,* and *will;* and different forms of the verb "to be," like *am, are,* and *is*)
    - plurals by adding -s to words
    - articles (e.g., *a, the*)
    - negatives (*not, can't, don't*), which are now used in the middle of the sentence, rather than at the beginning
    - conjunctions (*and*), and
    - questions with "wh-" words.

How Early Sentence Users interact

- By three years of age, Early Sentence Users can take a number of turns in a conversation, and conversations go on for longer.
- Children know that a pause in the conversation is a signal for them to take a turn.
- At first, it's easier to discuss something an Early Sentence User has initiated than it is to discuss something you initiate.

What Early Sentence Users understand

- Early Sentence Users understand many different concepts.
- They follow two-step directions.
- They follow simple stories in books.

Next steps

Early Sentence Users become Later Sentence Users, who are able to:

- use more grammatically complete sentences, and
- take even more turns in a conversation, both around topics they initiate and topics initiated by others.

Later Sentence User

I've learned to talk and take my turn.
My job now is to talk to learn.

Typically developing children are Later Sentence Users from three to five years. Later Sentence Users use long, complex sentences and can hold conversations for extended periods of time.

Why Later Sentence Users communicate

Children at this stage use language to think, learn, and imagine. For example, they use language to plan what they're going to do, anticipate what will happen next, report on things they experience or have experienced in the past, and to create imaginary situations.

Stories (narratives) become a regular part of the Later Sentence User's conversation – she describes events from her own experiences and tells imaginary stories.

At three years, children's stories are short (one to two sentences) and tell about very recent events – you often need to ask questions to find out exactly who or what the story is about. At four years, children's stories are longer (four or five complex sentences) and likely to be about an event in the past. The child at this stage knows how to tell a good story – she introduces it, provides background information (e.g., where it happened, who was involved), and gives details about what happened and how the story ended. At five years, the child adds more details about the setting and ends the story with a final outcome or some description or evaluation of the situation.

How Later Sentence Users communicate

- At this stage, most of the child's sentences are more than four words long.
- Grammar gradually becomes more complex and correct.
- Some grammatical errors continue as the child attempts to find a general rule that can be applied to all words in a certain grammatical context (e.g., "If we say, 'I called,' 'I shouted,' and 'I climbed,' why not say, 'I runned'? Or, if we say 'That's his,' 'That's hers,' and 'That's ours,' why not say 'That's mines'?").
- Children at this stage use complex sentences that link two or more ideas together. At first, they use *and* to link sentences, progressing to *and then, because, what, when, but, that, if,* and *so*.

- They produce sentences with verbs like *think, wish, wonder, hope, remember,* and *pretend.*
- They use pronouns (*I, you, she, we,* and *they*) correctly.
- At first, a Later Sentence User reverses the order of verbs and nouns to form questions (e.g., "What you are doing?").
- By three and a half years, questions sound more like adult questions (e.g., "What you are doing?" becomes "What are you doing?").
- They begin to use helping or auxiliary verbs (like *are, is, can, do,* and *will*) in questions, so that, for example, "You help me?" becomes "Will you help me?" and "She sick?" becomes "Is she sick?"
- At this stage, children use more advanced forms of negatives. By three and a half years, they use *don't, can't, doesn't,* and *isn't.* By four years, they use *no one, none,* and *nothing* and the past-tense forms *didn't, wasn't,* and *couldn't.*
- Vocabulary is up to 5,000 words!

How Later Sentence Users interact

- Later Sentence Users can take more turns in a conversation, and conversations are longer – even those on topics you initiated.
- They are very aware of the importance of pauses as a signal for change in speaker.
- Children at this stage say "Yeah" or nod to acknowledge what you're saying.
- They may not always give you a turn, especially if they're telling you something of great interest. Sometimes they don't respond to a topic you've introduced, or switch topics to something that interests them.
- Later Sentence Users persist when trying to get into a conversation.
- They call out or yell to get their listener's attention before starting to talk.
- They stay close to the listener and maintain eye contact to keep her attention.

What Later Sentence Users understand

- Later Sentence Users seem to understand everything.
- By five years, they follow stories and understand complex questions such as "What would happen if there was no rain?" and "How many ways can you think to sort buttons?"

Next steps

Later Sentence Users:

- continue to develop increasingly complex sentences
- become more adept at using language as a tool for thinking, learning, and imagining, and
- become more sophisticated story-tellers.

Language stages and conversational styles

Two children at the same language stage may interact very differently because of differences in their conversational styles. (See Chapter 1 for a more complete description of conversational styles.) For example, a Communicator with a sociable conversational style may initiate frequently with sounds and gestures and be very easy to engage in social interaction. However, a Communicator with a reluctant conversational style may initiate less frequently and interact mostly in response to your questions and commands. Even though both these children are Communicators, you will need to adjust the way you interact with them to respond to their different conversational styles. You will find out more about adjusting the way you interact in Chapter 3.

All of these children are Communicators, but they interact very differently because of differences in their conversational styles.

Shona has a sociable style and enjoys offering a taste of spaghetti to her teacher.

Yummy spaghetti!

Nicholas has a passive style. He observes the other children but does not participate in the activity.

Jessica has a reluctant style and initiates less frequently.

Austin has his own agenda and prefers to play on his own.

Summary

Communication begins at birth and continues to develop throughout childhood and early adulthood. In infancy, children learn that their behaviour has an effect on others. From that realization evolves intentional (but still nonverbal) communication, which forms the foundation for all future communication. Even in infancy, children discover the power and pleasure of social communication. Within their day-to-day exchanges with caregivers, they learn language. Spoken language develops and is refined between the ages of one and five years, by which time children are able to have lengthy conversations and use language to gain information, to think, and to imagine. Children who are language delayed take longer to achieve the stages of language development and their speech is frequently less mature than that of typically developing children. Some children with severe cognitive delays may not progress beyond one of the early stages of communication development. Others who are unable to develop speech because of motor difficulties will need to learn to use alternative means, like signs or picture systems, to express themselves.

Observation Guide 2: The child's stage of language development

This Observation Guide will help you identify:
- the child's stage of language development based on how and why s/he communicates (expressive language) and what s/he understands (receptive language), and
- her/his ability to engage in social interactions.

Child's name: _____

Age at time of this observation: _____

Child's first language: _____

Child's ability to speak English (if child is verbal): _____

Date: _____

For Discoverers and Communicators (before language develops)

A. How often and for what reasons the child communicates

Observe the child in many different situations over a period of days to see **how often** s/he communicates for the reasons listed below. Remember – Discoverers do not yet communicate intentionally. Caregivers have to **interpret** why they are communicating.

WHY ▼ HOW OFTEN ▶	Often	Sometimes	Rarely	Never
To protest				
To request an object or action				
To request a social routine				
To call for attention				
To respond to you when you talk to her/him				
To request comfort				
To show off or draw attention to self				
To draw attention to people, things, or events (comment)				
To label (says a word, use a picture or sign)				
To request information (by using questioning intonation)				

Please note: All Observation Guide pages may be photocopied.

B. The child's stage of language development

When the child communicates, note **how** s/he sends her/his message and **why** s/he is communicating – then check the column where the HOW and WHY intersect.

HOW \ WHY	To protest	To request an object or action	To request a social routine	To call for attention	To respond to you when you talk to her/him	To request comfort	To show off or draw attention to self	To draw attention to people, things (comment)	To label (uses a word, picture, or sign)	To request information (by using questioning intonation)
Discoverer *										
Cries, fusses										
Looks										
Smiles										
Makes vowel-like sounds or a variety of consonant and vowel sounds										
Changes pitch/loudness of voice										
Makes body movements										
Changes facial expressions										
Laughs										
Reaches/moves towards										
Communicator										
Looks at person to make eye contact										
Points										
Gestures (e.g., waves, shakes head)										
Pantomimes (acts out what s/he wants to say)										
Combines pointing, eye contact, and making sounds										
Makes sounds that have special meaning										
Uses single words										

* Remember – you need to interpret for the Discoverer.

Please note: All Observation Guide pages may be photocopied.

C. How the child interacts

- ❏ makes sounds to take turns back and forth
- ❏ has a definite interest in getting your attention
- ❏ is easily engaged when you play games like Peek-a-Boo
- ❏ initiates games like Peek-a-Boo and Pat-a-Cake
- ❏ draws attention to her/himself and to things in the environment
- ❏ can share your focus and get you to attend to what s/he's interested in by using eye contact, sounds, gestures, and actions and by pointing
- ❏ interacts with you during play with toys

Summary of observations for Discoverers and Communicators

a) Child is a:

- ❏ Discoverer
- ❏ Communicator

b) Her/his ability to communicate and take turns seems to be:

- ❏ above age level
- ❏ at age level
- ❏ slightly below age level
- ❏ well below age level

Comments:

For First Words Users, Combiners, and Early and Later Sentence Users (after language develops)

A. How the child communicates (expressive language)

The child speaks using:

- ❏ single words
- ❏ two-word sentences
- ❏ three-plus-word sentences
- ❏ long, complex sentences

The child's grammar seems to be:

- ❏ at age level
- ❏ a little below her/his age level
- ❏ quite delayed

The child uses the following kinds of questions:

- ❏ statements with a rising intonation (e.g., "I have some?")
- ❏ Where, What, and Who questions
- ❏ Why questions
- ❏ When, How questions
- ❏ no questions heard

B. Why the child communicates

The child uses language to:

- ❏ make requests
- ❏ talk about the here-and-now
- ❏ talk about the here-and-now, as well as past and future events
- ❏ think, plan, negotiate, and imagine
- ❏ tell stories

Please note: All Observation Guide pages may be photocopied.

C. What the child understands (receptive language)

The child can understand:

- ❑ a few words that label familiar people and objects
- ❑ a fairly large number of words and simple directions (without any gestures or clues)
- ❑ many different ideas and concepts, two-part directions, and short stories
- ❑ abstract concepts, complex questions, stories with a plot

D. How the child interacts

Your conversations with the child:

- ❑ are difficult to keep going and rarely last for more than one or two turns
- ❑ last longer when the child initiates them
- ❑ are very short, but s/he will respond to your comments/questions
- ❑ last for about three or four turns each, and longer if s/he initiated the conversation
- ❑ can go on for quite a long time

Please note: All Observation Guide pages may be photocopied.

Summary of observations for First Words Users, Combiners, and Early and Later Sentence Users

a) Child is a:

❑ First Words User

❑ Combiner

❑ Early Sentence User

❑ Later Sentence User

b) How the child communicates (expressive language) seems to be:

❑ above age level

❑ at age level

❑ slightly below age level

❑ well below age level

c) Understanding (receptive language) seems to be:

❑ above age level

❑ at age level

❑ slightly below age level

❑ well below age level

d) Social interaction seems to be:

❑ above age level

❑ at age level

❑ slightly below age level

❑ well below age level

Comments:

Please note: All Observation Guide pages may be photocopied.

References

Bloom, L. & Lahey, M. (1978). *Language development and language disorders.* John Wiley & Sons.

Bowerman, M. (1979). The acquisition of complex sentences. In P. Fletcher & M. Garman, (Eds.), *Language acquisition* (pp. 285–306). Cambridge: Cambridge University Press.

Brown, R. (1983). *A first language: The early stages.* Cambridge: Harvard University Press.

Bruner, J. (1974/1975). From communication to language – A psychological perspective. *Cognition, 3,* 255–287.

Bruner, J. (1975). The ontogenesis of speech acts. *Journal of Child Language, 2,* 1–19.

Carter, A.L. (1979). Prespeech meaning relations: An outline of one infant's sensorimotor morpheme development. In P. Fletcher & M. Garman, (Eds.), *Language acquisition* (pp. 71–92). Cambridge: Cambridge University Press.

Clark, E. (1979) Building a vocabulary: Words for objects, actions and relations. In P. Fletcher & M. Garman, (Eds.), *Language acquisition* (pp. 149–160). Cambridge: Cambridge University Press.

Crystal, D. (1986). *Listen to your child.* Middlesex: Penguin Books.

Garman, M. (1979). Early grammatical development. In P. Fletcher & M. Garman, (Eds.), *Language acquisition* (pp. 177–208). Cambridge: Cambridge University Press.

Griffiths, P. (1979). Speech acts and early sentences. In P. Fletcher & M. Garman, (Eds.), *Language acquisition* (pp. 105–120). Cambridge: Cambridge University Press.

McLean, J., & Snyder-McLean, L.A. (1978). *A transactional approach to early language training.* Columbus, Ohio: Charles E. Merrill.

Olswang, L., Stoel Gammon, C. & Coggins, T. (1987). *Assessing linguistic behavior: Assessing prelinguistic and early linguistic behavior in developmentally young children.* Seattle: University of Washington Press.

Owens, R.E. (1984). *Language development.* Columbus, Ohio: Bell & Howell.

Prizant, B.M. (1988). *Early intervention: Focus on communication assessment and enhancement.* Workshop presented in Toronto, Ontario.

Reilly, J.S., Zukow, P.G. & Greenfield, P.M. (1984). Facilitating the transition from sensorimotor to linguistic communication during the one-word period. In A. Locke & E. Fischer (Eds.), *Language Development* (pp. 107–131). London: Croom Helm.

Schaffer, H.R. (1984). *The child's entry into a social world.* London: Academic Press.

Smutny, J.F., Veenker, K. & Veenker, S. (1989). *Your gifted child.* New York: Ballantine Books.

Tamir, L. (1984). Language development: New directions. In A. Locke & E. Fischer (Eds.), *Language Development* (pp. 13–20). London: Croom Helm.

Trevarthen, C. Hubley, P. (1978). Secondary intersubjectivity: Confidence, confiding and acts of meaning in the first year. In A. Lock (Ed.), *Action, gesture and symbol: The emergence of language.* (pp. 183–229) New York: Academic Press.

Umiker-Seboek, D.J. (1979). Preschool children's intraconversational narratives. *Journal of Child Language, 6,* 91–109.

Vygotsky, L. (1962). *Thought and language.* Cambridge: MIT Press.

Wetherby, A., Cain, D., Yonclas, D. & Walker, V. (1986). *Intentional communication in the emerging language of normal infants.* Miniseminar presented at the American Speech and Hearing Association Annual Convention, Detroit, Michigan.

Wetherby, A. (1991a). *Profiling communication and symbolic abilities: Assessment and intervention guidelines.* Presentation at Toronto Children's Centre, Toronto, Ontario.

Wetherby, A. (1991b). Profiling pragmatic abilities in the emerging language of young children. In T, M. Gallagher, (Ed.), *Pragmatics of language: Clinical practice issues* (pp. 249–281). San Diego, CA: Singular.

Get Every Child in on the Act – So All the Children Can Interact

Teachers in child-care settings have to ensure that every child has opportunities to interact with others throughout the day.

Sociable children create these opportunities for themselves. But children who haven't developed the necessary communication and social skills need help so they, too, can get in on the act – and interact!

In Part 2, you will read about getting every child in on the act and helping each one take part in interactions with you and with peers.

Chapter 3, "Let the Child Lead," contains practical information on how to facilitate interactions with even the most withdrawn and hard-to-reach children.

In Chapter 4, "Taking Turns Together: Helping Children Become Conversation Partners," you'll discover natural ways of developing children's abilities to take turns during interactions and conversations.

In Chapter 5, "Encourage Interactions in Group Situations: Adapt Your Activities and Routines," we take a look at how to promote interaction and conversation during those busy routines and group activities.

Chapter 6, "Get Yourself Out of the Act: Fostering Peer Interaction," describes the kind of physical environment that encourages peer interaction and what you can do to help socially isolated children become more involved with their peers.

It's not that difficult to get children in on the act. What they need is a stimulating environment, a genuinely interested conversation partner, and many opportunities for meaningful communication.

Chapter 3

Let the Child Lead

When teachers give children a chance, children initiate more frequently.
Teachers can then follow the children's lead.

A. Children who lead get the language they need

Children who initiate frequently and engage their teachers in social interactions create the ideal conditions for their own language learning – when their teachers are responsive.

Let's look at what happens when Rhumi, aged two, picks up a feather and shows it to Nina, her teacher.

Rhumi: *Look Nina!* (Rhumi establishes joint attention.)

Nina: *Oh, you've got a feather!* (Nina is responsive and provides Rhumi with the name of the object.)

Rhumi: *Fedder.* (Nina has given Rhumi simple, clear information about the object of her interest, so Rhumi pays close attention and then imitates the word "feather.")

Nina: *Yes, it's a feather, from a bird.* (Nina's response has given Rhumi a correct model for the word "feather," as well as some new information.)

Rhumi: *Bird? Outside?* (Rhumi requests more information.)

Nina: *Yes, this feather came from a bird outside.*

Nina may not realize it, but she is being very, very responsive. Rhumi initiated the interaction and Nina responded – promptly, warmly, and with interest. She's following Rhumi's lead, talking about what Rhumi is most interested in. As a result, **interaction** happens quite naturally. In addition, Nina provides Rhumi with **information** fine-tuned to her language level. This way, Rhumi can understand and learn from Nina's words. The result? Rhumi's language learning is flourishing. It's easy to see that *children who lead get the language they need.*

Language learning, however, doesn't always happen this naturally. It won't happen naturally, for example, if the teacher tries to provide **information** without making sure that **interaction** has first been established. If she tries to use Rhumi's interest as an opportunity to test the child's knowledge of birds and feathers, or to teach her the colours of feathers, Rhumi will lose interest – and the opportunity for learning will be lost. Even a sociable child can be turned off by a teacher's efforts to teach or test her when all she wants to do is to share her interest about a feather.

Rhumi has no trouble initiating conversation, but many children do, especially those with language delays. When teachers don't have much of a lead to follow, interaction is even harder to establish. And we've seen the breakdown in communication that results from the child contributing too little and the teacher either contributing too much or not spending much time interacting with the child at all.

When there is a breakdown in communication, the child can't repair it. Only you, the adult, can open the lines of communication and create opportunities for children to initiate.

Letting go of the lead

Letting the child lead may sound simple, but it's easier said than done.

For some teachers, the difficulty isn't so much in finding opportunities to let the child lead, but in changing long-standing patterns of interaction, as well as changing ideas about what a teacher's role really is. Teachers are expected to teach. Traditionally, that role has been thought of as "pouring" information into children, filling their brains with words, concepts, and knowledge. More recently, this approach has changed: teaching has become more child-centred. Letting go of the lead is part of a child-centred approach to teaching, which involves allowing children to choose conversation topics and building on their interests. Letting go of the lead is an important part of being a responsive conversation partner.

It's hard to let go of the lead . . .

. . . but look at how much fun it can be.

There are good reasons to let go of the lead and to encourage children to initiate. Children gain a great deal when teachers let go of the lead, including:

- a sense of the power and pleasure of communication
- increased self-esteem and self-confidence
- the desire to initiate in other situations, and
- many more opportunities to learn language.

Take the focus off getting the child to talk

Many teachers work with children who *can* talk but seldom do. It can be frustrating to interact with these children. Trying to make them talk by asking them questions or having them imitate words, however, won't solve the problem! Children are very sensitive to such pressure. They know when you are genuinely interacting with them and when you're interacting just to get them to talk. And if your focus is solely on getting a child to talk, you risk losing her.

The motivating force for communication comes from within, from the desire to connect with others and feel the satisfaction that results from that connection. Therefore, your challenge as a teacher is to create environments that encourage children to communicate because they *want* to communicate. Talking because someone else wants you to talk is not communication.

Pressuring a child to talk makes him talk less!

A child who seldom initiates needs time just to play with you and establish a connection. At first, she may not talk at all. As long as you follow her lead, however, and she interacts by looking at you and sharing in an activity, she is experiencing a purpose for communication – social contact. If you are patient and take the focus off talking, she will talk eventually – because she has something she really wants to say. Then, the stage is set for language learning.

Surprise! When the pressure is off...

Mine b'igger!

...and the child has something to say, he says it.

B. Observe, Wait, and Listen

Letting the child lead begins with:

Observing

Waiting

Listening

Observing, waiting, and listening are the keys to encouraging children to communicate with you. They are very effective tools for opening the doors to interaction – even with the most reluctant communicators.

Observe

Observing means paying close attention to a child so you can see exactly what she's interested in or what she's trying to tell you.

As adults, we are more tuned in to sound than to nonverbal communication. Babies and children who make enough noise – by making sounds, saying words, or crying – will get our attention. But some children, especially those with reluctant or passive conversational styles, haven't figured out how to use their voices to get attention. Nor have they developed the confidence to use them. For these children, communication may be very subtle. If you take the time to observe, however, you'll be able to see what they're "saying."

 Debbie was on the floor with Jerome, a very quiet 11-month-old. She tried to play with him, but felt she was getting nowhere – he just banged his blocks and made no sounds at all.

Observe closely, Debbie! After Jerome banged his blocks, he looked at you three times to see your reaction. That's communication!

Children with severe delays or limited motor abilities may have difficulty making sounds or moving their bodies. You must be a very keen observer to notice subtle movements or changes in body position or facial expression. These may indicate a child's interests or her attempts to get your attention. Observation Guide 2, in Chapter 2, will help you to recognize these subtle initiations, which are the beginnings of communication.

Karen is showing a picture book about animals to three-year-old Stephanie, a Discoverer with severe cerebral palsy. Stephanie seems to have a passive conversational style. She has very limited head movement and poor control of her arms for reaching or pointing. She also has difficulty making sounds. Since Stephanie can't point to the pictures or answer Karen's questions, Karen isn't sure if Stephanie is really interested in the book.

Observe closely, Karen! Stephanie's eyes widen and she smiles and extends her legs each time you show her that picture of a dog. She really is interested in the book. While you can't be sure why she likes that picture, you can show it to her more often – and find other pictures of dogs to see if she likes those too.

Stephanie, who has cerebral palsy, shows she is interested in the picture of the dog by smiling and extending her legs.

Wait – give the child a chance to initiate!

Waiting is a powerful tool because it gives the child an opportunity to initiate.

When you wait, you give the child time to initiate or to get involved in an activity. You are, in effect, giving her this message: "You're in control – I know you can communicate and I expect you to communicate. So, you decide what you want to do or say. I'll give you all the time you need."

Laura was trying to get Margie, a very shy three-year-old, to talk during a sensory activity with shaving cream. So she asked lots of questions: "What colour is it, Margie? How does it feel? What are you going to do with it?" Margie didn't respond.

Wait, Laura! Give Margie time to explore the materials and to initiate! To wait, you need to:

- stop talking
- lean forward, and
- look expectant.

When Margie initiates (and she will, when she's given the chance to play with the shaving cream in her own way), Laura needs to follow her lead, and then wait again to encourage her to initiate.

Waiting not only encourages children to initiate; it also gives them the time to respond to questions and requests.

Studies of adult-child interactions have shown that adults give children approximately one second in which to respond to questions. After one second, the adult repeats or

When you don't rush in,
When you observe, listen, and wait,
You let the child initiate!

rephrases the question or provides the answer. Only one second! Most children need much longer than one second to process questions and figure out responses. In fact, we may not want to encourage quick responses in children: some studies have shown that children who are reflective and think before responding do better in school than those who respond quickly and impulsively.

Waiting is one of the most important strategies to use with children who are language delayed and may not be able to keep up with the normal pace of conversation. These children may interact far more frequently and willingly when given time to initiate. As well, they are far more likely to respond to a question or comment when you give them enough time. Often, we don't expect children with delays to respond. As a result, we may wait barely a moment for a response before answering the question ourselves, thereby depriving children of the opportunity to express themselves. It's important not to overdo the Helper role when interacting with children with language delays – helping too much tells children that we don't expect them to communicate.

If you need to remind yourself to wait, think of the wait-and-see approach:

- Count to 10.
- Keep your hands off the activity.
- Look expectant and lean forward.
- Don't talk until the child initiates or shows what she is interested in.

Of course, once the child initiates, you'll respond with interest and enthusiasm. Then you'll wait again for the child to respond!

Listen

Listening means paying close attention to what the child is saying so that you can respond appropriately.

When you listen to a child, you let her know that what she says is important – and that's a good reason for her to continue the conversation.

Active listening involves not interrupting a child and not assuming that you understand what she is trying to say before she has finished speaking.

Four-year-old Christine was making a collage with cooked coloured noodles. She picked up a tiny piece of noodle, which was curled into a "U" shape, and glued it on to her paper. Then she showed it to her teacher, Amy.

"That's a sleigh," said Christine.

Amy, not really listening, said, "Yes, and what colour is it?"

"Red," answered Christine – and turned away.

Listen closely, Amy! Christine said something wonderfully imaginative, which you missed. If you'd listened and then said, "A sleigh! A tiny sleigh for all the ants at Christmas time!" you would have had a long conversation with her.

It's hard to talk when the "listener" isn't really listening.

Remember: Observe, Wait, and Listen is a strategy that should be used throughout an interaction, not just at its beginning. If you continue to OWL throughout an interaction, you encourage the child to stay engaged with you. You can then continue to respond to her initiations.

It's fun to have conversations when the teacher really listens!

C. Be face-to-face

In an interaction, get down to the child's physical level. Make sure you're face-to-face so that you can look directly into each other's eyes.

Why is this so important? For a child, being face-to-face with you adds a special quality to the interaction. It brings you closer to her, physically and emotionally, and makes her feel that you're really with her. Face-to-face contact is especially motivating for children with reluctant or own agenda conversational styles. When you position yourself face-to-face with a "hard-to-reach" child, she may surprise you by interacting for a long time. You'll notice a Discoverer's subtle sounds, facial expressions, and actions more easily if you can look directly into her eyes.

Here are a few ideas for face-to-face positioning:

- You sit on the floor; the child sits on a little chair.
- You lie on your stomach; the child (especially an infant) sits on the floor.
- You lie on your side with the child sitting on the floor.
- You sit on the floor with your knees bent up; a baby can sit on your knees.

If a child needs to sit in a special seat or wheelchair insert for physical support, you may need to be creative to find a face-to-face position. You may need to find a chair for yourself at just the right height, or perhaps find another seat for the child, one that will place her at a better level for interaction.

There's nothing like being face-to-face.

D. Follow the child's lead

When you follow a child's lead, you pick up on her interests and go with them. No matter how difficult a child may be to interact with, we have to believe that she has something to share, something to say. She just needs the right circumstances. So begin with a positive outlook: instead of focusing on what a child can't or doesn't do, focus on what she could or might do – if you followed her lead.

The best way to follow a child's lead is to become interested in what interests her. You can respond to any sort of initiation from the child: a look, a smile, an offer of a toy, a finger pointed toward an object of interest, a comment, or a question. If a child does not initiate to you directly, follow her lead by building on her actions.

He doesn't look at me or make any sounds or respond to his name....

Instead of being frustrated by what the child can't do . . .

For example, you could join in on her play with a toy. What's most important is that you react immediately and warmly to her interest, and that you show your own interest in her topic. The exact way you choose to respond to a child will depend upon her language stage and what she "tells" you.

*...focus on what he might be able
to do if you followed his lead.*

To follow a child's lead, you can:

- ◆ Imitate
- ◆ Interpret
- ◆ Comment
- ◆ Join in and play

These strategies aren't used one at a time: you'll find yourself using them together in various combinations throughout an interaction. Think of them as items on a buffet: pick, choose, and combine as necessary.

Imitate

Imitation is one of the most motivating strategies you can use to encourage a child to interact with you. When you imitate, you follow a child's lead by doing exactly what she does and says. You copy her actions, sounds, facial expressions, or words.

Many teachers have been surprised by so-called "unresponsive" children who become animated and interactive when they are imitated. Imitate a child with a reluctant, passive, or own agenda conversational style and you may see a different child emerge. Although you are likely to get bored with the game long before the child does, try not to stop or change the game too soon. What's boring for an adult may be just the beginning of a great time for a child.

Imitation takes different forms for children at different stages of communication development.

Discoverers enjoy it when you imitate their body movements, actions, facial expressions, and especially their sounds and babbles. They often imitate you right back!

Communicators are delighted when you imitate their actions and sounds. They will continue to perform the action or sound you have imitated to keep you engaged.

First Words Users will get a great deal of pleasure when you imitate their actions, sounds, and especially their first attempts at words. They will be far more likely to continue a conversation once you have imitated them.

Imitation is used less often with Combiners and Early or Later Sentence Users. Even children with more advanced language skills, however, respond positively to seeing you do what they do, especially if they have reluctant, passive, or own agenda conversational styles.

Observe, Wait, and Listen, then imitate – babies think it's really great!

Interpret

As a caregiver, your task is to interpret a child's message by putting into words what you think she means. This is a powerful way of letting the child know that she has been heard and understood.

Interpreting for the Discoverer: "give meaning to the message"

A Discoverer does not yet understand language and has not yet developed the ability to send messages directly to you. Therefore, you need to interpret her behaviour as if it were meaningful and intentional – with an enthusiastic comment. Even though the child may not understand what you're saying, you're treating her as if her behaviour is intentional. She'll discover that her behaviour can make things happen, and that her sounds, cries, looks, and body movements do indeed communicate.

For example, if an infant looks at a toy, follow her line of vision to see what she's interested in and say, "Oh, you like that bunny!" Then give the toy to her. If she sneezes, you could say, "Oh dear! What a big sneeze!" If she makes a sound while she's waiting to be taken out of her stroller, you could say, "Yes, I know. You want to get out of your stroller." If she picks up her coat, you could say, "You have your coat. You want your coat 'on'."

When Mira picks up her coat, her teacher, Rhea, interprets her behaviour to mean that Mira wants to put her coat on.

You have your coat. You want your coat on.

Interpreting for the Communicator:
say it "as she would if she could"

Interpreting is used somewhat differently with Communicators, who use sounds and gestures to send intentional messages directly to you. To learn how to send messages with words (or signs or pictures if she is unable to develop speech), a Communicator needs you to interpret her messages by "saying it as she would if she could." When you interpret by providing the words, the Communicator hears a language model she can learn from.

When a child finds it very difficult to produce words, interpreting her message will include a combination of:

- ◆ "saying it as she would if she could" and
- ◆ using an appropriate sign, or pointing to or handing over a picture card.

This combination provides the child with a language model that she can learn from as well as a nonverbal means of communication that she can use to communicate in the more immediate future.

Instead of telling the child what you'll do . . .

. . . let him hear you "translate" his message, saying it as he would if he could.

Interpreting for the First Words User:
say it "as she would if she could" until she can say it herself

A First Words User continues to communicate with sounds and gestures while she learns to use words. Continue to interpret her nonverbal messages by "saying it as she would if she could" or, for children with speech difficulties, by demonstrating an alternative way to communicate, like using a sign or picture.

Remember to talk slowly and clearly and to wait after you are finished. Maybe you'll get lucky and the child will repeat your words or actions!

Alexander's oral motor difficulties make it hard for him to say words. His teacher interprets his message by "saying it as he would if he could" and showing him another way to communicate — by pointing to a picture.

Comment

We all like to feel that we are being listened to. Children are no exception. When you comment in response to a child's initiation, she knows that you have received her message and that you are interested in it – and in her. At the same time, you provide her with information she can learn from.

Many teachers respond to a child's initiation by asking a question rather than by making a comment. While it may seem that a question or a direction has a better chance than a comment of getting a response back from a child, too many questions and instructions can turn a child off, especially if she feels she is being tested and pressured to respond. Comments, on the other hand, express your interest and entice a child to interact with you. They can also provide interesting information to which a child will want to respond. If a child doesn't respond to a comment, you can always change the comment to a question or rephrase what you have said. Since comments don't require as clear-cut a response as questions and directions, children may take time to learn how to respond to them. With practice, however, they will learn.

Respond in a way that shows the child you're interested.

When commenting, do:

- respond immediately – or you may lose your opportunity
- reflect what the child is interested in – or you may lose the child
- respond with warmth and enthusiasm – and you will build the child's confidence and desire to interact; and
- wait to see if the child will respond to what you have said. Some children need time to think before responding.

When commenting, don't:

- respond by saying "good job" or "good talking." This ends conversations.
- talk for too long. Say something briefly and then wait for the child to respond.

Sarah showed Maria that her doll's hair was wet. Maria followed her lead but asked a testing question, which Sarah didn't want to answer.

Sarah didn't want to respond to an instruction either.

This comment captured Sarah's interest, and she wanted to respond to it.

Join in and play

When children are playing, the best way to follow their lead is to join in, especially if you act like a kid yourself! The kind of kid you become will depend on a child's language stage and conversational style. While you may find that joining in and playing can be a challenge, it can be very helpful for children who are Discoverers or who have reluctant, passive, or own agenda conversational styles.

When you join in and play with a child who has a reluctant conversational style, you build on her interests and take the focus off talking. The main focus becomes playing together and having fun – and this often opens the door to conversation.

A child with a passive conversational style (most often children with language delays who are Discoverers) may produce few actions or potential initiations to follow. You may need to begin by creating opportunities to encourage the child to take the lead. Suggestions found later in this chapter on "Help the Child to Take the Lead" may be helpful.

Joining in and playing may be the best way to encourage a child with an own agenda conversational style to become interested in you.

Joining in with a Discoverer

A Discoverer may be a young infant or an older child with a significant language delay. Since Discoverers have a limited number of interests and have not yet learned to share these interests with you, it's often difficult to join in and play with them. Sometimes, a Discoverer may be so interested in manipulating a toy or object that she may seem to ignore your efforts to get her attention. Don't take this behaviour personally! All it means is that she is able to focus her attention on only one thing at a time and has difficulty with joint attention, being unable to focus on both a person and an object at the same time.

You need to look for opportunities to work yourself into a Discoverer's activities. This may mean gently intruding on her solitary play and turning it into a positive two-way interaction. Some children may not be too happy about of your intrusions at first. With some playful persistence on your part, however, solitary activity can be turned into interaction.

> **You can help a Discoverer learn to share her interests in an object or activity with you and develop joint attention if you:**
> - Respond to even the briefest eye contact
> - Get her attention by being very interesting and imitate whenever possible
> - Talk animatedly about what she is doing, use "fun" words to get her attention, and point to the toys
> - Build on her focus by making the game more interesting
> - Turn a chance action into a game
> - Play the "you give it to me and then I'll give it to you" game

Respond to even the briefest eye contact

There are many steps on the road to developing joint attention. The most important one is when a child who is playing with a toy or another object begins to look up at an adult – even for just a second. This moment is the beginning of sharing experience: it's as if the child is saying, "See this?" or "Are you still here?" Get excited when the child looks up at you. Respond with an animated comment, as if she had actually said something to you. You could say, "That's a nice block to chew," or "Yes, I'm watching you" – whatever comes to mind in response to that fleeting look.

Get the child's attention by being very interesting and imitate whenever possible

If a child is engrossed in her play and isn't looking up at you at all, you have to make yourself interesting enough to get her attention. Imitate her sounds and actions – that often encourages her to imitate you back. You can also call her name or make a fun, interesting sound (e.g., sing a song, whistle, make noisy blowing sounds, imitate the sound of the toy she's playing with) to remind her that you are there. She might then look up at you. Once she does, be ready to move on to the next step.

Talk animatedly about what the child is doing and point to the toys

Use lots of intonation as you talk animatedly while the child continues to play with a toy. For example, use a tone of excitement and anticipation if something interesting is about to happen with the toy. If a block is about to fall, you can exclaim, "Uh oh . . . it's going to FALL!" Comment animatedly if a toy makes a noise, "Ooh! What a big noise!" The child may look at you briefly when you do this, which is exactly where this process of joint attention begins. You should also point to objects as you make comments like, "Oh, there's the big block!" or "Look, the bunny popped up!" so she knows which object you're talking about.

These comments draw the child's attention to you and to the activity. The pointing helps the child focus on both the object and you – the person doing the pointing. Eventually, she will learn to follow your point, another key step on the road to joint attention.

An excellent way of getting a child's attention is to use "fun words" in an animated way. Fun words appeal to children because they are fun to listen to and often easy to imitate. For example the following fun words are bound to elicit a smile from Discoverers: "Uh oh" (when something falls or disappears), "Boom!" (when something bangs), and "Shhhh" (for sleep or quiet).

Michael is a two-year-old who is significantly delayed in his development, including his language development. He plays well with a pop-up animal toy on his own but does not respond at all to Nina, his teacher, when she tries to join in on the activity. Nina gets onto the floor and lies on her stomach across from Michael. She makes encouraging comments as Michael pushes the buttons, like, "Oh, you're pushing that button! Push hard!" and reacts with exaggerated surprise, saying "Pop!" each time another animal pops up. Soon, Michael looks up at Nina after she says, "Pop!" Then he begins to anticipate Nina's reaction by looking at her as soon as he pushes the button. Nina says an animated, "Pop!" and Michael smiles with delight. By joining in with Michael as he plays and using "fun words," Nina is helping him develop joint attention.

Build on the child's focus by making the game more interesting

Join in the child's play by building on her focus so that you become as interesting or more interesting than the toy.

First observe the child carefully. Once you see what she does with the toy:

- **imitate her actions.** Rather than expecting the child to share her toy with you, try imitating with a similar toy. Or, you can try imitating the toy's action with your hands (e.g., move your hands up and down to mimic the pop-up action of a jack-in-the-box). If a child is interested in lining up or stacking objects, you can try adding your own object to the stack or line-up.

- **move the toy as if it was alive** (e.g., pretend to make a toy animal jump up and down, or "zoom" a block up in the air in a playful manner).
- **make yourself part of the toy** (e.g., if the child is interested in a cup, put the cup on your head and playfully let it fall off. Use a "fun" word like "Oops!").

1. Maria observes Alexa taking blocks out of a container and casting them aside.

2. Maria playfully takes one of the blocks that Alexa has thrown aside.

3. Alexa watches as Maria makes herself part of the toy by placing the block on her head.

4. Alexa laughs aloud when Maria pretends to sneeze, causing the block to fall off her head. Maria was able to successfully turn Alexa's solitary play into a two-way interaction by building on her focus and developing a fun game.

Turn a chance action into a game

Sometimes, the best way to join in with a Discoverer is to create a game from a chance action the child performs by doing something interesting or imitating what the child says or does.

Jodi was feeding Rafael, an eight-month-old baby. As she leaned in close to give him a spoonful of cereal, he reached out and tapped her cheek. Jodi grabbed his fingers and pretended to eat them, and then let go. Rafael smiled and reached out again. Once more, Jodi grabbed his fingers, pretending to eat them – "Num num num!" This game went on for many minutes, much to Rafael's delight.

Creative games, created from simple random actions, have the potential to teach the child a great deal about joint attention – and about how much fun teachers can be to interact with.

Play the "you give it to me and then I'll give it to you" game

When a child is holding an object, you can join in by putting out your hand to ask her to give it to you. You may have to take the object from her and then hand it right back. This give-and-take game can go on for hours. It's very motivating for the child once she figures out exactly how to play. You can make the give-and-take game fun by exclaiming loudly every time the child hands the toy back to you.

The child learns some vital things from this game: she learns to reach, which is the first step towards the development of a meaningful reaching gesture. She also learns that she can interact with you and an object at the same time – the beginning of learning to share experiences.

Regardless of whether the Discoverer is a six-month-old infant or a language-delayed two-year-old, this give-and-take game is an important part of learning to communicate.

Joining in with a Communicator

You can join in with a Communicator if you:
- Play alongside the child and wait to see if you're invited in
- Imitate what the child does
- Join in by playing a game the child knows well

Play alongside the child and wait to see if you're invited in

Join in on a Communicator's play by first sitting beside her and waiting to see if you're invited to join in. The invitation may be very subtle, like a smile, a change in body position, or a look. As soon as she initiates, join in.

Observe, wait, and listen as you join in so you know what the child's focus is. Don't be tempted to change the focus and to start doing something different to try to distract her from what she is doing. The rewards of joining in are great when you build on a child's focus. She will be delighted to interact with you and the play may continue for a long time.

Imitate what the child does

Imitating is one of the most powerful ways of joining in with a child. Often, when you imitate a child, she will immediately imitate you back, starting a game that continues back and forth for quite a while. For example, if you see a Communicator dropping objects into a container (an activity they love to do), get some of your own pieces and take your turn dropping blocks into a bucket alongside her. She may begin to notice what you are doing and may watch to see if you drop your block into your bucket after she drops hers. If you're patient, she may even begin to use your bucket or offer you hers.

Join in by playing a game the child knows well

Some "hard-to-reach" children can be engaged quite easily if you play a game they love to play. Even older children with language delays will be delighted if you play "I'm gonna get you" or roll the ball back and forth with them. These games are easy to play because they are so simple and repetitive (see Chapter 4 for more information on Social Routines) and because they are active and lots of fun. At first, joining in may involve you setting up the game so a child can join in with you. Soon, however, the child will be the one to start the game and get you to join in with her!

Jake now knows how to start the hide and seek game – and how to get Nancy to join in.

Joining in with First Words Users, Combiners, and Early Sentence Users

When you join in the play of children who are developing language and engaging in "pretend" play, you have many opportunities to encourage and extend the play. At these stages, you may not want to simply imitate a child's play. Instead, become a kid yourself! Play a pretend role alongside the children. The more fun you are to be with, the longer the children will interact with you – and the more opportunities you'll have to provide them with language models that match their interests.

So, join in, act a bit like a kid, and have fun. But remember not to take over the play. Continue to observe, wait, and listen to encourage children to keep initiating.

Joining in with a Later Sentence User

A Later Sentence User is able to talk about more abstract topics that are not part of the "here and now." At this point, conversations may really take off: you may find yourself discussing a topic that has nothing to do with the play activity at hand. This is just fine – it's a sign of the Later Sentence User's increasingly sophisticated use of language. At these times, joining in the play may not be as important as just sitting with the child and "chatting." Remember – go with the flow and talk about what the child is interested in.

Conversations can really take off with Later Sentence Users.

E. Watch turn-taking take off

When you observe, wait, listen, and follow the children's lead, you'll have more fun with them and your interactions will last much longer. You'll discover that you and the children are responding, quite spontaneously, in turn to one another. You are, in fact, taking turns.

Turn-taking is a bit like two people taking turns on a see-saw. In a conversation, however, the two people are taking turns sending and receiving messages. The turns may involve talking, but they don't need to. A turn can be a look, a sound, a point, a sign, a word, a sentence, a story, or a combination of any of these.

Children gain a great deal from the playful, spontaneous interactions they have with you when the turns just keep on going. They are not only learning language, but discovering what it takes to be a conversation partner (and it takes a lot!). Helping children become more effective turn-takers will be discussed at greater length in Chapter 4.

When you observe, wait, and listen, and
follow the child's lead, turn-taking takes off.

F. Help a child take the lead – give a reason to communicate and then wait

Sometimes, observing, waiting, and listening to a child isn't enough to encourage her to initiate. Children with passive, reluctant, or own agenda conversational styles may need you to engineer the environment to motivate them to interact and communicate. Engineering is most often needed by children with significant language delays.

The rule of thumb for giving a child a reason to communicate is: set up the situation, let the child initiate, and then set up the situation again to see if you can get more initiations.

Build in opportunities for children to initiate and communicate in group activities:
- Place something you know the child likes within her view, but out of reach
- Introduce hard-to-operate toys that encourage the child to ask for help
- Do the unexpected
- Offer things bit by bit
- Offer choices
- Wait and see what the child will do: avoid the helper role

Place something you know the child likes within her view, but out of reach.

For example:
- Place a favourite toy on a shelf out of the child's reach.
- At snack time, place food like Cheerios or crackers in a clear container that is hard to open.
- During a gluing activity, offer a glue bottle that is hard to open.

Once you've set up the situation, lean in, look expectant, and wait quietly for the child to let you know that she wants the object. She may look at the object, reach for it, lean in its direction, or simply look excited when she sees it. Interpret her actions immediately! Say, "Oh, you want the jack-in-the-box!" as you give it to her.

Introduce hard-to-operate toys that encourage the child to ask for help

Hard-to-operate toys encourage interaction since children need your help to make them work and they are very motivated to seek that help. Depending upon a child's abilities, you can either demonstrate the toy and wait to see if she'll ask you to repeat the action, or offer the toy to the child and wait to see if she'll ask for help.

You can try wind-up toys, squeeze toys, pop-up toys, spinning tops, music boxes and other noise-makers, balloons, or bubbles.

Wind-up toys are usually motivating enough to get even the most reluctant communicator to initiate. Activate a wind-up toy so it moves or jumps for a few seconds (you don't want it to be activated for too long). When it stops, WAIT! Lean in, observe, and wait for the child to let you know she wants the object to move again. Depending on her stage of communication development, she may reach for it, wriggle excitedly, pick up the object, touch it, or just look at it. Say, "More jumping!" and quickly wind up the toy again a few times.

Jennifer is a two-year-old Communicator with a developmental delay. She sometimes requests with sounds and gestures. However, she has a passive conversational style and rarely initiates any communication at preschool. Her teacher, Melanie, has noticed that Jennifer seems interested in watching the other children play with bubbles but does nothing to join in with the activity.

Use the bubbles to give Jennifer a reason to communicate, Melanie! Sit face-to-face with her, blow a bubble, and wait to see what she does next. If Jennifer wants another bubble, she may move her body, look at you, make a sound, reach, or smile – all initiations you can follow by blowing another bubble.

Jennifer watches Melanie blow the bubbles but she does not initiate, so . . .

. . . Melanie waits expectantly and asks, "More bubbles?" to encourage Jennifer to communicate.

Do the unexpected

Doing something unexpected may attract a child's attention and get a reaction. For example:

- Do something silly like putting her hat on your head. Wait to see what she does.
- Make mistakes on purpose, like offering a child an article of clothing that belongs to someone else. You can also try putting a clothing item where it doesn't belong. Think about what a child might do if you put his shoe on his hand! Offer the child some food he doesn't like or doesn't expect, like a carrot on a cracker instead of cheese. Watch for his reaction.

When you do the unexpected, you may have to wait expectantly for a number of seconds to give the child a chance to react. It's important not to talk too much while waiting – and not to give up waiting if the child doesn't respond immediately. Given time, most children *will* respond. If a child initiates non-verbally, interpret by saying what you think they would say if they could: "That's Sarah's hat! It's not Jenny's hat – it's Sarah's hat!"

Offer things bit by bit

Make it easy for a child to make lots of requests by not giving her too much of anything all at once. She can request juice six times if you give her only a little at a time. If you're handing out utensils for playdough, give her one utensil and wait for her to request the next one.

Offer choices

Rather than giving the child something, let her choose – and communicate in the process. It is best to start with only two choices at a time, initially offering one thing the child really likes and one thing the child dislikes. Hold the choices up in front of the child and wait for her to respond. You could:

- offer a choice of foods at snack time
- let the child choose which clothing item to put on first – hat or mitts? – or
- offer a choice of toys.

Wait and see what the child will do: avoid the helper role

Try to avoid jumping in too quickly when a child needs assistance in familiar daily routines. Instead, wait and see what the child will do or ask for. For example, wait and see what the child will do when:

- a button or shoelaces need to be done up
- she wants to go out and the door needs to be opened
- the light needs to be turned on
- she's standing at the sink about to wash her hands, but the tap has not been turned on, or
- something has been dropped on the floor.

G. Set a limit on limits

It might seem strange that the topic of setting limits finds its way into a chapter called "Let the Child Lead." It might seem that setting limits has little bearing on language development. Yet the ways in which limits are set, and the situations in which they are set, can have a significant impact on both teacher-child interactions and on a child's interactions with her peers.

This discussion is not about behaviour that is obviously unsafe, aggressive, or disruptive. Rather, it's about those behaviours that drive many teachers crazy. It's about the different attitudes teachers bring to limit-setting, based upon their backgrounds, cultures, personalities, moods, and day-to-day stresses. It is also about putting children in situations that demand more from them than they are able to give. It's about encouraging natural curiosity, spontaneity, and exploration – and about not expecting too much. It is about letting children lead whenever possible. It is about creating situations that **prevent** misbehaviour and that provide more opportunities for positive interactions.

A child may want to initiate, but if she expects a negative response, she won't take the risk.

Let's consider Zoë, a four-year-old with a very loud voice. She is playing with some children in the dramatic play area. Although she doesn't realize it, her voice can be heard right across the room. Joyce, her teacher, tells her to use her "inside" voice, which Zoë does for a few seconds. But she soon gets caught up in the play again, and her voice goes up once more.

Joyce comes over to the dramatic play area and says to her: "Zoë, I asked you to use your inside voice and you didn't. So you'll have to go somewhere else, where you can play quietly."

Zoë is devastated. She walks around the room, head bowed, not really understanding why she is being punished. She had no idea her voice was so loud. She avoids Joyce. And because she feels so unhappy, she doesn't even play with the other children.

Here lies the connection between limit-setting and language development: children can become intimidated and disheartened in an environment that imposes too many unnecessary limits. Intimidated and disheartened children initiate less. And teachers who impose unrealistic limits spend a lot of time dealing with behavioural issues and less time having positive interactions with the children. The overall result is dejected children, fewer positive social interactions, and less language learning.

It all boils down to realistic expectations

Every day, children behave in ways that may appear to be inappropriate. Before you reach this conclusion about a child's behaviour, ask yourself: "Are my expectations realistic?"

It's important to consider the child's age, stage of cognitive and language development, and the overall situation.

Situation 1: Flour power!

Akila, aged four, is playing with flour at the sensory table. She brushes the flour off her hands in an effort to clean them. As she does, she creates a puff of "smoke." What a surprise! She immediately does it again, but this time she claps her hands together for greater effect. Behold – a nice, big puff of "smoke!" The other children see Akila's play and immediately join in, filling the air with huge puffs of "smoke" and the room with shrieks of laughter. Sue, the teacher, says, "Please stop that. You're getting flour all over the floor."

Instead of putting a stop to the children's play, ask yourself, "Are my expectations realistic?

Sue asked herself: "are my expectations realistic?"

She wasn't sure, so she gave herself these two tests:

1. The three good reasons test: Have I got three good reasons for stopping this activity?

(This test doesn't apply when children's safety is involved.)

Sue's reasons for not allowing the flour play:

       a. It makes a mess (not a good enough reason).

       b. The children are noisy (not a good enough reason either).

       c. Uh . . . (can't think of another reason!)

2. The "why are they doing this?" test

The children are enjoying the cause-and-effect of clapping their hands and creating puffs of smoke. This is very normal (and desirable) behaviour.

Alternative solution:

Allow the behaviour. Sue could follow the children's lead by joining in or by commenting on what they are doing.

Sue could follow the children's lead.

> Look at that huge puff of smoke!!

Afterwards, Sue could get the children to help clean up the mess on the floor.

Situation 2: Waiting and waiting . . . to go outdoors

It's the middle of winter and the toddlers are being helped into their boots and snowsuits for outdoor play. Some of them are all bundled up and ready to go, but they can't go until the others are ready. As they wait, they get hot, sweaty, and restless. One child pushes his neighbour and another pulls off his friend's hat. The crying starts. Sylvie, one of the teachers, tells the children to settle down and wait till everyone is ready.

It's hard for children to stay calm when they have to wait to go outside

Sylvie asked herself: "Are my expectations realistic?"

In this case, no. Toddlers can't be expected to wait patiently, especially when they are so warmly dressed.

Alternative solution:

Avoid putting children in situations where they can't cope. Sylvie splits up the children: those who are dressed first go ahead with another teacher. Not only does this reduce negative interactions, but it increases opportunities for positive interactions. (Adapting routines to encourage interaction will be discussed in more detail in Chapter 5.)

Situation 3: "But I'm not finished yet!"

Four-year-old Bihnle has been sitting at a table where, for the last 15 minutes, she has been drawing a very detailed picture. Mark, her teacher, tells her to tidy up because it's circle time. At first, she ignores him, trying hard to finish the last bit of the picture. Mark sees that she's not helping to tidy up, and he tells her to stop what she's doing right away and go and help the other children. Bihnle bursts into tears, saying, "But I'm not finished yet!"

Mark asked himself: "Are my expectations realistic?"

In this case, no. Adults also find it extremely difficult to leave an activity in which they are engrossed. And concentration and persistence are positive qualities – ones that need to be recognized.

Alternative solutions:

Prevent the situation. Give the child lots of warning before the transition occurs.
Recognize the child's feelings. If Bihnle is still not finished when the time is up, Mark could say, "It's hard when you want to finish something and you don't have the time."
Accommodate the child when possible. Mark could let Bihnle join the circle when she has finished her picture. Or he could put the picture in a place where she could come back to it later, perhaps after her nap.

Situation 4: "You Can't Catch Me!"

Ricardo, aged two, is walking back to his room from the washroom with Christina, his teacher, and two other children. As they walk through the preschool room to get back to the toddler room, he runs and hides behind a partition. Christina calls him back, but he smiles mischievously and stays put. She tells the preschool teacher that she'll be back for Ricardo and takes the other two children back to the toddler room. When she comes back for Ricardo, she takes his hand and says, "I don't like it when you run away from me." Ricardo pulls away and protests loudly.

Christina asked herself: "Are my expectations realistic?"

Well, it seems unrealistic to expect toddlers to do everything they are told. And here Ricardo was obviously initiating a game.

Alternative solution:

Avoid a confrontation: try playful distraction. Christina hides on the other side of the partition, and says, "Where's Ricardo?" Then she jumps out, peers over the partition, and squeals, "There he is!" Ricardo is delighted. He giggles and crouches low as Christina hides again. The game continues for a few more turns. Then Christina says, "I'm going to catch you! You'd better run!" and she pretends to chase him all the way back to their room.

Ricardo and Christina gain a happy interaction and a moment of closeness – and Ricardo still ends up where he's supposed to be.

Situation 5: All in a stew

Rashid, aged 18 months, is not very impressed with his lunch. He tries some stew, but he can't seem to sink his teeth into it. He picks up some meat and throws it onto the floor. Heather, his teacher, sees this and says, "You're obviously not hungry." She picks him up from behind without warning, takes him to his cot, and lays him down. As she walks away, Rashid starts to cry.

Heather asked herself: "Are my expectations realistic?"

Not for an 18-month-old. Rashid still has a lot to learn about table manners! And Heather can use this situation to show him what he should do with his food when he doesn't like it.

Alternative solution:

Set limits in a positive manner:

1. Tell the child what he should do, rather than what he shouldn't (e.g., "Leave your food on your plate, Rashid. See? On the plate.").
2. Give a reason for the limit (e.g., "You make a mess when you throw food on the floor. A big mess!").
3. Reinforce appropriate behaviour (e.g., "Good, Rashid! Your food is on your plate.").

Summary

When teachers let children lead by observing, waiting, listening, and following their lead, they encourage children to initiate and participate actively in interactions. When teachers imitate children, interpret their messages, make relevant comments, and join in and play, interactions are more fun, and therefore longer, with more turn-taking. And when teachers set limits only when necessary, interactions in the classroom remain positive, frequent, and enjoyable for everyone.

References

Bondurant, J.L., Romeo, D.J. & Kretschmer, R. (1983). Language behavior of mothers of children with normal and delayed language. *Language, Speech and Hearing Services in Schools, 14*(4), 233–242.

Bruner, J. S. (1975). The ontogenesis of speech acts. *Journal of Child Language, 2,* 1–19.

Craig, H. K. (1983). Applications of pragmatic language models for intervention. In T. M. Gallagher & C. A. Prutting (Eds.), *Pragmatic Assessment and Intervention Issues in Language* (pp. 101–127). San Diego, CA: College-Hill Press.

Deci, E.L. (1980). *The psychology of self-determination.* Lexington, Mass: Lexington Books.

Deci, E.L. & Ryan, R.M. (1985). *Intrinsic motivation and self-determination in human behavior.* New York: Plenum Press.

Duchan, J.F. (1984). Clinical interactions with autistic children: The role of theory. *Topics in Language Disorders, 4*(4), 62–71.

Fey, M.E. (1986). *Language intervention with young children.* San Diego, CA: College Hill Press.

Girolametto, L. (1986). *Developing dialogue skills of mothers and their developmentally delayed children: An intervention study.* Unpublished doctoral dissertation. University of Toronto, Toronto.

Girolametto, L. (1988). Improving the social-conversational skills of developmentally delayed children: An intervention study. *Journal of Speech and Hearing Disorders, 53,* 156–167.

Harris, J. (1984). Teaching children to develop language: The impossible dream. In D.J. Müller (Ed.), *Remediating children's language: Behavioral and naturalistic approaches* (pp. 231–242). San Diego: College Hill Press.

Hendrick, J. (1984). *The whole child.* St Louis: Times Mirror/Mosby.

Hubbell, R.D. (1977). On facilitating spontaneous talking in young children. *Journal of Speech and Hearing Disorders, 42,* 216–231.

Hubbell, R.D. (1981). *Children's language disorders: An integrated approach.* Englewood Cliffs, NJ: Prentice Hall.

Lieven, E.M. (1984). Interactional style and children's language learning. *Topics in Language Disorders, 4*(4), 15–23

Lock, A. (Ed.). (1978). *Action, gesture and symbol: The emergence of language.* New York: Academic Press.

MacDonald, J.D. (1982a). Communication strategies for language intervention. In D.P. McLowry, A.M. Guilford & S.O. Richardson (Eds.), *Infant communication: Development, assessment and intervention* (pp. 83–146). New York: Grune and Stratton.

MacDonald, J.D. (1982b). *Language through conversation: A communication model for language intervention.* Nisonger Center, Ohio State University.

Mahoney, G.J. (1975). Ethological approach to delayed language acquisition. *American Journal of Mental Deficiency, 80* (2), 139–148.

McDonald, L. & Pien, D. (1982). Mother conversational behavior as a function of interactional intent. *Journal of Child Language, 9,* 337–358.

McLean, J., & Snyder-McLean, L.A. (1978). *A transactional approach to early language training.* Columbus, Ohio: Charles E. Merrill.

Newhoff, M. & Browning, J. (1983). Interactional variation: A view from the language disordered child's world. *Topics in Language Disorders, 4*(1), 49–60.

Prutting, C. (1982). Pragmatics as social competence. *Journal of Speech and Hearing Disorders, 47,* 123–134.

Schaffer, H.R. (1984). *The child's entry into a social world.* London: Academic Press.

Snow, C.E. (1984). Parent-child interaction and the development communicative ability. In R.L. Schiefelbusch & J. Pickar (Eds.), *The acquisition of communicative competence* (pp. 69–107). Baltimore: University Park Press.

Snow, C.E., Midkiff-Borunda, S., Small, A. & Proctor, A. (1984). Therapy as social interaction: Analyzing the contexts for language remediation. *Topics in Language Disorders, 4,*(4), 72–85.

Sugarman, S. (1984). The development of preverbal communication: Its contribution and limits in promoting the development of language. In R.L. Schiefelbusch & J. Pickar (Eds.), *The acquisition of communicative competence* (pp. 23–67). Baltimore: University Park Press.

Wells, G. (1981). *Language through interaction.* New York: Cambridge University Press.

Wells, G. (1986). *The meaning makers: Children learning language and using language to learn.* Portsmouth, New Hampshire: Heinemann.

Learning Language and Loving It

Chapter 4

Taking Turns Together: Helping Children Become Conversation Partners

Children learn the rules of conversation by participating in interactions.

A. Adults help children learn the rules of conversation

Conversations with children begin at birth, long before infants understand any words. While these conversations may be one-sided at first (i.e., you do most of the communicating), they provide the foundation upon which all of a child's future conversations will be built. Within these early conversations, children hear their caregivers talk, and contribute to these conversations using the communication skills available to them. Through this back-and-forth exchange, children learn to communicate and, ultimately, to use language. Your task as an educator is to help children learn how to interact and have conversations, starting from birth.

Learning to take part in conversations is a complex process. Conversations are like a game for two or more players – a game made complicated because of its many rules. The only way inexperienced players (infants and young children) can learn these rules is by playing the game with a more experienced player (like you). Once they learn the basic rules, their ability to participate in conversations improves, dramatically increasing their opportunities for learning language.

These are some of the rules of the "conversation game":
- Initiate interactions, or respond when others initiate.
- Take a turn at the appropriate time.
- Give the other person a chance to take a turn.
- Pay attention to the speaker.
- Continue the conversation by taking additional turns on the topic.
- Send clear messages.
- Clear up misunderstandings.
- Stick to the subject (not as easy as it sounds!).
- Initiate a new topic, when appropriate.

Although we expect children to have difficulty following all these rules, it's important to note that adults have difficulty following them, too! Think of the adults you know who talk too much or who interrupt when you're trying to speak. They consistently break the rule of giving others a turn. People who don't look at you during a conversation break the rule of paying attention to the speaker (making you feel uncomfortable in the process). When someone changes the subject abruptly or mumbles, he or she is breaking the rules of sticking to the subject and sending clear messages.

As the more experienced conversation partner, your task is twofold: first, to ensure that a child has frequent opportunities to interact and, second, when interacting with him, to help him stay in the game and learn its rules. In Chapter 3, you learned how to get an interaction going by following the child's lead. In this chapter, you will learn how to keep that interaction going. This skill is important for all children, but especially for reluctant communicators and for children who are language delayed.

Support children in taking turns

The strategies you use to support children as they learn the conversation game are like the scaffolds that hold up a building while it is under construction. As construction progresses, the walls and supporting structures take shape. As the building begins to support itself, the scaffolds are gradually removed until they disappear entirely. Adults use conversational scaffolds when they interact with children, taking their turns in ways that make it easy for children to take theirs.

In the beginning, adults use lots of supports to ensure that children take their turns successfully. For example, we accept any of a child's actions, sounds, or facial expressions as his turn, even though he does not yet understand what he is supposed to do. As he becomes a more experienced conversation partner, we use fewer and different supports, always ensuring that we make it as easy as possible for him to take his turn. If he can't take a turn because he doesn't understand what we've said to him, we say it again slowly or change our words, making sure that he can take his turn and that he stays in the conversation.

Many children with language delays, even those who are Sentence Users, still need adults to support them during conversations since their limited conversational and comprehension skills can make it difficult for them to know when and how to take a turn.

> Children can contribute so much more when you support them in interactions.

Teachers can help children become equal partners in conversations.

B. Laying the foundation for conversations: Treat Discoverers like turn-takers

Infants' brains are wired for language learning. Only by being engaged in interactions, however, can they begin to learn. Without realizing it, adult caregivers engage Discoverers (whether they are infants or young children with language delays) in interactions by treating them like turn-takers. At this early stage, anything at all qualifies as a turn – a widening of the eyes, a grimace, a yawn, a sound, or even a wriggle! By being treated like a turn-taker, the Discoverer enters the wonderful world of interaction.

> **You can lay the foundation for conversations if you:**
> - Talk to Discoverers as if they can talk to you
> - Set the stage for conversations: Help the child develop joint attention
> - Make social routines part of your everyday interactions
> - Make turn-taking in social routines easy for the Discoverer
> - Create social routines in response to the child's interests, sounds, and actions

Talk to Discoverers as if they can talk to you

Watch a caregiver interact with a very young infant and you'll see how she treats almost anything the baby does as if it were an attempt to communicate. When the baby burps, she says, "Oh, what a big burp! Now you feel better!" When he startles in response to a loud noise, she says, "What was that big noise?"

When the caregiver responds, she doesn't speak the way she would to an older child. Rather, she speaks with lots of animation, exaggerating her intonation and facial expressions in order to hold the child's attention and get him to respond again. The principle of "talking to the child as if he can talk to you" applies not only to typically developing infants but to any Discoverer who has yet to discover his power to affect others.

You will notice that when caregivers talk to Discoverers, they ask lots of questions. For example, if you sneezed and an infant looked at you in surprise, you would quite instinctively say "Did I scare you?" rather than "I scared you!" Even though infants at this stage of language development don't understand the meaning of the words, the question's rising intonation pattern seems to be interesting for them to listen to and helps keep their attention.

When you treat a Discoverer's behaviour as if it were intentional, you are establishing a pattern of turn-taking long before he has any idea what turn-taking is about. You are giving him a turn, even though he doesn't know it. This interaction starts out as a very one-sided affair because you take most of the turns.

As an infant develops, you expect more and more from him. By seven months, he has become more interactive and can make a variety of babbling sounds. Now, you can have long "conversations" with him, making sounds back and forth to one another. Once the infant can do this, you hold out for those kinds of sounds when you're trying to get him to take a turn, no longer accepting burps or coughs as turns.

Matthew has a developmental delay and is at the Discoverer stage. While he doesn't yet send direct messages, his teacher treats him like a turn-taker and interprets his actions as meaningful.

Set the stage for conversations: Help develop joint attention

Very early on, Discoverers get the idea of how face-to-face interactions work. They learn to look at you, make sounds back and forth, and they love to play face-to-face games like Peek-a-Boo and Pat-a-Cake. Interactions involving toys and other objects, however, take longer to establish. That's because the child is not yet able to establish joint attention. He can either pay attention to you or to the object, but not to both. Chapter 3 pages 85–88, describes strategies you can use to join in with a Discoverer and help him develop joint attention. For example, to get a child interested in a teddy bear, you first have to get the child's attention, so you might have to:

 ◆ call the child's name a number of times
 ◆ make funny faces
 ◆ shake the bear in front of him
 ◆ playfully touch him with the bear again and again, or
 ◆ say, "Here comes the teddy!" and zoom the bear in from the side.

You can see that you may have to take many turns before getting a response. However, as soon as the child shows some interest by looking at or reaching for the bear, you treat this response as his turn. Then, once again, you take a number of turns to try to hook him into taking another turn, using animation, facial expressions, gestures, and exaggerated intonation. Gradually, he comes to recognize and respond to these cues more consistently, resulting in interactions that can go back and forth for several turns.

The need to help Discoverers develop joint attention applies to children with and without language delay. Sometimes, an older child who is language delayed will be at the same stage of communication development as a very young infant, as you will see with Mila in the description below.

Mila is a two-year-old Discoverer with a significant developmental delay. Her teacher, Miriam, finds it very difficult to engage her in interactions. The one activity Mila loves, however, is when Miriam blows bubbles for her and she tries to catch the bubbles as they fly away. When she wants Miriam to blow more bubbles, Mila doesn't look at her – she just grabs the bottle or the wand and makes sounds. Now Miriam wants to encourage joint attention in this natural, interactive situation, so Mila can learn to use eye contact both to request more bubbles and to share her excitement.

Therefore, Miriam will need to:

- *be face-to-face with Mila to make it easy for her to look at her*
- *pause after blowing the bubbles to give Mila a chance to take a turn*
- *get directly in her line of vision when Mila's pauses, and as soon as Mila makes even fleeting eye contact with her, say "More bubbles! OK!" and blow more bubbles*
- *follow Mila's focus of interest by pointing to the bubbles she tries to catch and commenting on them animatedly, making sure she is close enough for Mila to make eye contact with her*
- *draw Mila's attention to one particular bubble (which, for example, may have landed on the ground), in an effort to get Mila to look at what she points to*
- *imitate her actions and sounds, which may motivate her to make eye contact with her, and*
- *continue to pause expectantly to encourage Mila to take more turns.*

Miriam helps Mila develop joint attention by asking "more bubbles?" and waiting expectantly for Mila to look at her. Miriam then enthusiastically interprets her look as a request to continue.

While you can't *teach* a child to establish joint attention, you *can* support interactions in ways that encourage its development. You have to work hard to make yourself an interesting and animated conversation partner, tuned in to the child's interests. And you have to make it easy for the child to tune in to you.

It can be hard work to engage children who are new to the conversation game, but the effects can be quite dramatic. When a child becomes an active and willing conversation partner, he will experience the power and pleasure of social interaction. You, no longer feeling frustrated, can begin to view him as a conversation partner with potential. When you set up an interaction so that the child becomes an active participant, both of you will enjoy being together.

> When you set up an interaction so that the child becomes an active participant, both of you will enjoy being together.

Make social routines part of your everyday interactions

Infants and children who are inexperienced turn-takers learn a great deal from familiar, repetitive, predictable interactions that contain clear cues as to when to take a turn. These interactions or "social routines," like Peek-a-Boo and Pat-a-Cake, are an important part of children's earliest social interactions. Not only are they fun, but they give children opportunities to interact with you just for the pleasure of your company. Through these carefully supported interactions, children learn the basics of turn-taking and are exposed to simple, repetitive language that helps them learn their first words. Even a child with a significant developmental or language delay will be able to take turns within a suitable social routine. If a child is too old for Peek-a-Boo and Pat-a-Cake, you can create routines to accommodate his age and interests, and build in opportunities for him to take his turn.

Social routines make turn-taking easy for children at the early stages of communication development because:

- the routines have a specific way of being played
- they involve only a few actions, sounds, or words
- the turns are very predictable and repetitive
- each person's turn is clearly defined, and
- there are obvious cues that "tell" the child to take a turn.

Social routines occur in two contexts:

- **simple turn-taking games** introduced by the adult (e.g., Peek-a-Boo, Pat-a-Cake, giving objects back and forth), and
- **repetitive, playful turn-taking activities** that an adult creates during everyday routines like mealtimes, bath time, getting dressed, or going to the toilet. These routines always build on the child's interests, sounds, or actions.

Make turn-taking in social routines easy for the Discoverer

Games like Peek-a-Boo, Pat-a-Cake, and songs like "Row, Row, Row Your Boat" are an important part of a Discoverer's earliest social interactions. Because initially he has no idea of what he is supposed to do, you have to do most of the work. First, you have to get his attention. So ham it up, be a clown, and make sure you're interesting to look at and listen to. You really have to be something of an entertainer at the beginning!

You help Discoverers take turns in a social routine if you:
- Get the child's attention
- Play the game or sing the song from beginning to end a few times
- Cue the child to take his turn
- Treat any reaction – like a wriggle, a smile, a kick, a burp, a sound, or a stare – as if the child has taken his turn
- Take his turn for him if he doesn't respond, then continue with the game
- Once he knows the game well, expect him to take a consistent turn

Get the child's attention

Be face-to-face, call the child's name in an animated way, and greet him. If the game involves a toy, show it to him.

Play the game or sing the song from beginning to end a few times

Play the game a few times to get the child familiar with it, without expecting him to do anything specific. Be sure you are animated and interesting so that he pays attention to what you are doing. Once he becomes familiar with how the game is played, he will be better able to take his turn.

Cue the child to take his turn

The next time you play the game, pause at an appropriate spot and look expectantly at the child, as if to say, "It's your turn to do something!" For example, if you have been blowing "raspberries" on a baby's stomach, pause before blowing the next one and wait expectantly to cue the child to do something to tell you to do it again. If you have been singing a song, stop at the end of the song, look expectant, and wait for him to let you know that you should continue.

Treat any reaction – like a wriggle, a smile, a kick, a burp, a sound, or a stare – as if the child has taken his turn

When the child realizes that by kicking his feet or making a sound he's having a definite effect on your behaviour, he'll do it again – deliberately.

Take his turn for him if he doesn't respond, then continue with the game

Even if the child doesn't take his turn, keep the game going. If you wait a few seconds and the child doesn't respond, continue playing the game. If he seems uninterested in the game, try a new one.

Liam loves the tickling game.

Once he knows the game well, expect him to take a consistent turn

When you have played the game over and over again and the child has come to know it well, he'll begin to get excited in anticipation of the "fun" part. For example, just before the "Weeweewee all the way home" in "This Little Piggy Went to Market," he'll wriggle with excitement because he knows the best is about to come – and that wriggle will be his turn.

*After tickling Liam several times, Lena stops and **waits expectantly** with her hand in mid-motion to **cue** Liam to take a turn. Liam opens his eyes wide and wiggles his body in anticipation of what's to come. Lena interprets Liam's wiggle as "I'm so excited – do it again!" And the game continues.*

An older Discoverer with a language delay also benefits from social routines. When Shona waits expectantly while playing "This Little Piggy," Habib takes a turn by shaking his foot in anticipation of having his toes wiggled.

Create social routines in response to the child's interests, sounds, and actions

In Chapter 3, page 86, you learned how to join in a Discoverer's play by building on his focus and making the game more interesting. You can:

- imitate the child's actions and sounds
- pick up a toy that interests the child and move it as if it were "alive"
- make yourself part of the toy
- turn a chance action into a game, or
- play the "you give it to me and then I'll give it to you "game.

These situations can be turned into social routines that then become excellent opportunities for you to encourage turn-taking. The key is to wait expectantly after your turn. That way, you cue the child to react in a way that you can interpret as a request for you to take another turn.

Felicia imitates Jordan when he bangs two blocks together.

Then Felicia asks "Bang, bang?" and waits expectantly to cue him to take another turn.

C. Building conversations: Expect more consistent, specific turns from Communicators

---

A Communicator is a relatively experienced turn-taker. At this early stage, he has learned the following important rules of conversation:

- Pay attention to the speaker.
- Take a turn at the appropriate time.
- Give the other person a chance to take a turn.
- Continue the conversation by taking additional turns.

By the age of 10 months, a Communicator has developed joint attention (see Chapter 3, page 85) and is able to take turns on a shared topic. His opportunities for learning about the world through interactions are now endless and your interactions with him become more varied. Before now, it was hard to play together with toys because he couldn't attend to both you and the toy. Now, you can either join in his play or get him to join in yours. You can show him interesting things, like how a jack-in-the-box works or where to put the piece of a puzzle, as long as he's interested. You no longer have to work so hard to get and keep a conversation going.

Jason keeps looking at Lucy, his teacher. He's making sure they're both still focused on the playdough. His ability to maintain joint attention makes playing and interacting with him so much easier for Lucy!

Give the Communicator plenty of practice with social routines

Social routines play a critical role in helping Communicators learn to take the lead in interactions. They also provide opportunities for Communicators to practise their developing turn-taking skills and to learn new words. Communicators can take specific turns in social routines, like making a particular sound or performing a certain action. As with Discoverers, Communicators' social routines can occur either in games you introduce or in activities where you build on the child's interests, sound, or actions.

Help the Communicator practise turn-taking in social routines by:
- Knowing what turn you expect him to take
- Cueing him to take his turn
- Varying the routine's actions or words, especially when his interest begins to fade
- Creating new routines by building on his interests
- Supporting his attempts to initiate routines

Know what turn you expect the child to take

In any social routine, you have to think about what turn the child is able to take – and then expect that turn each time you play the game.

A Communicator can take his turn by performing actions that are part of a routine – he'll rock back and forth to tell you to sing "Row, Row, Row Your Boat" again or he'll make sounds at the right time to tell you to continue singing a song. If you don't continue the routine, he gets very upset and sends stronger, more urgent messages until you oblige.

To help a Communicator take his turn, remember the following points:

- **A child will enjoy taking a turn that involves performing a "fun" action in the game.** Games that involve familiar actions, like raising arms for "hooray," or miming actions, like brushing teeth or beeping the horn of the bus (in "The Wheels on the Bus Go Round and Round") are examples of "fun" actions a Communicator will be able to perform in a game.

- **The easiest verbal (word) or vocal (sound) turn for a child to take is the last word or sound in a sentence.** It is easier for a child to fill in a sound or word at the end of the sentence than it is at the beginning or the middle. This is because the first part of the sentence gives the child the cue for what's coming next. Therefore, you let the child fill in the "blank" at the end of a sentence by pausing before that last word. For example, in the song "The Grand Old Duke of York," two sentences end with the words "up" or "down": "And when they were up they were . . . **up** / And when they were down they were . . . **down**." It is logical to expect that the child will fill in the blank for the words "up" and "down" at the *ends* of those sentences.

- **Expect imperfect pronunciation of words:** Communicators will learn many of their first words from their favourite social routines. If you repeat a routine frequently, you will help a child make the connection between the words and the actions. Once he has made that connection, he is likely to try to say the word. Young children have difficulty pronouncing words with certain sounds and sound combinations. For example, in "Row, Row," a Communicator may pronounce the word "dream" as "dee" or "deem," which is perfectly normal. Don't be tempted to correct the child – accept his turn and keep the game going.

Cue the Communicator to take his turn

Wait expectantly

Sometimes a child needs you to let him know that it's his turn – especially before the routine is familiar to him. You can let him know by pausing at an appropriate spot and waiting expectantly. Waiting provides him with a clear cue, telling him that you have finished your turn and he should take his. Waiting expectantly is not exactly the same as the kind of waiting described in Chapter 3, which gives the child time to initiate. When you wait expectantly, you send a very strong message that says, "I expect you to take your turn and I am waiting in anticipation!"

Waiting expectantly involves using very strong body language. When you stop at the part of the routine where you expect the child to take his turn, you:
- move in closer
- lean forward and look directly into his eyes, and
- look animated and expectant.

Waiting expectantly works wonders!

Use animated questions or comments

A simple comment or question, said with a rising intonation and followed by expectant waiting, can also effectively cue a child to take a turn.

Melanie is playing Peek-a-Boo with Shonelle, a two-year-old Communicator with a language delay. Melanie covers her head with a blanket and says, "Where's Melanie?" in an animated voice and then waits expectantly. Shonelle recognizes Melanie's question and expectant pause as cues for her turn. She responds by pulling the blanket off Melanie's head and laughing. Melanie then takes her turn and says "Boo!"

At this stage, Melanie does not expect Shonelle to actually answer the question, "Where's Melanie?" with words. Instead, she uses the question to cue Shonelle to take a turn by performing actions.

Don't take the child's turn for him if he can take it himself

Don't assume that a child needs you to perform all the actions in the routine. Give him a chance to pull the blanket off your head during Peek-a-Boo or make a sound when you stop singing a song. When given a chance to take a turn, he may surprise you.

A Communicator knows what to do . . .

. . . when you play Peek-a-Boo!

Vary the routine's actions or words, especially when the child's interest begins to fade

Once the child knows the routine very well, change it slightly so that he learns to take turns in a different situation. For example, put the child's name in a song he already knows – he'll love it! Or change the words of the song or routine to capture something he is doing. For example, if he's banging on a box, you could sing, "Bang, bang, bang the box . . ." to the tune of "Row, Row, Row Your Boat."

> Row, row, row michael's boat gently **DOWN** the stream . . .

Same song, but this one has my name in it, and I love being upside down!

Create new routines by building on the Communicator's interests

Children will be delighted when you create new routines, especially when these occur in response to their actions or sounds.

Eric likes putting hats on Kara's head . . .

> The hat's on my head!

. . . so she turned his actions into a new social routine.

Kevin is a 17-month-old Communicator who is developmentally delayed. He has a passive conversational style and usually initiates only to protest.

Today he is fascinated by a large rubber ball and keeps turning it over and over. Wendy, his teacher, notices that he is very excited when he finds the ball's blow hole. She pokes her finger into the hole, and says animatedly, "Look at the hole! Pokey, pokey, pokey!" Kevin is delighted by her poking action and by the sound of the word "Pokey." He reaches for her hand and pulls it back toward the hole, telling her to do it again. She repeats "Pokey, pokey, pokey!" And so the "Pokey, pokey" social routine is born.

When you turn a child's sounds or actions into a game by imitating them, you give him the feeling of being an initiator. "Wow, she's following me!" he'll think – and he'll do it again.

Support the Communicator's attempts to initiate routines

Support the child in his attempts to initiate interactions by himself. For example, get into position for a well-known routine with the child, but do not start it. If he is familiar enough with the game, he should do something to get it going. And as soon as he does – play!

Support the Communicator in everyday conversations

Reduce conversational overload

Communicators begin to take more turns in conversations by using gestures, sounds, and/or eye gaze. However, because they can't talk yet, it's easy for the adult to do too much of the talking, take too many turns, or say too much when taking a turn. Remember: keeping the conversation balanced is critical.

- Don't dominate the conversation by taking all the turns. Give the child a chance to take a turn by slowing down so he has time to absorb your words or actions. Pause and wait expectantly after each of your turns to cue him to take his.
- When taking your turn, say only one thing and then cue the child to take a turn. Children can typically understand more than they can say. So, although your turns will often be a little longer than the child's, don't say too much.

Slow down – the baby's getting dizzy!

Ask questions the Communicator can answer with a gesture or a sound

Children learn to answer questions through practice. They can answer in many ways, even before they can speak. When asking Communicators questions, it's important to remember that questions are there to help them take another turn in a conversation on a particular topic – not to test their knowledge. Children should enjoy the conversation and should want to answer the question in order to learn from it. For example:

- If you ask, "Do you want to play with the blocks?" a child can nod for yes or shake his head for no.
- If you ask, "Where's the bird?" he can gesture "gone" with his hands up in the air.
- If you ask, "Where did your ice cream go?" he can point to inside his mouth.
- If he is able to say a few words, ask questions that enable him to use his words. If he can say "Mummy," you may ask, "Who's here?" when his mother walks into the room.

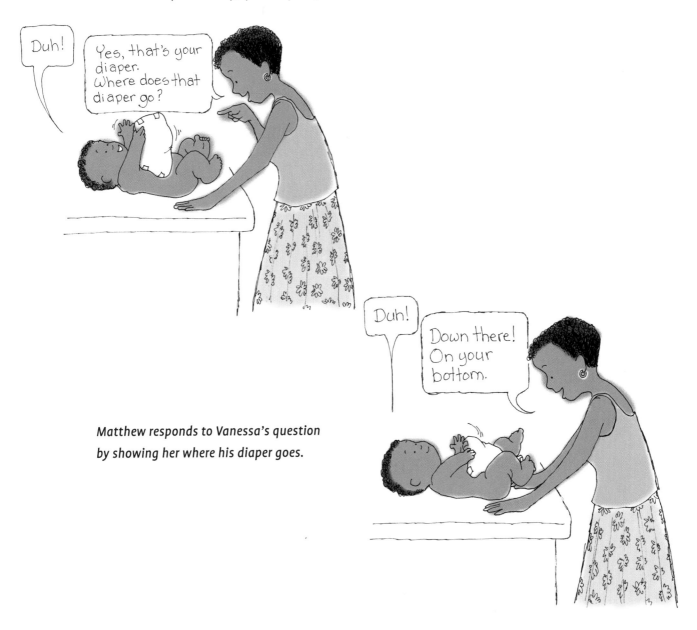

Matthew responds to Vanessa's question by showing her where his diaper goes.

D. Taking turns with words: Support First Words Users

First Words Users begin to take turns with words, often using words to replace sounds, actions, or gestures they might have used at an earlier stage. If a child has difficulty saying words at this stage, he may continue to take turns with sounds and gestures, but also add signs or pictures.

A few weeks ago, Kelly took turns in Peek-a-Boo only with sounds and actions. Now, Kelly starts the game and says "PeeBoo" for her turn. Lois's repetition of "Peek-a-Boo" every time they played this game has paid off!

Use social routines: Follow the leader with First Words Users

The First Words User is no longer a spectator in the game. He can now initiate social routines and take turns with words. He takes over your role, expecting *you* to respond. For example, he covers his face with his hands to start playing Peek-a-Boo or holds out his hands and says, "Row, Row" to tell you to sing "Row, Row, Row Your Boat." Now that he can initiate a social routine, *he* will run the show, and you will adopt the role he used to play.

Becoming the initiator is a great social achievement for the child because he has realized that he needs both to initiate *and* respond in interactions. He has learned one of the most important rules of conversation, the rule of "give-and-take," which he will use for the rest of his life.

Now Kelly starts the game, and Lois her teacher is the responder.

Where's Kelly?

Use comments and questions to cue First Words Users to take their turns

First Words Users are becoming more experienced conversationalists and they can participate in conversations about everyday things. However, they still rely on your support to stay in the conversation. Comments, questions, and waiting expectantly are your most effective tools for communicating your interest to a child at this stage and cueing him to take another turn.

Comments and questions work differently for First Words Users than they do with Discoverers and Communicators. At the earlier stages, questions and comments keep a child's attention or cue a nonverbal turn. First Words Users, however, can understand and say some words. By providing them with comments or asking them questions they can understand, you help them take another turn with words.

Because First Words Users are just learning to have conversations, they don't respond as easily to comments as they do to comments followed by questions – or to questions alone. With more experience, they will learn to respond to comments alone, which involves a more sophisticated form of turn-taking. In the meantime, you may find yourself using lots of questions to help a First Words User stay in the conversation. Remind yourself during interactions and conversations that your aim is to communicate and exchange information with the child, and to connect and enjoy each other's company. You also want to have a conversation on one topic for as many turns as the child will take. You're not aiming to teach or test the child. As soon as you teach or test, your focus is no longer on exchanging information, and the child will likely lose his desire to interact with you.

Use questions and comments that show your interest and create anticipation

The tone of your questions and comments conveys your interest and motivates the child to respond. A question like "what have you got?" or a comment like, "Wow, look at your bunny!" followed by an expectant pause can cue this child to take another turn.

Sharon's question lets Joshua know she's really interested in what he's showing her – and it will encourage him to respond.

Use questions and comments that are easy for the First Words User to respond to and understand

Since they are easy to understand and respond to, questions that require "yes/no" answers, and simple "Who?" "What? and "Where?" questions help keep the conversation going with First Words Users.

When you know something about a child's life and family, you can use this knowledge to help him participate in conversations – like Tanya does in the following example with Christian, a three-year-old First Words User with a language delay. By skillfully asking questions and making comments that both follow Christian's lead and cue him to take another turn, she keeps the conversation going.

Christian: *(pointing to the phone)* *Da!*

Tanya: *That's a phone!* (comment acknowledges his interest) *Do you have a phone at home?* (Yes/No question cues another turn)

Christian: *(Nods enthusiastically)*

Tanya: *Do you talk on the phone?* (Yes/No question follows his lead and cues another turn)

Christian: *Nona (his grandmother)*

Tanya: *Oh, you talk to Nona* (comment confirms child's message). *And do you talk to Gabriel?* (another relative – Yes/No question cues another turn)

Christian: *(Nods)*

Tanya: *And when you talk to Nona, do you say, "Hi! Hi Nona!"?* (Yes/No question follows Christian's lead and cues another turn)

Christian: *Hi!*

Tanya: *Yes! You say, "Hi!"* (comment confirms child's message) *Where's Nona?* (a simple "Where?" question cues another turn)

Christian: *Go. (Gestures "gone")*

Tanya: *Yeah, Nona's gone* (confirms child's message). *She's at home* (adds some new information).

And so on . . .

Tanya supports the conversation with comments and questions to acknowledge what Christian has said and to cue him to take another turn. She makes it possible for Christian, who can say only a few words, to have a real conversation!

Ask questions to check that you have understood the First Words User's message

When it's hard to understand what a child says, you probably find yourself asking "checking" questions to see if he meant what you think he meant. Caregivers often use these questions with First Words Users who are language delayed, since their speech may be difficult to understand.

Mary asks several questions to figure out what Andrea means. Finally, after Andrea shows her teacher what she wants, Mary gets it right!

Ask questions that allow the First Words User to make choices

Questions that offer choices are motivating for the child to respond to and are easy to answer because the response is contained in the question. Some examples are: "Do you want milk or juice?" "Do you want to play on the slide or the swings?"

E. Becoming equal partners in conversations: Encourage Combiners and Early and Later Sentence Users to "hold their own"

By the time children become Combiners and Sentence Users, they have learned the basic rules of conversation. But there's still a long way to go! They have to learn to "hold their own" in conversations and to exchange information by contributing their thoughts and ideas – just like more mature speakers do.

To "hold their own" in conversations, children must learn to:

- send clear messages
- clear up misunderstandings (including being aware of whether the listener understands the message or needs more information, and letting the speaker know if they don't understand something)
- begin and end conversations appropriately
- keep the conversation going for longer periods, and
- contribute to the conversation by adding information that is on topic and related to the speaker's previous turn. This involves sticking to the subject, which requires children to pay attention to what the speaker says and then respond appropriately.

Learning all these skills may sound like a huge task, but children learn to do these things as they interact with others during everyday activities and conversations. They learn a lot about conversations from other people's responses to their comments and questions, from the models provided by their conversation partners, and, of course, from the way you set up conversations and support them.

Combiners and Early or Later Sentence Users with language delays, however, may continue to have difficulties taking turns in a conversation, even though they may be speaking in sentences. The way you set up conversations and support them is critical to their success as conversation partners.

Encourage conversations during play

Playtime with toys and sensory-creative materials provides many opportunities to encourage conversations with Combiners and Early or Later Sentence Users. When you and a child play together with toys, you can both see the topic of the conversation. Since he doesn't have to explain or describe what he is referring to, he has fewer conversational demands to fulfill. Conversations during play or sensory-creative activities, therefore, take the pressure off a child who is still learning how to have verbal conversations – and make it easier for him to have a conversation with you. This strategy is especially helpful for children with language delays or for those who have difficulties with speech production and communicate with signs, gestures, or pictures.

During playtime, a child may take a turn nonverbally by doing something with a toy or the play materials. He may even stop interacting for a while as he becomes engrossed in some aspect of the play. Again, this makes it easier for him to participate in conversations.

Children gain valuable experience by taking turns in verbal conversations during play activities, and you can keep the conversation going even longer by being a creative play partner. Introduce children to activities or ideas that you think will appeal to them. Once you have introduced an activity, give children lots of time and space to get involved with its materials in their own way – and then follow their lead. Build on their interests to keep the activity exciting and to give you both more to talk about.

Letting the car run down the ramp was fun for a while . . .

. . . but making a bridge for the car to go under gives both you and the child more to talk about.

Some other ideas for playing creatively in the above situation include:
- making a wall with blocks for the car to bump into
- changing the angle of the ramp and seeing the effect on the speed of the car
- using different-shaped objects (e.g., balls, blocks, pegs) to see how they go down the ramp, or
- creating a pretend play scene using miniature people and cars.

As children become Sentence Users, they become better at carrying on conversations with you about abstract topics not associated with objects you can both see (e.g., they can talk about what they did yesterday, or what it would be like to go to the moon). Conversations like this get them ready for the kind of language they will be expected to use when they get to school. Chapter 8 has more information on how children begin to use language to learn about the world.

Playing with the toy spaceship reminds Mario of a movie he saw – and the conversation really takes off!

Cue Combiners and Early and Late Sentence Users to take their turns

Use comments and questions followed by expectant waiting to communicate your interest to Combiners and Sentence Users, as well as to cue them to take another turn. Pausing after a comment or question also ensures that a child has an opportunity to respond.

Continue the conversation with . . .	Avoid stopping the conversation with . . .

• comments that build on the child's interest (often followed by a question)
 	
• questions that:
  • match the child's language stage
  • ask about the child's focus of interest
  • stimulate children's creative thinking
  • show your interest, and
  • request information you don't know.
	• questions that are:
	  • too complex
	  • too simple or concrete
	  • intended to test the child's knowledge, and
	  • rhetorical and don't really require a response.

Include comments, not just questions, in your conversations with Combiners and Sentence Users

Often, adults don't use enough comments in their conversations with Combiners and Sentence Users. Perhaps we feel that by asking children questions, we have a better chance of getting a response. It's true that when children are learning to have conversations, they don't respond as easily to comments as they do to questions. However, they need to learn to respond to comments in order to become effective conversation partners. And when you use comments as well as questions to cue a child's turns, he is less likely to feel that you are "trying to make him talk." This is especially important for children with language delays or reluctant conversational styles.

Amy wanted her teacher, Natalie, to show an interest in the bears on her sweater, but Natalie responded with a series of questions to see if Amy could name them . . .

*. . . so Amy decided to end the conversation! Amy would have been more likely to stay in the
conversation if Natalie had commented, "Amy, you have bears on your sweater!"*

You can use comments both to get a conversation started (they act as leading statements;
see Chapter 3, page 82) and to cue another turn by giving children interesting information
that they'll want to respond to.

Combine a comment and a question

Often, the best way to keep the conversation going with Combiners and Sentence Users
is to share a child's interest, curiosity, and enjoyment by:

- first, making a **comment,** which acknowledges the child's message, and
- then, asking a **question,** which helps the child take another turn.

Let's imagine that Joey, a four-year-old Early Sentence User with a language delay,
runs up to show you a white stone he found in the playground.

Joey: *Look me find!*

You: *Oh, you found a beautiful stone!* (comment first) *Where did you find it?*
(ask a question to cue him to take another turn)

Joey: *Dere (points toward the fence).*

. . . and the conversation continues.

Use questions to continue, not control, the conversation

You can continue the conversation with questions if you match your questions to the child's stage of communication and if the questions build on the child's interests.

Match your question to the child's stage of communication:
Ask questions he can answer

Children's understanding of questions develops over time, and they must learn to respond to a variety of questions. In order for a child to successfully answer a question, however, it must be appropriate to his language stage.

Questions that begin with "who," "what," "where," "when," "why," and "how" are generally more difficult to understand than questions that require a "yes/no" answer. "How?" and "when?" questions are the most difficult for young children to understand. And when you ask children "why?" questions, they may answer "Cause," without really understanding what they are being asked.

You can't avoid asking children questions they don't understand, nor should you try to. However, you should be aware of the types of questions that will frustrate children or end the conversation because they are inappropriately complex.

If you ask a child a question like "How are you getting home today?" which he doesn't understand, communication breaks down. You can repair the breakdown by changing the question to one that he *can* answer, like, "Who's picking you up today?" or even "Is Mummy picking you up today?" Communication breakdowns often occur with children with language delays when it is difficult to judge their level of understanding. Be prepared to simplify questions whenever a child doesn't seem to be able to respond.

Many teachers agree that open-ended questions are the best kind to ask older children. However, sometimes open-ended questions are too broad for a child to answer, and must be narrowed down before he can respond.

> What happened when you went to the doctor, Nicki?

Nicki can't answer this question because it's too open-ended. So Tania has to change the question . . .

When Tanya asks more manageable, focused questions, Nicki can take her turn.

When you narrow down an open-ended question, you support the conversation by providing a more appropriate cue to help the child take another turn and keep it going.

In the following example, Lucienne and José, an Early Sentence User, are playing with a toy farm. Lucienne begins with an open question, which José cannot answer. She then asks questions that narrow the focus. She also makes comments, which confirm what José says, and encourage him to take another turn. In this way, she supports the conversation and keeps it going.

José: *This is a farm.*

Lucienne: *What should we do on the farm?* (open question)

José: *I dunno* (question was too broad).

Lucienne: *Well, here is the farmer and here is the cow. What can the farmer do with the cow?* (question that narrows the focus)

José: *He could milk him.*

Lucienne: *Yes, he could milk the cows so we have milk to drink* (comment that confirms what José has said). *I'm going to help the farmer milk the cow* (comment that builds on José's interest and encourages him to take another turn).

José: *I wanna milk him too!*

. . . and the play continues.

These Later Sentence Users would have shared their thoughts if they had been asked a question more appropriate to their language stage. If their teacher had combined a comment and a question and said, "What a great tower. Who is the tower for?" they would have taken another turn in the conversation.

Match your questions to the child's interest: Ask sincere questions about what the child is interested in

When you ask questions that are sincere (because you really don't know the answer) and build on a child's focus, he is more likely to respond.

Judy asks a sincere question and then waits for Laura to answer.

Questions that test a child's knowledge, however, can stop a conversation dead in its tracks!

Let's go back to Joey, the four-year-old Early Sentence User with a language delay. He runs up to show you a white stone he found in the playground. "Look me find!" he exclaims. If you ask questions like, "What colour is it?" "What shape is it?" "How does it feel?" or "What's this called?" you won't capture his excitement. Nor will you acknowledge and confirm his interest and encourage another turn. Testing questions like the ones above pressure a child and keep him from talking about things of real interest to him – such as where he found the stone, whether he's ever seen a stone like it before, and what he wants to do with it.

Ask interesting questions that have no "right" answer to stimulate children's creative thinking

We don't ask children enough questions that stimulate creative thinking and problem-solving skills – both areas of critical importance for academic success.

Too many of the questions we ask children are "fact" questions that have only one right answer. These questions test a child's memory and his ability to label or simply provide the "right" answer. Questions like "What do we call a person who delivers mail?" or "Who remembers what makes flowers grow?" don't even begin to tap children's abilities to think creatively.

"Figuring-out" questions require more thought and reasoning on the child's part than fact questions. Questions like "How are balls the same as oranges?" involve some analysis on the child's part and some understanding of higher-level concepts, but they still require a closed-end, "right" answer.

Creative questions get creative answers!

Creative questions encourage children to be creative because there are no right or wrong answers. Instead, children are free to come up with their own original, imaginative ideas. Questions like "What could we do about it?" "What might happen if . . . ?" "Suppose that . . ." or "What would you do if that were you?" challenge the child to think of more than one answer and encourage the kind of thinking that develops creativity and problem-solving skills.

(In Chapter 8, the section titled "Helping children become better story-tellers" contains information on the kinds of questions that help children provide necessary information when they tell stories.)

Avoid rhetorical questions that limit a child's response

Questions that don't really require a response are wonderful for Discoverers, who react to your tone of voice, but not for Combiners and Sentence Users, who have something to say.

If a three-year-old shows you a tower he has built and you respond by saying, "That's a big tower, isn't it?" you haven't done much to keep the conversation going. A better response would be a comment to follow the child's lead (e.g., "That's a really big tower!") followed by a question (e.g., "Who lives in that tower?") to cue the child to take another turn in the conversation.

Encourage Combiners and Sentence Users to let you know when they don't understand

One of the rules of the conversation game is that the listener is expected to let the speaker know when the speaker's message is unclear. Early on in their conversational lives, children learn to request clarification from the speaker, getting him or her to repeat or rephrase a misunderstood or improperly heard comment or question. Very young children may look at you quizzically when they don't understand you, or they may say "Huh?" or "What?" When they request clarification, you repeat your message in a way that they can understand.

Some children with language delays don't request clarification. They may not realize that they don't understand what has been said. Even if they do, they may do nothing about it. As a result, they are at a serious disadvantage in all aspects of learning, including language learning. In later years, children who don't request clarification can end up confused, bored, frustrated, and passive in school, and this pattern may continue unless they are taught to request clarification.

You can help young children learn to request clarification by modelling the request in a small group.

Roberto is a three-year-old Combiner with a language delay. He has a reluctant conversational style and doesn't request clarification when he can't understand what is said to him. It is snack time, and he is sitting in a group with three other children and their teacher, Lenore.

Sandy, aged two-and-a-half, shows his cracker to Lenore and says something that no one can understand. Lenore looks at the children, making sure she has a confused look on her face. She gestures "I don't know" with her hands up in the air as she says, "I didn't understand what Sandy said. Roberto, let's ask Sandy 'What?'" (She leans forward.) "Sandy, what?" Sandy (with a bit of luck) repeats what he said, and then Lenore says "Oh! Your cracker is broken. See Roberto, Sandy's cracker is broken!"

This modelling process can begin when children are Combiners, and it should continue to be used with Early and Later Sentence Users. For these children, you should model more socially appropriate questions, such as "What did you say?" or "What do you mean?"

When children don't request clarification, they place total responsibility for a successful conversation in the hands of their partner, causing problems in both adult-child and child-child interactions. Failure to request clarification is often seen in children with reluctant or passive conversational styles, and it may have lifelong consequences.

Encourage Combiners and Sentence Users to stick to the subject

Have you ever had conversations with a child who doesn't stick to the subject? Have you wondered what you should do about it? Well, children need to know that they have strayed off topic, and you can help them realize that they have broken a conversational rule by redirecting them back to the original topic.

Shari is talking to Thomas, a four-year-old Early Sentence User with a language delay, about his cousin's new puppy. Let's look at how she redirects him when he strays from the topic.

Thomas: *The puppy bited me.*
Shari: *Oh no! Where did he bite you?*
Thomas: *My Dad took me home.*
Shari: *Where did the puppy bite you? Can you show me where?* (Redirects the topic)
Thomas: *Here. (Shows his arm)*
Shari: *On your arm. Wow, I can see the teeth marks. And did your dad take you to the doctor after the dog bit you?* (Acknowledges the child's statement once he answers the original question)
Thomas: *Yeah, I go to doctor and I was crying.*
Shari: *It must have really hurt. Is it better now?*

If the child says something that is totally unrelated to the topic, don't "just go along with it." Let him know that he's done something to cause a breakdown in communication. Look confused and tell him that you don't understand or that you were talking about something else – he can only learn to play the conversation game when someone lets him know the rules.

Chapter 8 has more information on how to help children retell events that have happened in their lives.

Help Combiners and Sentence Users learn to give and take turns in a group – especially those children who don't give anyone else a turn!

When you interact with children in small groups, the turn-taking is often unequal. Often, one child dominates the conversation, talking a lot, interrupting others, and answering for them. Just as often, another child seems unable to find his way into the conversation.

You can help children understand what kind of turn-taking behaviour is and is not appropriate in a group situation. Spell it out for them. Tell them whose turn it is, that they must wait for their turn, and that they can't butt in or answer for another child. Chapter 5 has more information on how to draw in the reluctant turn-takers at the same time.

Maya, a junior kindergarten teacher, is sitting with a group of five four-year-olds at the snack table.

Tom: *Maya, I've got a new racing car at home. It goes so fast!*

Brett: *(Interrupting)* *My Dad bought me . . .*

Maya: *Brett,* (holds up her hand as if to say "Stop") *Tom was talking, so it's his turn. Tom, tell me about your new car.*

Tom: *It goes so fast. It goes vrooom! Like that.*

Maya: *Wow! It sounds like it's faster than a racing car. Does it look like a real racing car?*

Tom: *Yeah, it is like a real one.*

Maya: *You're lucky, Tom.* (Turns to Brett) *Okay, Brett, now it's your turn.*

Brett: *My Dad bought me a truck wif big wheels, and a man can sit inside.*

Maya: *Does it make a noise when you drive it?*

Brett: *Yeah, a big noise, and you know what else?*

Maya: *What?*

Brett: *I saw a real truck like that at a farm . . . (keeps talking for a while)*

Maya: *Brett, it's time to give someone else a turn to talk.* (Turns to a quiet child) *Shannon, do you ever play with trucks or cars at home?*

Shannon: *(Looks at teacher shyly)*

Brett: *She don't play wif trucks. I got even more trucks . . .*

Maya: *Brett,* (holds up her hand as if to say "Stop") *I asked Shannon a question, so it's her turn to talk.*

Helping children learn the rules for group conversations may seem like directing traffic, but it can go a long way to helping them understand how group conversations work.

F. Making time for one-to-one interactions

From time to time, children need your undivided attention. Although it's not easy, it is possible to sneak some one-to-one interactions into your busy day.

Take turns on the run

Every minute counts! A brief conversation is better than no conversation at all. When *a child* initiates an interaction:

- stop what you are doing for a moment
- get down to his level, and
- respond warmly to him.

When *you* initiate an interaction:

- say something inviting (e.g., "You made a really big tower!")
- wait for a response
- take a few turns with the child; and then
- let the child know you have to leave before you go.

Instead of rushing off . . .

Those are nice shoes!

. . . stop and chat for a minute.

You've got beautiful new shoes!

Make the most of the quiet times

It may be early morning
Or afternoon when it's late,
But quiet times are the best times
To communicate.

Make the most of those quiet times when you have only three or four children in your room. Rather than use these times to tidy up or to prepare materials, spend some time with the children who really need one-to-one interactions.

Going home late isn't so bad if I get all this attention!

Let them help you

All children love to help. Cleaning paintbrushes, wiping dirty tables, or handing out cups at snack time are all special treats for children. So instead of rushing through some of your chores, let one or two children help you. There's so much to talk about when you work together.

It's a real treat for a child to help with chores.

Summary

Children learn to become conversation partners by taking part in many, many interactions with supportive adults. To help children become conversation partners, teachers need to support conversations in ways that make it easy for children to take their turns. Infants and children with significant language delays need a great deal of support, whereas children whose conversational ability is more advanced need less. Supports include: playing social routines with a child and pausing to indicate that he should take his turn; using questions and comments appropriately; redirecting a child who strays off topic; and spelling out the rules for taking turns in a group situation. Teachers can also enhance children's conversational skills by making time for one-to-one interactions.

References

Bates, E., Camaioni, L. & Volterra, V. (1979). The acquisition of performatives prior to speech. In E. Ochs & B. B. Schieffelin (Eds.), *Developmental pragmatics* (pp. 111–129). New York: Academic Press.

Berko Gleason, J. (1989). *The development of language.* Columbus, Ohio: Merrill.

Bruner, J.S. (1975). The ontogenesis of speech acts. *Journal of Child Language, 2,* 1–19.

Bruner, J.S. (1983). *Child's talk: Learning to use language.* New York: Norton.

Cazden, C.B. (1983). Adult assistance to language development: Scaffolds, models, and direct instruction. In R.P. Parker and F.R. Davis (Eds.), *Developing literacy* (pp. 3–18). International Reading Association.

Cross, T.G. (1984). Habilitating the language-impaired child: Ideas from studies of parent-child interaction. *Topics in Language Disorders, 4*(4), 1–14.

Donahue, M. (1985). Communicative style in learning disabled children: Some implications for classroom discourse. In D. N. Ripich & F. M. Spinelli (Eds.), *School discourse problems* (pp. 97–124). San Diego: College Hill Press.

Foster, S. (1985). The development of discourse topic skills by infants and young children. *Topics in Language Disorders, 5* (2), 31–45.

Girolametto, L. (1986). *Developing dialogue skills of mothers and their developmentally delayed children: An intervention study.* Unpublished doctoral dissertation. University of Toronto, Toronto.

Girolametto, L. (1988). Improving the social-conversational skills of developmentally delayed children: An intervention study. *Journal of Speech and Hearing Disorders, 53,* 156–167.

Hart, B. (2000). A natural history of early language experience. *Topics in Early Childhood Special Education, 20:1,* 28–32.

Hendrick, J. (1984). *The whole child.* St Louis: Times Mirror/Mosby.

Kaye, K. & Charney, R. (1980). How mothers maintain "dialogue" with two-year-olds. In D. Olson (Ed.), *The social foundations of language and thought* (pp.211–230). New York: Norton.

Lucariello, J. (1990). Freeing talk from the here-and-now: The role of event knowledge and maternal scaffolds. *Topics in Language Disorders, 10*(3), 14–29.

MacDonald, J.D. (1989). *Becoming partners with children: From play to conversation.* San Antonio, Texas: Special Press.

MacDonald, J.D. & Gillette, Y. (1984). Conversational engineering: A pragmatic approach to early social competence. *Seminars in Speech and Language, 5,* 171–184.

McDonald, L. & Pien, D. (1982). Mother conversational behavior as a function of interactional intent. *Journal of Child Language, 9,* 337–358.

Mirenda, P.L. & Donnellan, A.M. (1986) Effects of adult interaction style on conversational behavior in students with severe communication problems. *Language, Speech and Hearing Services in Schools, 17,* 126–141.

Newson, J. (1978). Dialogue and development. In A. Lock (Ed.), *Action, gesture and symbol: The emergence of language* (pp. 31–42). London: Academic Press.

Owens, R.E. (1984). *Language development.* Columbus, Ohio: Bell & Howell.

Prizant, B.M. (1988). *Early intervention: Focus on communication assessment and enhancement.* Workshop presented in Toronto, Ontario.

Ratner, N. & Bruner, J. (1978). Games, social exchange and the acquisition of language. *Journal of Child Language, 5,* 391–401.

Sachs, J. (1984). Children's play and communicative development. In R.L. Schiefelbusch & J. Pickar (Eds.), *The acquisition of communicative competence* (pp. 109–140). Baltimore, MD: University Park Press.

Spinelli, F.M. & Ripich, D.N. (1985). Discourse and education. In D. N. Ripich & F. M. Spinelli (Eds.), *School discourse problems* (pp 3–10). San Diego: College Hill Press.

Terrel, B.Y. (1985). Learning the rules of the game: Discourse skills in early childhood. In D. N. Ripich & F. M. Spinelli (Eds.), *School discourse problems* (pp 13–27). San Diego: College Hill Press.

Trevarthen, C. & Hubley, P. (1978). Secondary intersubjectivity: Confidence, confiding and acts of meaning in the first year. In A. Lock (Ed.), *Action, gesture and symbol: The emergence of language* (pp. 183–229). London: Academic Press.

Verbey, M. (1992). *Improving joint engagement in parent-child interaction: Reanalysis of an intervention study.* Unpublished master's thesis, University of Toronto, Ontario.

Warr-Leeper, G. (1992). *General suggestions for improving language.* Presentation at Clinical Symposium on "Current Approaches to the Management of Child Language Disorders" University of Western Ontario, London, Ontario.

Wells, G. (1981). *Learning through interaction: The study of language development.* New York: Cambridge University Press.

Wells, G. (1986). *The meaning makers: Children learning language and using language to learn.* Portsmouth, New Hampshire: Heinemann.

Encourage Interactions in Group Situations: Adapt Your Activities and Routines

Encouraging all children to get involved in interactions begins with a small group and you.

A. Interact with every child in the group: you can if you SSCAN

We know that it is critically important for every child to engage in interactions with teachers and peers throughout every day. We also know, however, that these kinds of interactions don't always happen, or that they don't happen often enough. In every group of children in your classroom, you will notice that some children aren't really part of the group. Although they may be there physically, they aren't involved in the activity at hand, nor are they engaged in interactions with you or anyone else. These are the children who need your help the most. They need you to draw them in so they have the same opportunities to learn language and develop social skills as the other children. The first step in helping these children is to consider *why* they are left out of the group. Then, we can develop a plan to include them.

Sometimes a teacher doesn't realize that a child is being left out.

Children may be left out of group interactions because:

- their social and language skills are less developed than their peers' and they lack the confidence and/or the ability to get your attention in a group of confident, interactive children

- they have limited verbal skills, and you may miss their efforts to initiate interactions with you if their initiations are nonverbal, subtle, or unclear (this includes children who use pictures or signs)

- they may not fully understand what is said to them if they are language delayed or still learning English, or

- delays in their motor development make it challenging for them to participate physically in activities.

Encouraging all children to get involved in interactions begins with you and a *small* group of children – no more than four. The smaller the group, the better able you will be to observe all the children and help each one become involved. (See Chapter 11, pages 385–386, for information on how to encourage participation and interaction in large groups, like circle time.) There are a variety of small group activities that provide many, many opportunities for you to draw in each child and help her interact. For example, reading to a small group, taking a few children to the bathroom, playing at the sand table, and sitting at the lunch table are all potentially interactive small group activities. The focus of this chapter is interaction between you – the teacher – and the children in a small group. (In Chapter 6, you will learn more about how to help children interact with their peers.)

The secret to interacting with every child in a group is to remember that you **CAN** if you **SSCAN** – and if you take the time to focus on each child.

The letters of the word "SSCAN" can help you put this technique into practice:

Small
groups are best

Set up
an appropriate
activity

Carefully
observe each
child's level of
participation and
interaction

Adapt
your response to
each child's needs

Now
keep it going!

Small groups are best

How many children should be included in a group?

When possible, limit the group size to three or four children. When the group is small, interactions are far more relaxed and you can give each child much more attention.

Who should be grouped together?

It's important to group children who will be a good "mix." Think about children's conversational styles and ability to communicate. If a child has a language delay or a reluctant or passive conversational style, it will be difficult for her to be with a group of very sociable, verbal children. On the other hand, a group of children who all have reluctant conversational styles would also be unbalanced and would not provide appropriate models to each other. A successful group often results from a mix of conversational styles.

Shaida is a preschool teacher. She is concerned about Sara, a three-year-old Communicator with a language delay. Sara has a reluctant conversational style and rarely initiates interactions with teachers or peers. When she does, her sounds and subtle use of pointing often go unnoticed in the noisy classroom.

Sara is a child with a language delay and a reluctant conversational style. Shaida needs to help her get involved in the group.

Shaida is planning a group activity in which she can help Sara participate and interact.

First Shaida has to decide how many children will be in the group. She decides on four children, including Sara. Now she must decide which children to include in the group. Let's see what Shaida is thinking ...

"Emily has a more reluctant conversational style, but she does interact when she gets settled into an activity. She's an Early Sentence User, who will provide Sara with good language models. And she won't dominate the conversation, which will give Sara a chance to get involved."

Emily

"Jordan is an Early Sentence User and he's very sociable. I'll include him."

Jordan

"I don't think I'll include Daniel this time because he tends to have his own agenda. I would have to spend too much time trying to keep him at the table and involved in the activity. That would take too much time away from Sara."

Daniel

"Wilson would be a good one to include in this group. He's sociable, quite verbal (he's a Later Sentence User), and doesn't dominate in a group activity."

Wilson

Set up an appropriate activity

Select an activity that will encourage all the children in the group to participate. This isn't easy when the children in your group are at different stages of language and cognitive development and when some children have limited motor skills.

When deciding which activity to use with a small group of children, the activity should:

- Interest all the children
- Match each child's abilities
- Not involve too many materials
- Allow you and the children to be face-to-face

The activity should interest all the children

Children participate in activities that interest them. Therefore, select an activity that will appeal to all the children in the group.

The activity should match each child's abilities

The main goal of a small-group activity is to enable all children to participate, including children with delays. Children who lack confidence or who are developmentally delayed are more likely to participate in open-ended activities that do not pressure them to create a specific product. For example, four young children who are given gluesticks and a variety of paper and fabric scraps – and no specific instructions – will produce four wonderfully different creations, if given the chance. The value of the activity lies in the *act of creating the product,* rather than in the product itself.

If you have children with special needs in your group, you may need to adapt the activity to enable them to participate. It's best to start out with as few adaptations as possible so they can participate in the activity with minimal modifications. You can increase adaptations as necessary.

Adaptations of activities for individual children may involve:

- providing some physical assistance
- having different expectations for what the child will do in the activity
- modifying the materials
- setting up a different and more developmentally appropriate activity alongside the other children's activity

Least Adaptation

Most Adaptation

If a child requires accommodation because of difficulties with motor skills, you may find it helpful to consult with an occupational or physical therapist.

When planning adaptations for a child with special needs, it is important not to highlight the child's differences and make her appear less competent than the other children. One way to minimize differences is to make appropriate materials available to all the children.

Rhona has adapted this activity so all the children can participate. Gillian and Simon enjoy sailing boats in the water. Anthony also likes sailing but gets physical assistance from Rhona. Melissa has a developmental delay and is not yet pretending (see Chapter 9), but can use the cups provided to participate in her own way.

The activity shouldn't involve too many materials

Activities that involve too many materials reduce children's likelihood of interacting and communicating. Children will spend more time exploring and familiarizing themselves with the materials than they will interacting with others.

The activity should allow you and the children to be face-to-face

Your physical position in the group is critically important. Some children don't need to be face-to-face in order to interact with you. Others, especially children with reluctant and passive conversational styles, need that face-to-face contact in order to initiate at all. You should position yourself directly across from these children so that it's easy for you to make eye contact with them – and for them to make eye contact with you. When you're directly across from a child, you'll also be able to pick up her initiations, which might be as subtle as glancing at you or leaning over slightly to see what someone is doing.

Shaida is now ready to select and set up an activity for her group of children. She remembers that:

The activity should interest all the children

Sara loves to play with the cash register. She likes pushing the buttons and seeing the money disappear into the slots. Shaida has seen Sara "buy" things with play money, so she knows that Sara understands the concept of buying and selling objects. Shaida decides to set up a store, which she knows will appeal to Sara, as well as to the other children.

The activity should match the children's abilities

All the children, including Sara, are able to manipulate the toys in the "store" and understand the concept of pretending to buy and sell objects. To encourage them all to participate, Shaida won't give them directions about what to do in the store. First, she will see what they do and then she'll respond.

The activity shouldn't involve too many materials

Shaida will put enough objects and groceries in the "store" that each child has something to play with, but not so many objects that the centre becomes cluttered. When children have too many toys to choose from, they frequently switch focus, which reduces the likelihood of interaction.

The activity should allow you and the children to be face-to-face

Shaida will create a space so she can sit against the wall and be face-to-face with most of the four children at any one time.

> When you observe a small group of children participating in an activity, focus on each child for a number of seconds to observe each child's:
> ♦ Level of involvement in the activity
> ♦ Interest in the activity.

Observing children's level of involvement in an activity

Think about each child's involvement in the activity along a continuum of three elements:

♦ **Attention:** is the child showing interest in the activity, attending and reacting to what you and the other children do?

♦ **Participation** (in activities that involve physical handling of materials): is the child actively participating in the activity and handling the materials?

♦ **Interaction:** is the child interacting (initiating and responding) with you and with the other members of the group?

Just like climbing a ladder, a child must master one rung at a time: first attending, then participating, and finally interacting. You can't expect a child to interact before she can attend and participate. Similarly, if a child is attending to the activity, but not participating or interacting, then the goal is to help her participate before expecting her to interact.

A child's attention, participation, and interaction may vary depending on her ability to attend, on how interesting the activity is, and on how motivated she is to interact with you and others. It is also very important to remember that a child's involvement in any activity depends on how much she *understands*. If she has difficulty understanding what you say during the activity, she is unlikely to attend and participate.

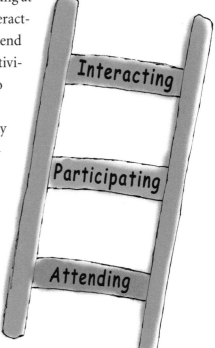

Climbing the ladder to interaction

Different levels of involvement: climbing the ladder to interaction

The child who is interacting with you and/or with any of the other children

It is easy for children who are sociable to get your attention, especially because they are the easiest ones in the group for *you* to interact with.

The child who is participating, but not interacting

Some children with reluctant conversational styles participate in activities but do not try to compete with the other children for your attention. They will not initiate unless they have your full attention and see you waiting expectantly for them to communicate.

The child who is attending, but not participating

This level of involvement can be typical of children who have reluctant conversational styles. They often do not know how to join in and are very dependent on others to tell them what to do or how to do it.

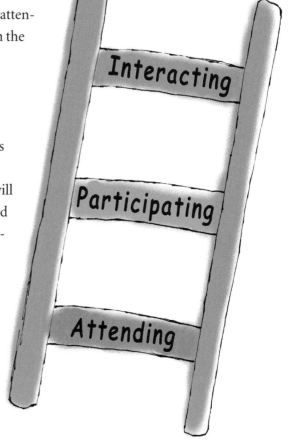

The child who is not attending

A child who does not pay attention may typically be delayed in development and/or have a passive or own agenda conversational style.

Observing children's interest in the activity

A child's interest may not be obvious – observe closely to see what aspect of the activity she's interested in. If she's playing with playdough, is she interested in poking and pulling it, or is she using it to pretend? Is that snakelike object she rolled a snake in her mind, or is it something else? Don't jump to conclusions – take the time to be sure you know what her focus is.

Let's go back to Shaida playing "Grocery Store." Shaida carefully observes the children to determine if they are attending, participating, and interacting. Let's see what Shaida's thinking...

"Emily has a reluctant conversational style. She's **participating**, but she may need some encouragement to **interact** with me and the other children."

wanna buy some cereal?

"Jordan really wants to **interact** with me."

Emily

Jordan

Push the buttons.

Wilson

Sara

"Wilson is so sociable and interested in **interacting** with the other children. He's making a real effort to get Sara involved."

"Sara is **attending**, but she's not **participating** or **interacting**. She's going to need some help to get involved because she has such a reluctant conversational style."

Adapt your response to each child's needs

Once you have observed each child's level of involvement and interest, your goal is to get all the children to interact with you and, if possible, with each other. (We'll discuss interaction with peers more fully in Chapter 6.)

Where you begin and how you respond to each child will depend on:

- ◆ her level of attention, participation, and interaction, and
- ◆ what interests her.

Aim to foster **attention** for children who are not paying attention, **participation** for children who are not participating, and **interaction** for children who are not interacting.

Begin by following each child's lead, spending a little time with her and engaging her in a "mini-conversation." Since each child may have a different focus, following the leads of all the children in a group can be challenging. It's as if each child is doing a different dance while you are trying to be each one's dancing partner. You have to be really quick on your feet to follow so many different steps!

Sometimes a conversation with one child will be interrupted as another child adds something to the topic. As long as all the children stay engaged in the conversation, these "group" conversations are fine. In fact, group conversations provide children with opportunities to experience participation in a group discussion, a skill that becomes increasingly important when they go on to school.

Jay, a child with a reluctant conversational style, is attending but he doesn't know how to join the group so he can participate. His teachers first goal is to get him involved in the activity so he can participate.

How to adapt your response for each child's level of involvement

The Child is . . .	The Goal is . . .	How to Adapt Your Response
• Not attending • Not participating • Not interacting	Help the child attend and become aware of what the activity has to offer.	• Change or adapt the activity if you think it doesn't appeal to the child or if she doesn't seem to have the skills needed to participate in it. • Make your language easy to understand (see Chapter 7). • Call her by name in an animated voice and offer her the materials. • Change position so that you are face-to-face. • Do something interesting with the materials and then wait to see what she does.
Attending, but . . . • not participating • not interacting	Encourage the child to use the materials and get involved in the activity	• Invite the child to join in. Use her name and an animated voice. • Give her a place to sit and some materials to play with. • Change position so that you are face-to-face. • Wait expectantly to see what she will do. Sometimes children just need time to relax and get involved in the activity. • Suggest a role in the game or something she could do with the materials. Demonstrate if necessary. • Comment about something you know she likes or has done in the past in a similar activity. • Make your language easy to understand (see chapter 7).

Attending, participating, but . . .
• not interacting
	Encourage the child to initiate to you or the other children.	• Sit face-to-face and observe what the child is doing. Wait! Follow the child's lead by:
		  • imitating what she is doing with the materials, and
		  • joining in the play, using your own materials.
		• Make your language easy to understand (see chapter 7).
		• Respond promptly to any initiation – and watch for subtle initiations like small gestures, quick looks, or soft sounds.
		• Use questions and comments (see Chapter 4, page 133–140) to keep her in the conversation.

Attending Participating Interacting	Engage the child in extended interactions, then continue to SSCAN the group. Ensure that one child does not control your attention in the group.	• Use sincere questions and comments to keep the child in the conversation. • If she is drawing your attention away from the other children, use gestures (e.g., hold up your hand, gently touch her arm) or give a verbal cue, like "I'm talking to Sara now. Please wait until I'm finished."

Let's go back to Shaida playing "Grocery Store" and see how she decides to adapt her response to each child's needs.

Jordan is interacting. Shaida follows his lead and extends the conversation.

Emily is participating but not interacting. Shaida encourages interaction by following Emily's lead and by using sincere comments and questions.

Sara is attending but not participating. Shaida encourages Sara's participation by making her the shopkeeper. She then encourages Sara and Emily to interact by suggesting that Emily pay Sara for her groceries. Shaida then tells Sara exactly what to do with the play money.

Wilson encourages Sara's participation by helping her fulfill her role as "shopkeeper." Shaida may be able to fade out here and let the children interact. This strategy will be discussed further in Chapter 6.

Now keep it going!

Once you have SSCANned the group and interacted with each child, start the process again. Observe each child carefully, adapting your response according to how involved she is in the activity and what seems to interest her most. This process continues for the duration of the activity. By the end of the activity, each child should feel included and involved, and should have had the opportunity to interact with you – and, possibly, with some of the other children – several times.

SSCAN the entire room

When you SSCAN the entire room, you may notice children who are not engaged in activities or interactions. These children also need help getting in on the act!

Elisa SSCANs the room and notices that
Patrice is sitting alone doing nothing . . .

. . . so she invites her to join in and play.

Now Patrice is in on the act!

SSCAN is an important strategy that you can use in group situations throughout the day. Let's look at opportunities for group interaction in sensory-creative activities and daily routines. In Chapter 9, we will look at group interaction during pretend play.

B. Plan to SSCAN during sensory-creative activities

Sensory-creative group activities offer children unique opportunities to explore, experiment, and create in an environment where it's okay to make a mess! At times, teachers may leave children alone to explore sensory materials, particularly when they have reached preschool age. At other times, teachers sit with children and capitalize on their desire to share their discoveries, sensations, and creations.

The fun isn't just in exploring, but in sharing the pudding
and experience with you.

Plan to SSCAN during sensory-creative activities and you can set the stage for children to explore and create – and share in the fun and wonder of their experiences.

 ## Small groups are best

- No more than four children.
- If you have more than four children, consider having two tables and splitting your time between the two.

 ## Set up an appropriate activity

- Let the children help prepare the materials – children love to mix paint and play-dough and hand out materials.
- Provide materials appropriate to children's stages of development. If they are very young or delayed in their development, they may still be putting things in their mouths. Provide safe materials!
- Try to have materials that are open-ended and encourage the children to be creative. Rather than setting a specific task like, "Let's all make snakes," or "Make a snowman like this one," allow each child to paint or create whatever she wants.
- Have more than enough materials for each child, but not so many things that the children are overwhelmed and distracted.

- Be well prepared. Have all the materials ready so you don't have to leave the table.
- Limit the number and type of props to encourage children to use their imaginations. For example, children ages three and up will make many imaginative creations out of playdough if they are *not* given tools, such as cookie cutters, that have a specific purpose. Provide open-ended tools, like sticks, stones, and strips of cardboard, to encourage creative and imaginative use of materials.
- Have your own materials, so you never have to take materials from a child.

Carefully observe each child

- Place the least interactive children across from you so you can be face-to-face and observe any subtle initiations.
- At the beginning of the activity, wait, wait, wait! Give children lots of time to explore the materials in their own way before you do or say anything at all. This is the moment to sit silently and observe what they do, or to handle the materials silently on your own.
- Observe each child's level of involvement – is she attending, participating, and interacting?
- Observe what each child seems most interested in – does she like to mix the finger paint, let it drop onto the paper, or use her hands to make patterns on the paper?

When children are given opportunities to explore
and create, each child will do it in a different way.

Adapt your response to each child's needs

- Once you have identified a child's levels of attention, participation, and interaction, and her focus of interest, have a mini-interaction or conversation with her. Follow her lead by imitating her actions, commenting, or joining in on her play — and making it fun!

- Once you've had a mini-interaction with one child, move on to the next child, identifying her level of involvement and following her lead. In this way, you share your attention with each child in turn.

- When a child initiates during a painting activity, for example, respond with interest and use sincere questions and comments to keep the conversation going. Try to stay away from testing questions, like "What are you making?" or "What colour is that?" which can end conversations very quickly. (See Chapter 4, pages 133–140, for more information on questions.)

- If a child is not participating, consider changing the activity. A change may be indicated if the child cannot easily manipulate the materials, if she doesn't like touching them, or doesn't seem to have the skills she needs to use them.

- Be aware of paying too much attention to the very sociable children, who may initiate constantly.

*Make a **comment** that shows your interest.*

Imitate what the children do and say, but use your own materials.

I'm Slimer and I'm gonna slime you!

I'm coming too!

I'm a slimey ghost too! Let's go and find some kids to slime!!!

Yeah, let's cover them with slime!

Join in on the children's **make-believe.**

 Now keep it going!

C. Plan to SSCAN during daily routines

"Get dressed quickly so we can go outside."
"Hurry and eat your snack so we can go and play."
"Not so much talking! Wash your hands and go and eat."

Does this sound familiar? Do you spend much of your time during routines trying to keep everyone on track?

There's no arguing that daily routines can sometimes challenge the patience of the most patient teacher. On the days when there's lots of crying (the children's, not yours!) and when nothing goes according to plan, it may seem best to get the routine over with as quickly as possible. On days like these, you may be right!

There has to be a better way to get children ready for outdoor play.

Although routines can be stressful both for you and the children in your classroom, they can promote positive relationships and language learning. Every routine has the potential for some interaction, no matter how brief. With some creative planning and flexibility, routines can provide another set of group situations where you can plan to SSCAN, making them more relaxing and interactive for everyone.

Four factors that make or break interactions during routines

The amount of interaction that occurs during a daily routine depends upon the:
- Number of teachers and children
- Physical environment
- Timing and pacing of the routine
- Role the teacher plays

The number of teachers and children

During a routine, teachers become stressed and children become restless and rowdy when there are too many of them and too few of you to help them. In all the noise and confusion, opportunities for positive interactions get lost. It becomes more challenging to notice the subtler initiations of a child with a language delay.

Consider the following solutions:

- **Have all teachers available to help.** Many directors of child-care centres or preschools organize staff schedules so that all teachers are available during the busy routines of the day.
- **Split up the group.** Smaller groups make for less noise and confusion and make "turns-on-the-run" possible. For example, when dressing children for outdoor play in the winter, it helps if one teacher goes ahead with the group that is ready first. If there is a child with special needs who is particularly sensitive to noise and confusion, or who needs more time, consider having a teacher dress her, take her to the bathroom, etc., before or after the other children.

Cut down the waiting time – take out the children who are ready.

To make time for interaction, try to stagger routines.

- **Stagger the routine.** If the toddlers don't all go to the bathroom at the same time and the infants don't all eat at 11:30 a.m., you'll have fewer children to contend with and many more opportunities for interaction.

The physical environment

A well-designed physical environment will increase opportunities for interaction.

Consider these aspects of your environment:

- **The place where the routine is conducted.** Sometimes a lack of space makes interaction difficult. For example, if all the toddlers are putting on their snowsuits in a small area, they are more likely to push and shove one another than they are in an area with more space.

If you have a child with special needs, who uses adaptive equipment like a wheelchair or walker, make sure that the space is large enough to comfortably accommodate him.

Lack of preparation and a line of high chairs is a recipe for disaster.

- **The equipment.** The equipment you use can make or break a routine. For example, there will likely be less interaction at one large lunch table with 10 children and two teachers than at two smaller tables with five children and one teacher each.
- **How you set up the environment.** Let's take a look at mealtimes again. Ideally, teachers should plan and prepare everything in advance so that they can sit and interact with the children. One child-care centre invented the "runner" system to deal with the problem of teachers constantly leaving the table to get food or drinks for children. One teacher, the "runner," is responsible for bringing the food (and anything else) to each table, where it is served by another teacher. It helps to have a small cart or table for serving bowls and supplies beside each table so that the teacher can serve the food from her seat. Except for the "runner," all teachers sit and interact with the children in a relaxed atmosphere.

Semi-circles, a table for supplies beside the teacher's chair, and plenty of preparation makes the difference. Now there are opportunities for interaction.

There will be less crying and more interaction when the babies sit at the table.

- If a child needs any special equipment during a routine, such as a seating insert or a picture communication system, make sure it is set up before you start the routine.

The timing and pacing of the routine

Consider these aspects of timing and pacing routines:

- **The time of day.** There are busy times of day – and then there are *busy, busy* times of day! Some routines have to involve all the children in the classroom at the same time, but others can be staggered. For example, toddlers can have bathroom routine as they arrive in the morning.
- **The pacing and amount of time it takes to complete the routine.** Hurried routines produce harassed teachers and frustrated children. And if routines are not well planned, children spend too much time waiting for the rest of the group. Try to have well-organized routines that allow for a slower pace and more interaction. Particularly with infants, routines like diaper-changing and feeding provide nurturing one-to-one interactions. These routines should not be rushed.

In the long run, a well-organized routine that allows for interaction won't take any longer than a rushed, poorly planned routine. And if some waiting on the children's part is unavoidable, teachers should be prepared to keep them occupied with stories, songs, or other activities.

The role the teacher plays

In the end, the success of a routine depends on you and your responsiveness to the children. If you take the time to observe and listen to them, to respond to their initiations and to pay some attention to each child, your routines won't be routine – they will be some of the best times of the day.

Instead of talking to other teachers . . .

. . . sit with the children and have a conversation.

Some shared thoughts on the dreaded "dressing-for-outdoor-play" routine

Many teachers in the northern hemisphere say that getting children dressed for outdoor play on cold, wintry days is the most difficult of all their daily routines. While teachers and children who live in warm climates have been playing in the sun, these teachers have been developing some creative solutions to make the routine more organized, more interactive, and less traumatic.

About improving interaction . . .

"When helping children get dressed, we remind ourselves of the importance of interacting with each child by thinking of the beginning, middle, and end of the conversation. The beginning involves responding to the child's request for help, offering our help, or just seeing how she is doing. The middle involves either responding to her initiation or talking to her about something we think will interest her. The end involves 'closing' the conversation by saying something like, 'You're all ready to go and play. Now I'm going to help Simon.' It's important to do all three."

"We realized that we were often dressing children from behind and were not even looking at the child we were helping! Even when we *were* in front of the child, we kept on looking around the room, talking to other children and ignoring the child we were with. Now we dress the child face-to-face and make an effort to interact as much as possible with the child we are helping."

About preventing children from getting hot and bothered . . .

"We leave jackets and hats off till everyone has their snowpants, boots, and scarves on. Only then do we put on jackets and hats – that way the children don't get so terribly hot and irritable."

"There are some children, especially in the infant and toddler rooms, who just hate to be dressed up in their snowsuits, and so we leave them till last. We let them look at a book or watch the others getting ready until we can help them. Then we dress them, trying to keep them calm by talking to them. As soon as these children are ready, we head out – fast!"

About taking the time to encourage self-help skills . . .

"When it gets cold enough to wear snowpants outside, we spend some time in small groups showing the toddlers how to put on their snowpants. This is done at the end of playtime, while some of the children are still playing. In this way, we can spend time with those children who need to be guided through each step of putting on their snowpants. It really pays off later!"

Summary

Working with groups of children presents teachers with the challenge of interacting with every child on and off throughout every day. Teachers have many ways to provide children with the attention and interaction they need in a group situation. SSCANing enables teachers to monitor involvement and interest levels of all the children in the group and to encourage participation and interaction from all children. Interactions during daily routines can be further maximized by adapting the ratio of teachers to children, the physical environment, the timing and pacing of the routine, and the role the teacher plays. There are many ways for creative teachers to make routines less stressful and rushed – and, as a result, more interactive.

References

Day, D. (1983). *Early childhood education: A human ecological approach.* Glenview, IL: Scott, Foresman.

Gonzalez-Mena, J. (1986). Toddlers: What to expect. *Young Children, November,* 47–51.

Hendrick, J. (1984). *The whole child.* St Louis: Times Mirror/Mosby.

Striker, S. (1986). *Please touch.* New York: Simon and Schuster.

Yardley, A. (1973). *Young children thinking.* London: Evans Brothers.

Chapter 6

Get Yourself Out of the Act: Fostering Peer Interaction

Playing with a mate helps children learn to communicate.

A. Interactions with peers: A vital part of learning to communicate

Let's take a look at André, whom we met in Chapter 1, during outdoor play a few weeks after his arrival at Sunshine Child Care Centre. We find him and another little boy squealing with delight as they take turns climbing onto a step and making a big show of jumping down to the ground.

We can see that the two boys are definitely interacting – they take turns jumping off the step, they look at each other as they jump, and then they laugh gleefully. They are obviously experiencing the special pleasure that comes from sharing an experience with a playmate.

Playing with peers is a wonderful, magical part of childhood. It's also a very important part of a child's life, because what children learn from interacting with peers has an enormous impact on both their social and language development.

Peer interactions differ from adult-child interactions in many ways. One important difference relates to how the two conversation partners keep the interaction going. In adult-child interactions, the adult uses various strategies to help the child stay in the conversation. Because peers can't support a child's continued participation in an interaction the way an adult can, children have to learn to hold their own during interactions with peers. When an interaction with a peer goes wrong as a result of a conflict, a lack of interest, or a misunderstanding, children have to know how to get things back on track. This is called "repairing" a breakdown in communication – and interactions with peers provide many opportunities for developing this skill.

Children need to take part in playful peer interactions.

Through peer interaction, children also develop the ability to see things from another person's point of view. They learn to make compromises, to resolve conflicts, and to share, collaborate, and cooperate with others. They also learn how to negotiate and assert themselves, which is an important skill. And all this is accomplished through the use of language. In order to become well-adjusted human beings, children need to interact with other children; even at the toddler stage, interactions with caregivers can't replace interactions with peers.

As children's play skills develop, peer interaction becomes increasingly dependent upon language. Some types of play can't succeed unless children have adequate language skills. In sociodramatic play, for example, children must be able to use language to plan, explain, negotiate, and create imaginary situations. Children learn these language skills, which involve using certain kinds of vocabulary, grammatical forms, and ways of expressing oneself, during play with other children. Peer interactions also require well-developed verbal conversational ability. Children have to be able to initiate interactions, respond when others initiate, send clear messages, continue the conversation, clear up misunderstandings, and stick to the subject. Between three and five years, it becomes obvious that the children who interact most often with their peers are the ones who have excellent language skills.

> Through peer interaction, children develop the ability to see things from another person's point of view. They learn to make compromises, to resolve conflicts, and to share, collaborate, and cooperate with others. They also learn how to negotiate and assert themselves, which is an important skill. And all this is accomplished through the use of language.

From three years of age onwards, children should demonstrate most of the following behaviours with peers:

- getting a peer's attention
- being the leader in an activity
- imitating a peer
- expressing affection toward a peer
- expressing hostility toward a peer
- following or refusing to follow a peer's request
- negotiating an acceptable solution, and
- playing in a group for a relatively long time.

B. Observing peers at play

Peer interaction usually takes place within play situations. Therefore, it is helpful to look at:
- the types of play children engage in and
- how much social interaction takes place during the play.

Types of play

A. Functional Play	
Begins in the first year of life and peaks between two and three years.	Functional play reflects Piaget's category of sensorimotor play, during which the child performs repetitive motor movements, such as manipulating and exploring toys and objects, in the environment. Examples of functional play are: • performing various actions on a toy (e.g., banging or shaking blocks, or putting objects into a container and then taking them out) • cause-effect actions (e.g., switching lights or music boxes on and off, acting on busy boxes, seeing the effects of one's actions on sand, water, playdough, etc.) • using objects according to their real functions (e.g., pushing a car back and forth) • motor activities (e.g., running and jumping)
B. Constructive Play	
Begins in the second year of life and peaks between three and four years. It is still seen in five- and six-year-olds.	During constructive play, the child uses materials to create or construct something from a plan he has in mind. He may use the same materials as he used for functional play, but he now uses them to build something. For example, he uses blocks to make a building or a tower. During constructive play, a child may spend a great deal of time on one activity, concentrating on achieving his goal.
C. Dramatic Play	
Begins in the second year of life and peaks between six and seven years.	The child pretends during dramatic play. At first, pretending consists of acting out real-life situations alone, using realistic props. In time, pretending progresses to cooperative make-believe play in groups, where the child uses language to create the play setting and story. He depends less on objects, and the objects he uses in the play may look nothing like those they are supposed to represent.
D. Games with rules	
Begins at about age six and continues throughout adulthood.	Children play games according to a set of rules accepted by the players (e.g., checkers, tag, and kickball).

How much social interaction takes place during the play?

As you observe a child at play, notice how involved he is with the other children or how aware he seems of their presence. It is important to keep in mind that, even at the kindergarten level, children still spend some time playing alone.

No social interaction

Solitary-functional play

A. Non-play behaviour

During free play, if you look around the room, you may notice some children who aren't playing at all. A child may be:

- **unoccupied:** he doesn't play, but may watch others briefly or glance around, not focusing on one activity for very long.
- **an onlooker:** he observes groups of children, without attempting to join in, although he may speak to them. Being an onlooker differs from being unoccupied because the child shows a definite interest in what the other children are doing and positions himself close to them.

B. Solitary Play

The child plays alone, using toys different from those used by children nearby.

Minimal social interaction

Parallel-constructive play

C. Parallel Play

Children play independently, but alongside one another, using the same toys and materials. They may look at each other's materials, make eye contact, or imitate the actions of other children, showing a definite awareness of each other's presence. Parallel play is thought to provide children with the right conditions to move on to more interactive forms of play.

A lot of social interaction

Cooperative group-dramatic play

D. Group Play

- **associative play:** children play with each other, each child pursuing his own interests within the same activity. They talk about what they are doing, exchange materials, and follow each other around. They are involved in a similar type of play activity because of a common interest in the activity, not because of a desire to play cooperatively.
- **cooperative play:** children play together in a group that is organized to achieve some goal, as in sociodramatic play or when playing a formal game. There is a sense of group cohesiveness, with one or two leaders assigning roles and responsibilities. The children cooperate and collaborate to accomplish the goal. Older and more mature children will be seen to engage in more associative and cooperative play.

C. Peer interactions improve with age

As children mature and develop a wider range of play, social and language skills, their play with peers becomes more and more interactive. Therefore, we need to know what kinds of play we can expect from children at different ages and stages. The three stages outlined below (infants, toddlers, and preschoolers and kindergartners) reflect the age groupings in early childhood and child-care settings in Ontario, Canada.

Infants (up to 18 months)

We can expect:

- Some unoccupied and onlooker behaviour
- Solitary-functional play
- Solitary-dramatic and constructive play (in the second year), and
- Some group functional play (in the second year).

Infants haven't yet developed the skills to engage in extended give-and-take interactions with a peer. They interact with other children far less often than older children do, and these interactions are usually brief. Therefore, we can expect mostly individual play from them. However, infants do interact with their peers in functional play activities, like pushing a car back and forth to each other or running after one another.

Caregivers of infants have described how babies little older than a year enjoy "running" from one side of the room to the other in a small group or how they all bang on the table at lunch (teachers' favourite!). It's obvious that these activities are social because the children actually look at one another, smile, and laugh together; during the running activity, they wait for each other before changing direction.

Infants enjoy interacting with peers during (noisy) functional play activities!

Toddlers (18 to 30 months)

We can expect:

- Some unoccupied or onlooker behaviour and
- Solitary functional play.

There is a definite increase in:

- Solitary dramatic and constructive play
- Parallel functional, constructive, and dramatic play, and
- Group-functional play (in the third year).

Toddlers still engage in solitary play, but they spend about half their playtime in parallel play activities. Group play consists primarily of group-functional play, but the toddler now has a larger repertoire of interactions that can be shared with peers. These include imitating another's actions (e.g., one child imitates another in throwing all the books off the bookshelf – this game would be cut short, needless to say!); playing turn-taking games like run-and-chase and ball games; rough-and-tumble games; and performing actions on the same toy.

Of course, in addition to these positive interactions, there are countless struggles to get the same toy or to become involved in the same activity. These can involve a fair amount of hitting, pushing, scratching, and even the odd bite! Toddlers still have a lot to learn about life from the other guy's point of view.

Parallel-dramatic play is a common sight in the toddler room.

Preschoolers and kindergartners (3-5 years)

We can expect decreases in:

- Unoccupied behaviour
- Solitary functional and dramatic play, and
- Parallel functional and dramatic play.

There is a definite increase in:

- Mature solitary or parallel constructive play and
- Cooperative group sociodramatic play.

Solitary and parallel play decrease from ages three to five, but they don't disappear. While solitary-functional and solitary-dramatic play should decrease, we still expect to see preschoolers and kindergartners engaged in solitary- or parallel-constructive play such as building, constructing, or drawing. Even at four-and-a-half years, children spend about a third of their time in parallel play, which offers them the opportunity to be near their peers without having to be actively involved with them.

You can see a qualitative difference in the parallel play of children approaching school age: it becomes more complex and involves more constructive play. It is quite common to see four- and five-year-olds sitting side by side doing puzzles, constructing with Lego, drawing, or making something at the sand table. Children with the ability to concentrate on a construction or creation for a long time are thought to show independence, creativity, and perseverance.

Solitary-constructive play is a common sight in the preschool room.

Group play often grows out of parallel-functional play: children start off by examining and manipulating sensory materials like sand and playdough and then proceed to play with the materials associatively or cooperatively. Parallel-functional play gives less sociable children the opportunity to work their way into a group by first playing alongside peers and then trying to gain entry into the group's play.

Group play, particularly cooperative group play, increases between three and five years of age. Three- to three-and-a-half-year-olds spend approximately one quarter of their time in group play and interact with their peers more frequently than with their teachers. Cooperative dramatic play becomes one of their preferred activities. By five years of age, children create pretend play scenarios and can interact with their peers for long periods of time.

Complete Observation Guide 3 (at the end of this chapter) to help you identify children's abilities to interact with their peers and to develop a plan of action to get socially isolated children involved in peer interactions.

D. When is a lack of peer interaction cause for concern?

By the time children reach three years of age, any difficulty with peer interactions becomes increasingly obvious. While you can expect preschoolers to engage in some solitary- and parallel-constructive play, they should participate more and more in cooperative group play and in verbal conversations with peers. Not every child is outgoing and sociable, but most children do develop relationships with their peers after the age of three and are able to maintain social interactions for at least a short time. In fact, by the age of three, children in group settings should interact more with peers than with teachers.

Peer interactions at the preschool stage require many high-level skills, one of which is well-developed verbal conversational ability. Children who seldom initiate or respond during peer interactions are breaking the basic rules of conversation and are likely to end up being ignored by their peers (see Chapter 4, page 108 for information on the rules of conversations). As well as knowing the rules of conversation, children need to know when and how to use those rules. For example, a child may be able to initiate peer interactions, but if he does so by dumping a truck on top of another child's block construction and saying, "Let's play with my truck!" he's not going to get a positive response!

Until children learn to analyze social situations and adjust their behaviour accordingly, there is an awful lot of conflict during peer interactions.

As adults, when we engage in social interactions, we constantly analyze the situation, decide what kind of behaviour is appropriate to that situation, and make the necessary adjustments as the conversation continues. This is a complex process, and it takes years to develop and refine.

Children begin to learn this process during interactions with their peers. They have to learn to consider not only the situation as a whole but also the needs, feelings, and points of view of others. For example, if a four- or five-year-old child wants to join a group of children, he might start out by asking if he can play. If he is refused permission, he might ask again in a more pleading tone or, depending on the situation, he might state aggressively that he has a right to join in, or even suggest a role for himself. If he is still refused permission, he might argue or stay close to the group and try to edge his way in. This kind of ongoing behavioural adjustment enables children to find solutions to problems with peers and to keep interactions going. Children need to be able to cooperate *and* assert themselves with peers.

Children with poor language and social skills, however, have difficulty initiating interactions with their peers and tend not to persist if their first attempt fails. Also, when a preschool child doesn't have the necessary cognitive and language skills to analyze a social situation, his interactive behaviour will often be inappropriate. This will result in rejection by peers, who may think of his behaviour as "mean" or "weird." Some children become aggressive and noncompliant when they are rejected by their peers, resulting in a cycle of poor relationships with peers and increasingly problematic behaviours.

Because a lack of peer interactions can have a negative effect on a child's social, intellectual, and language development in the long term, we should be very concerned about children aged three or older who are ignored or rejected by their peers.

Children over age three who have reluctant conversational styles and who engage only in solitary play need your help to move on to more interactive types of play. In other words, they need help getting in on the act.

Children over age two who spend large amounts of time unoccupied, or engaged in onlooker behaviour or in functional play activities, may also be cause for concern.

Children who are developmentally delayed or language delayed, who are learning English as a second language, and/or who lack age-appropriate social skills will also be at a serious disadvantage when it comes to peer interactions. If they don't have the language or social skills to interact with their peers, they will find themselves left out. And when they are left out, they can't learn the social and language skills that are normally gained through peer interactions. Children who are socially isolated can't learn complex social skills simply by being exposed to sociable children. They need support, guidance, and behind-the-scenes engineering. In many cases, some specific social skills will have to be taught to them.

It's not easy for some children to get in on the act.

E. Get socially isolated children involved in peer interactions

Children who are socially isolated can't go it alone. They need you to provide them with a physical environment that encourages peer interaction, and to create many opportunities for successful interactions with other children.

You can help children engage in peer interactions if you:
- Make the best use of the space in your classroom
- Encourage a variety of groupings
- Provide materials and activities that promote peer interaction
- Support children's interactions with peers

The information in this section is aimed primarily at children over age three. However, many of the suggestions can be applied to younger children who are having difficulties getting involved with their peers.

To help children learn to apply and generalize peer-related social skills, you may need additional information beyond the scope of this book. A number of programs and approaches are designed to improve children's social skills. Some are adult-mediated and some use peers as models, tutors, or social reinforcers. Since we know that social skills are unlikely to improve without help, it is a good idea to investigate the programs that are available in your community.

Rooms with large open spaces encourage noisy, boisterous behaviour and discourage extended, intimate peer interaction.

Make the best use of space in your classroom

The way you use space in your classroom affects group interaction. Classrooms that have shelves and tables lined up against the walls and a large open space in their centre discourage peer interaction.

Too much open space:

- Encourages running, fighting, and noisemaking
- Discourages intimate peer interactions
- Discourages quiet activities such as book reading, and
- Results in teachers spending too much time setting limits.

You can make the best use of space in your classroom if you:

- Create well-defined play areas: break up large, open spaces
- Make areas large enough for children to play comfortably
- Create private spaces
- Keep quiet and noisy areas separate
- Put areas that complement one another close together
- Create a clear pathway through the room

Create well-defined play areas: break up large, open spaces

Classroom environments encourage peer interaction when they have a variety of well-defined play areas that offer some privacy. Such environments reduce distractions and bring children closer together physically and socially.

If you have a room with a large open space in its centre, consider closing it up to increase peer interaction. Use shelving, couches, tables, or low partitions to break up the room. The house centre will then feel more like a house, and constructions in the block centre will be protected. The more privacy the area needs, the more enclosed sides it should have.

Activity centres or play areas need not all be at the edges of the room; well-defined areas in the centre will reduce open space and encourage group interaction. In addition, your partitions need not all be at right angles; placing furniture or partitions diagonally creates interesting spaces that attract children.

Use low partitions so that the children inside the play area can see the rest of the room, and the children outside can see what each play area contains. When you have made the changes, crouch down to see how it looks from a child's perspective!

Well-defined, secluded play areas promote peer interaction.

Make areas large enough for children to play comfortably

Close up large areas, but not too much! Small areas lead to crowding, which discourages group interaction. The amount of available space in each area should allow for free movement, without children bumping into one another. Block areas, for example, need a large space, as does the dramatic play area.

It's especially important to make an area large enough to accommodate children who engage in solitary or parallel play. This set-up provides these children with space to play, as well as with opportunities to work their way into the group.

Play areas should also adequately accommodate children with special needs who use adapted equipment or who have mobility challenges. Wheelchairs, individually designed seats, or adapted toys may all require extra space. Also, children with delayed motor skills or poor motor coordination may find it difficult to function in too small a space.

Create private spaces

Sometimes children need to get away from it all – to rest, to think, to dream, to relax for a while (sounds appealing doesn't it?). At home, they can often do this, but in early childhood settings, it's not that easy. Perhaps giving children a private place to go to will give them an opportunity to re-energize and come back to the group ready to play.

Private spaces can be anywhere – behind a partition or a couch, under a makeshift tent, or, best of all, in a large appliance box!

Keep quiet and noisy areas separate

The music area, for example, shouldn't be close to the book centre because the noise will discourage children from going to look at books. Book centres encourage interaction when they have comfortable seats for more than one child and when they are sheltered and quiet.

Put areas that complement one another close together

Some activity centres encourage more imaginative and cooperative play when they are close together. For example, if the block centre and dramatic play area are close together, children can use the blocks in their dramatic play.

Create a clear pathway through the room

To avoid children having to squeeze past tables or walk across established play areas, there should be a well-defined pathway that leads from one side of the room to the other. Knocking into other children or stepping on their toys won't encourage interaction!

Encourage a variety of groupings

Making the best use of space in your classroom will encourage children to come together in groups. Three kinds of peer groups can be identified in preschool settings: **pairs**, **casual groups**, and **cooperative groups**. Children benefit from being involved in each one. Planning a variety of activities in your classroom will encourage all three kinds of groupings.

Type of Peer Grouping		Where Group Occurs
Pairs	Because it is less demanding to interact with one child than with a number of children, preschoolers spend much of their time in pairs. Paired interactions are often brief, but some twosomes become "best friends" and are seldom seen apart.	◆ at tables for two ◆ in private spaces ◆ when games for two (e.g., checkers) are available
Casual groups	Casual groups form at less structured activity centres, where children come and go as they wish. Associative play is common in these groups, and interactions may not last very long. However, casual groups offer children the stimulation of interacting with peers in play situations that are relatively undemanding. Solitary or parallel play is also seen in these areas.	◆ at sensory-creative tables (during activities such as playdough, fingerpaint, water and sand play) ◆ in art areas ◆ in floor play areas ◆ at table toy areas
Cooperative groups	Cooperative groups are the most highly organized, stable, and socially demanding groups. Children often take on clear roles in cooperative groups, which consist of a small number of children, one of whom is the leader. The role of the leader is particularly obvious during sociodramatic play. Because participation in cooperative groups depends on a child's language and social skills, these groups are usually composed of children who are highly verbal and imaginative.	◆ in the dramatic play area ◆ in the block area ◆ in floor play areas

Cooperative groups attract children who are highly imaginative and verbal.

Provide materials and activities that promote peer interaction

Even in the most well-designed classrooms, some children end up playing alone. Once the classroom has been designed to make the best use of space and encourage a variety of groupings, the next step is to look at the materials and activities within it to see how they can be engineered to get isolated children involved with their more social peers.

> **You can promote peer interaction through materials and activities if you:**
> - Set up an environment that brings children together
> - Provide large pieces of equipment that encourage interaction
> - Adapt play activities to increase the likelihood of interaction
> - Provide toys for all developmental levels
> - Provide duplicate toys
> - Provide an appropriate number of toys – neither too many nor too few
> - Set up the environment so children are face-to-face
> - Encourage outdoor group interactions

Set up an environment that brings children together

Children are more likely to interact if they are near each other and engaged in the same activity. Your task is to bring children together to increase the likelihood of interaction.

Provide large pieces of equipment that encourage interaction

Certain large pieces of equipment create opportunities for interaction by bringing children together in a small space. Good examples of large play equipment include large stationary toy buses or cars with seats for two or more children, rocking boats with seats along the perimeter, indoor slides, large toy houses, and couches in the book centre.

Adapt play activities to increase the likelihood of interaction

Some play activities, like blocks, puzzles, playdough, books, and computers, tend to be associated with solitary play. However, you can set up these activities so that interaction is more likely. The first step toward interaction may involve parallel play, with a child playing by himself, close to his peers. Since parallel play often leads to social play, consider this a good first step. You can encourage interaction by:

- placing cars in the block centre to encourage children to "drive" through the block structures other children build
- providing a large floor puzzle rather than a small table puzzle so that children can work together on the same activity

- offering a limited number of tools in a playdough activity so children will need to share (you might need to join children in this activity to model and encourage appropriate requesting and turn-taking!), or
- bringing a solitary child closer to his peers by placing his favourite toy near them. Alternatively, attract peers to a child who usually plays alone by setting up a fun or novel activity that you know the more isolated child enjoys.

1. Michael spends much of his time playing alone, spinning the wheel on a miniature egg beater in the kitchen centre. Let's see what his teacher, Shandra, decides to do to encourage Michael to interact with his peers.

2. Michael is now at the water table with his favorite toy, playing alongside the other children.

3. Soon, Julia notices Michael stirring the water with his egg beater and joins in by offering him a bucket of water to mix.

Provide toys for all developmental levels

A child can interact with his peers in an activity only if he is physically and developmentally able to participate in that activity. Full participation can be challenging for a child who lacks the necessary cognitive, motor, language, and/or social skills. To successfully include all children, you need to provide materials that both lend themselves to social play and are appropriate to all ability levels.

Example: Accommodate children at functional and constructive stages of play

Children at the constructive play level may enjoy building houses and bridges. However, a child who is still at the functional play level does not use blocks to build things. Therefore, he will not be able to join in a "building a house" activity with his peers. However, this child may enjoy dropping blocks in a container and then taking them out. You may, therefore, be able to encourage him to play in the block area near his peers by placing some containers in with the blocks.

Example: Accommodate children who can pretend with and without realistic props

A child with a cognitive delay may not be able to participate in the dramatic play centre since he cannot pretend at the same level as the other children. He may need very realistic props while the other children may prefer open-ended props or may not need props at all. A mixture of realistic and open-ended props will accommodate the children's varied levels of make-believe – and will provide something for everybody. For example, if the play centre is set up as a restaurant, you could include props like real menus, a napkin holder, a waiter's uniform, and trays.

Provide duplicate toys

The first step to interaction may be to encourage a child to watch his peers and join in their activities. If he is able to use the same toys or materials as his peers, a child may be motivated to imitate them, moving from solitary to parallel play (i.e., playing near his peers with the same materials). This strategy can work particularly well in less structured situations, such as creative or sensory activities (e.g., painting, or sand and water play), or with table or floor toys.

Provide an appropriate number of toys – neither too many nor too few

The number of toys in an activity centre affects the amount of interaction in that centre. If there are too many toys, children will spend their time exploring the materials rather than interacting with each other. Too few toys, on the other hand, may lead to disputes over who gets what, resulting in conflict and disruption. Children with language delays will have particular difficulty handling such conflict due to their poor verbal negotiation skills, adding to their isolation in the room.

If there are too many toys, children will spend their time exploring the materials rather than interacting with each other.

Too few toys may lead to disputes over who gets what, resulting in conflict and disruption.

I want a cup too.

No, it's mine!

Set up the environment so children are face-to-face

Just as your interactions with children are enhanced when you are face-to-face with them, being face-to-face fosters children's interaction with each other. Therefore, arrange materials so that children are more likely to look at each other. To encourage face-to-face interaction, you could:

- ◆ pull tables, such as water or sand tables, away from a wall so that children play across from each other rather than beside each other
- ◆ seat children across from each other at lunch or creative tables, or
- ◆ make sure there is enough space in the block centre so children can play face-to-face rather than only side by side.

Encourage outdoor group interactions

Outdoor activities that involve running, chasing, jumping, and going down the slide enable children with good motor skills but limited social skills to interact successfully with their peers.

This kind of play is not very demanding for the less sociable child because it has few rules and involves little conversation. If the child is physically able to keep up, outdoor games can be extremely interactive.

Outdoor group-functional play provides opportunities for everyone to join in.

Let's make another train!

Support children's interactions with peers

Once you have made the best use of space in your classroom, encouraged a variety of groupings, and provided materials to increase the likelihood of interaction among children, you will still need to provide support to children who remain unengaged with their peers, or who can't maintain an interaction once it has started.

You can help socially isolated children interact with their peers if you:
- Are aware of too much teacher-child interaction
- Help children develop a "shared understanding" of themes and concepts used in the classroom
- Pair a socially isolated child with a more sociable child
- Assign a collaborative task
- Step in, set up, and fade out of activities
- Direct conversations away from yourself
- Set up a small group – and stay to play
- Raise the profile of the low-profile child

Be aware of too much teacher-child interaction

Children who have difficulty interacting with peers may spend a lot of time with you – perhaps too much. They may initiate interactions only with you because they are assured of getting a positive response. You may also find that – without realizing it – you spend too much time supervising and guiding a child who is developmentally delayed and/or socially withdrawn, because he seems to need all the teacher input he can get. "Hovering over" or "shadowing" a child, however, interrupts his opportunities for peer interaction, makes him too dependent on adults, and encourages other children to regard him as "different." If there is a low teacher-child ratio in a classroom, children with special needs may spend too much time with their teachers. Research has shown that the more adults there are in a classroom, the less peer interaction there is!

Help children develop a "shared understanding" of themes and concepts used in the classroom

Michael Guralnick has coined the term "shared understanding" to refer to a child's need to understand a concept, in the same way his peers understand it, in order to behave appropriately in a situation. For example, in order to participate in a dramatic play centre set up as a restaurant, a child needs to understand what a restaurant is; the purpose of restaurant equipment and materials like menus, coffee machines, and cash registers; and appropriate behaviour for cooks, serving staff, and customers. If he has never been to a restaurant, or has not yet developed an understanding of appropriate equipment, roles, and behaviours associated with restaurants, then a classroom activity based on a restaurant will be beyond his capabilities. A lack of shared understanding may result in inappropriate behaviour. Or, a child may avoid the activity entirely, becoming further isolated.

It's important, therefore, to help children develop a shared understanding of the concepts for any new activity. In the above example, if it is not possible to take the child to a restaurant, you can recreate a restaurant experience in the classroom, using it to help him develop an understanding of restaurants – and an "internal script" about them that he can follow during pretend play. You can use stories about visits to a restaurant or role-play a trip to one, using realistic props and guiding him through the experience.

Some children need a great deal of practice in order to develop a shared understanding of a situation or concept. Therefore, it's very important to get parents involved in reinforcing a child's learning about a new concept.

Pair a socially isolated child with a more sociable child

Pairing a sociable child with a socially withdrawn child can provide the less skilled child with some positive social experiences. This strategy works best if the children are the same age, and if the sociable child is willing to comply with your suggestion and is interested in the isolated child. In addition, the sociable child must have appropriate play skills and should play in the selected activity often.

When pairing peers, you need to set the tone for a friendly, cooperative interaction with phrases like, "You and Cory can play together with this new construction toy," "I want you two to help each other build something out of these blocks," or "How about you two find out together which of these three wind-up toys jumps the farthest?" This approach helps you avoid a situation in which the focus is on the child with well-developed social skills "helping" or "teaching" the less skilled child.

When paired with a child with poor social skills, the socially skilled child instinctively adjusts how he interacts so that he can engage his classmate. He is likely to simplify his language, use more repetition, and give instructions when necessary. In fact, he makes some of the same adjustments to his speech that caregivers make when interacting with young children.

Felix is a withdrawn four-year-old with a language delay. Tim is a sociable, verbal four-year-old. Because Felix interacts more with Tim than with anyone else, every now and again their teacher pairs up the two boys. On one occasion, she asks the boys if they want to go together to the "secret hideaway" (a large appliance box) and explore the "treasure box" (a box full of interesting ornaments and trinkets). Felix and Tim examine, share, and talk about the interesting objects they find in the box – and both boys have a lot of fun.

Assign a collaborative task

When a pair or small group of children completes an assigned task together, a great deal of conversation and collaboration can result. The best tasks are real-life ones, like cleaning up a spill with a broom and dustpan, making a sign for the classroom, setting up a new toy, or mixing the ingredients for a sensory activity. When you assign these tasks, each child should have a distinct role to play, and shouldn't need help in order to complete his task. The task should be set up so that a successful final product is possible only if each child contributes (this prevents the more competent children from doing it all themselves).

Collaborative tasks can bring about positive interaction and good feelings among the children in the group. The less social children feel more important and capable as a result. These tasks can accomplish a great deal, especially if they are assigned regularly so that the positive effects don't vanish as soon as the interaction is over.

There's a lot to talk about when you have a job to do together.

Step in, set up, and fade out of activities

If you ask a group of children if another child can play with them, it's too easy for them to say "No!" – or to say "Okay" and then ignore the child. To get in on the act, therefore, a child with delayed language or social skills will need some very skilful intervention from you.

By setting up an interaction, giving a socially isolated child a specific role to play, and then fading yourself out of the picture, you can help socially isolated children participate actively with their peers.

There are two ways to step in, set up, and fade out:

- ◆ set up interactions from inside the group – give the child a role to play while you are part of the play and
- ◆ set up interactions from outside the group – make suggestions without playing yourself.

Set up interactions from inside the group – give the child a role to play

When you set up interactions from inside the group, you must engineer a way of including an isolated child *while you participate in the play.* Your task is to give the child a role to play, using a gentle, playful approach so that your suggestions are interpreted not as instructions but as a positive addition to the existing play. By creating a desirable role for the isolated child within the existing play of a group of children, you increase the chances of that child being accepted into the activity.

You are in the dramatic play area, and you are playing "Store" with three children. You see Anna, who usually plays alone, making tea for her dolls nearby. You decide to try to get her to join the group.

"I see my friend Anna across the street!" you say to the children. "Hi Anna! We're so thirsty. Could we buy some drinks from you?" (It's important to continue playing a pretend role in this situation, to avoid being seen by the children as "the teacher" who is insisting that another child be admitted to their play.)

Anna's face lights up, and she comes over, bringing some cups with her.

"How much is the tea?" you ask.

"Five dollars," she replies.

"Okay! I'm so thirsty, I'll pay anything," you say. "Anybody here want a drink from Anna's store? She makes the best drinks in town!"

The rest of the group follows your example, and Anna "sells" everyone a drink. You talk to her (in your pretend role) as if she really were a "drink seller," and when she seems to have become part of the group, you leave.

"I have to catch my bus now," you say. "I'm going to visit my aunt. Thanks for all the lovely things, and thanks so much for the tea . . ."

Then you fade out of the picture.

Nicole usually plays alone. Even when she is at the water table with other children, she does not interact with them. Marta, her teacher, joins the group and creates a desirable role for Nicole as "hairwasher."

The other children then become interested in Nicole and begin to interact with her.
Then, Marta is able to fade out of the interaction.

Set up interactions from outside the group – make suggestions without playing yourself

Sometimes you can help a child join a group without joining the group yourself. By suggesting a desirable role for the child that enhances the play, you increase the chances of the other children accepting him into their play.

During free play, you notice Liam annoying the girls in the house centre. He keeps on driving his wagon into the wall of the "house," and they are getting very irritated with him. You know that he's doing it for attention and that he lacks the social skills to initiate interactions appropriately.

You approach him and make a suggestion quietly in his ear. He agrees and goes to get some toy tools, which he puts in his wagon. Then you both go back to the house centre and knock on the door. The girls say, "Who's there?"

Look at what happens . . .

Help the child find a role that adds some fun to the play.

Fade away when you see they're doing okay!

Sometimes, whether or not they are socially skilled, children need to be prompted or coached to look at and listen to each other to initiate and maintain an interaction.

Four-year-old Michael is building a tower in the block centre. Justice, a four-year-old Combiner with a language delay, is watching him closely. Obviously, he wants to play. Both boys will need some coaching for the interaction to work. Essie, their teacher, coaches Michael:

> *"Michael, can you look at Justice and ask him what he wants?"*
> *"What do you want?" Michael asks.*
> *Essie then coaches Justice: "Tell Michael you want the blocks."*
> *"Want blocks," Justice says.*
> *Essie then coaches Michael on how to reinforce Justice: "Michael, now you can say to Justice, 'Okay, we can play together,' and give him some blocks."*
> *Michael uses Essie's model to invite Justice to play with him. Essie's coaching makes Michael more aware of Justice as a play partner and provides Justice with a successful – and fun – play experience.*

Direct conversations away from yourself

In group discussions, children often direct more initiations to you than to their peers. When this happens, you become like an air-traffic controller – all incoming and outgoing conversation is routed through you!

Use your role as air-traffic controller to the children's advantage: redirect the conversation by drawing quieter children into the conversation and then fading yourself out. You can do this by asking questions, making statements that a child can confirm and expand upon, and acting as an interpreter for children who have difficulty making themselves understood. This strategy will be most successful if the children are physically near each other, share common interests, and are participating in a similar activity.

When directing conversations away from yourself and drawing in a quiet child, it's important that the child's peers notice and listen to him. Sometimes, you may need to prompt a quiet child to speak loudly enough to gain his listener's attention and to wait for the response. Even then, a child who is isolated in the classroom and typically plays on his own is often not noticed by his peers when he is encouraged to direct a comment to them. You may need to prompt the peer to respond with a comment like, "Look, Sean, Noah wants to give you a car."

Ryan, an Early Sentence User with a language delay, approaches his teacher, Gillian, and asks to play with the dinosaurs that two other children are playing with. Gillian decides to direct the conversation away from herself to Christopher, who is playing nearby with the dinosaurs.

Gillian knows that Ryan often speaks quietly and is not easily understood by the other children. She says, "Ryan, call Christopher and tell him in a loud voice so that he can hear you, 'I want to play too.'"

Even though Ryan speaks loudly, Christopher does not respond to him. Gillian prompts Christopher, saying "Christopher, listen to Ryan. He wants to play too." Christopher responds by giving Ryan a dinosaur and Ryan happily joins in the play.

You can direct conversations away from yourself in different ways:

Ways to Direct Conversations Away	What you do	When to do it	Example
Direct conversation away from yourself by providing a model of what to say	Tell the child exactly what to say to his peer	Works best if child is unfamiliar with situation or unable to say words on his own	"Tell Paul, 'Look at my hat.'"
Direct conversation away from yourself with direct suggestions (no model provided)	Tell the child to initiate to his peer without telling him exactly what to say	Works best if child can produce words on his own	"Show Paul that funny hat you were just wearing."
Direct conversation away from yourself with a hint or indirect suggestion	Make a more subtle suggestion to encourage the child to initiate to his peer	Works best if the child's language, cognitive, and social skills are well-enough developed for him to understand indirect suggestions	"I bet Paul would love to see your hat."

You can direct conversations away from yourself in different situations:

Purpose of Child's Initiation	Example	How to Redirect
Requests to play	If a child tells you he wants to play with blocks . . .	Say, "Tell Jordan, 'I want to play with the blocks.'"
Requests for materials	If a child asks you for glue . . .	Say, "Ask Jordan for the glue."
Requests for help	If a child asks for help with block building . . .	Say, "I think Jordan knows how to put those blocks together."
Requests for approval or praise	If a child shows you a picture he has drawn . . .	Say, "Show that picture to Jordan. I think he'll like it."
Comments	If a child starts to tell you about a movie he saw . . .	Say, "Tell Jordan what you saw in the movie. He went to see it last week."

By directing the conversation away from himself, the teacher is encouraging conversation among the children.

Set up a small group – and stay to play

Even when you step in, set up, and fade out, many children still can't go it alone. They don't yet have the skills to stay involved in interactions with other children. As soon as you leave, they are no longer part of the group. These children need you to stay and support them during the interaction.

Start off small – perhaps just you and the child alone. A small corner with a few toys won't seem so overwhelming to a socially withdrawn or delayed child. Or, join a small group of children who are already engaged in an activity, but make sure that the activity is appropriate to the child's level of play. If he engages primarily in simple pretend play or in constructive play, start with that. Sociodramatic play may be cognitively too demanding for some children, particularly if they are language delayed (see Chapter 9 for information on how to promote pretend play).

Once you and the child begin to interact, you can involve one or two children in your play or become involved in theirs. You can keep the interaction going a number of ways:

- by following the children's lead and joining in their play (e.g., if the children are playing with toy cars, you get a toy car and "drive" it along with them)
- by making suggestions that encourage interaction (e.g., "Let's drive our car over to Thomas's car and see what he's doing.")
- by offering props that will create interaction (e.g., "Let's make a tunnel for all the cars to go under."), or
- by giving the child toys that will keep him involved (e.g., "Here's a man who wants a ride in your truck.").

Children who rarely play with others may take a long time to warm up to their peers. At the beginning, there may be long periods of silence and little interaction. As long as these children are enjoying themselves and are exposed to other children, they can still benefit from such interactions.

Raise the profile of the low-profile child

Children often form negative impressions of their less able peers, and these impressions can be hard to change. But unless they do change, the less social child remains at a serious disadvantage.

 "She can't say anything," says Lara of Kelly, a language-delayed four-year-old. "I don't wanna play with him," says Mohammed about Brian, a developmentally delayed five-year-old. "He doesn't know how to play properly."

You can raise the profile of these less able children by helping their peers look at their disabilities in a different light.

> **Teacher:** *"You know, Lara, Kelly is still learning to talk and she's trying as hard as she can. Learning to talk is hard when you're just starting out. Some children learn to talk when they are small and others learn when they're bigger. It's like learning to ride a bike – my sister could ride a bike when she was five, but I only learned when I was seven!"*

You can encourage children to find ways to interact with the less able child – and make the idea seem fun!

> **Teacher:** *"There are so many games you could play with Kelly that don't need talking, Lara. She loves running games and playing with 'goop.' I'll bet you could think of some games you could play with her, and you can let me know if you need anything for them."*

When you give Lara the responsibility for initiating positive interactions, you give her the opportunity to change her negative image of Kelly.

You can also give less social children high-profile jobs, like setting up an art table. In addition, show them a new toy first so that they feel like the "expert" when other children come to play with it.

Changing children's perceptions of their peers is a challenge. But if you can effect some change, you have gone a long way to setting the stage for positive peer interactions.

Summary

Teachers can do many things to help socially isolated children take part in peer interactions. They can create environments that have well-defined play areas and stimulating activities. They can set up interactive situations that make it easier for children to join in with their more sociable peers. They can also set up small groups where they create roles for socially isolated children so that they are included in the activity. Teachers may also have to stay and play with children who cannot keep an interaction going without continuous support. In these situations, the goal is to help the children learn social skills, which they will then use independently. And teachers can make every effort to promote children's positive attitudes toward their less interactive and less verbal peers by raising the latter's profile.

Observation Guide 3:
The child's interactions with peers

Child's name: _____

Age at time of this observation: _____

Child's first language: _____

Child's ability to speak English (if child is verbal): _____

Date: _____

A. What types of play does the child engage in most of the time? (Record examples.)

- ❑ Functional
- ❑ Constructive
- ❑ Dramatic
- ❑ Games with rules

B. How much social interaction takes place during the play most of the time?

No social interaction
- ❑ Non-play
  - ❑ Unoccupied
  - ❑ Onlooking
- ❑ Solitary play
  - ❑ Functional
  - ❑ Constructive
  - ❑ Dramatic

Minimal social interaction
- ❑ Parallel play
  - ❑ Functional
  - ❑ Constructive
  - ❑ Dramatic

A lot of social interaction
- ❑ Group play
  - ❑ Functional
  - ❑ Constructive
  - ❑ Dramatic

Please note: All Observation Guide pages may be photocopied.

C. How does the child interact with peers?

		INITIATE			RESPOND		
		Requests	Comments	Questions	Requests	Comments	Questions
Child to Peers	Often						
	Sometimes						
	Rarely						
Peers to Child	Often						
	Sometimes						
	Rarely						

With which children does the child interact most frequently?

During which activities is the child most interactive with his peers?

A Planning Guide to Promote Peer Interaction

Begin by using Observation Guide 3 to identify and describe a child who does not regularly interact with his or her peers. Then, use the following questions to help you plan how to encourage this child to interact with his or her peers:

Develop an action plan

1. Are there appropriate peer groupings for the child to join?

- Is the environment set up to encourage the child to interact with other children?
- What is the best type of grouping for this child? A pair? Casual group? Cooperative group?
- Is there an opportunity for the child to join this type of grouping? If yes, when and where? If not, how can you create this opportunity?
- Are the children involved in the activity good conversational partners for the child? If not, can you change the make-up of the group? If yes, what role could the peers play in encouraging this child to interact?

Now, decide which grouping you will try and which children you will include.

2. Do the activities and materials promote peer interaction?

- Are there large pieces of equipment to draw the child to other children in a small space (e.g., cars, boats, slides, play houses, etc.)?
- Are there opportunities for outdoor group activities?
- Are there duplicate toys?
- Is there an appropriate number of toys?
- Do the activities encourage the children to be face-to-face?
- What materials are available? Do the materials need to be modified for this child so s/he can participate in the activity? If so, how?
- Are there opportunities for collaborative tasks?
- Does the child have a "shared understanding" of the themes and concepts used in the classroom? If not, how can you support him or her to acquire them?

Now, decide which activities and materials you will use.

3. Do you need to facilitate the child's interactions with his peers?

- ◆ Are there too many or too few teachers?
- ◆ Which teachers are present and what are they doing?
- ◆ Is there too much teacher-child interaction?
- ◆ Could a teacher:
  - step in, set up interaction from inside or outside of the group, and fade out?
  - direct conversations away from him/herself?
  - stay to play?
  - raise the child's profile?

Now, decide how you will support the child's interactions with his peers.

Try your action plan

You may need to repeat the activity several times to give the child a chance to become comfortable with the activity and his peers.

Evaluate your action plan

Observe how the child interacts with his peers in the new activity you have planned.

		INITIATE			RESPOND		
		Requests	Comments	Questions	Requests	Comments	Questions
Child to Peers	Often						
	Sometimes						
	Rarely						
Peers to Child	Often						
	Sometimes						
	Rarely						

Compare these observations with what you initially recorded on page 219. How successful was your activity?

If you were to do the activity again, how would you modify it? For example, would you encourage more participation from children, encourage more interaction among children, provide more or less prompting or structure, modify materials, or use different materials?

References

Adcock, D. & Segal, M. (1983). *Making friends.* Englewood Cliffs, NJ: Prentice-Hall.

Corsaro, W. A. (1981). Friendship in a nursery school: social organization in a peer environment. In S. R. Asher & J. M. Gottman (Eds.), *The development of children's friendships* (pp. 207–241). New York: Cambridge University Press.

Cavallaro, C.C. & Haney, M. (1999). *Preschool inclusion.* Baltimore: Paul H. Brookes Publishing Co.

Craig-Unkefer, L.A. (2002). Improving the social communication skills of at-risk preschool children in a play context. *Topics in Early Childhood Special Education, 22–2,* 3–13.

Field, T. (1981). Early peer relations. In P. Strain (Ed.), *The utilization of classroom peers as behavior change agents* (pp. 1–30). New York: Plenum.

Field, T., Roopnarine, J.L. & Segal, M. (Eds.), (1984). *Friendships in normal and handicapped children.* Norwood, NJ: Ablex.

Gallagher, T.M. (1991). Language and social skills: Implications for assessment and intervention with school-age children. In T, M. Gallagher, (Ed.), *Pragmatics of language: Clinical practice issues* (pp. 11–41). San Diego, CA: Singular.

Guralnick, M. (1982). Programmatic factors affecting child-child social interactions in mainstreamed preschool programs. In P.S. Strain (Ed.), *Social development of exceptional children* (pp. 71–91). Rockville, MD: Aspen.

Guralnick, M. (1986). The peer relations of young handicapped and nonhandicapped children. In P.S. Strain, M. Guralnick & H.M. Walker (Eds.), *Children's social behavior: Development, assessment and modification* (pp. 93–140). New York: Academic Press.

Guralnick, M. (1990). Peer interactions and the development of handicapped children's social and communicative competence. In H. Foot, M.J. Morgan & R.H. Shute (Eds.) *Children helping children* (pp. 275–305). New York: John Wiley & Sons.

Guralnick, M. & Neville, B. (1997). Designing early intervention programs to promote children's social competence. In M. Guralnick (Ed.). *The effectiveness of early intervention* (pp. 579–610). Baltimore: Paul H. Brookes Publishing Co.

Guralnick, M. (Ed.). (2001). *Early childhood inclusion: Focus on change.* Baltimore: Paul H. Brookes Publishing Co.

Hadley, P.A. & Rice, M. (1991). Conversational responsiveness of speech- and language-impaired preschoolers. *Journal of Speech and Hearing Research, 34,* (6), 1308–1317.

Hendrick, J. (1984). *The whole child.* St Louis: Times Mirror/Mosby.

Hildebrand, V. (1980). *Guiding young children.* New York: MacMillan.

Johnson, J.E., Christie, J.F. & Yawkey, T.D. (1987). *Play and early childhood development.* Glenview, IL: Scott, Foresman.

Katz, L.G. & McClellan, D.E. (1997). *Fostering children's social competence: The teacher's role.* Washington, DC: National Association for the Education of Young Children.

Kritchevsy, S., Prescott, E. & Walling, L. (1974). Planning environments for young children: Physical space. In G. Coates (Ed.), *Alternative learning environments* (pp. 311–320). Dowden: Hutchinson & Ross.

Levy, A.K. (1986). The language of play: The role of play in language development. In S. Burroughs and R. Evans (Eds.), *Play, language and socialization* (pp. 163–175). Cooper Station, NY: Gordon & Breach.

Loughlin, C.E. & Suina, J.H. (1982). *The learning environment: An instructional strategy.* New York: Teachers College Press.

Loughlin, C.E. & Martin, M.D. (1987). *Supporting literacy: developing effective learning environments.* New York: Teachers College Press.

Rice, M., Sell, M.A. & Hadley, P.A. (1991). Social interactions of speech- and language-impaired children. *Journal of Speech and Hearing Research, 34,* (6), 1299–1307.

Rice, M.L. & Wilcox, K.A. (1995). *Building a language-focused curriculum for the preschool classroom, Volume I: A foundation for lifelong communication.* Baltimore: Paul H. Brookes Publishing Co.

Sachs, J., Goldman, J. & Chaille, C. (1985). Narratives in preschoolers sociodramatic play: The role of knowledge and communicative competence. In L. Galda and A.D. Pellegrini (Eds.), *Play, language and stories: The development of children's literate behavior* (pp. 45–61). Norwood, NJ: Ablex.

Strain, P.S. (1982). Peer-mediated treatment of exceptional children's social withdrawal. In P.S. Strain (Ed.), *Social development of exceptional children* (pp. 93–105). Rockville, MD: Aspen.

Provide Information and Experience that Promote Language Learning

Social interaction with caring, responsive adults is crucial to children's development, but it isn't the only thing they need. Part 3 of this book is about providing children with information and experiences that help them develop spoken language, not only to satisfy their physical and social needs but also to think, problem-solve, imagine, and learn.

In Chapter 7, "Adjust the Way You Talk" you will find clear, practical suggestions for helping children at each of the six stages of language development. This chapter also addresses the needs of the second-language learner.

Chapter 8, "Create an Environment for Talking and Learning," describes how children (from about three years onward) learn to use more sophisticated language for planning, thinking, imagining, and learning. It provides a simple framework for encouraging such language use during daily interactions and conversations.

Chapter 9, "Promote Pretend Play: Imagine the Fun, Imagine the Learning," contains information on the development of pretend play and its relationship to language. This chapter has many illustrated examples of what you can do to promote pretend play and, in the process, foster language learning.

Learning Language and Loving It

Adjust the Way You Talk

Learning language is an active process spurred on by a child's search for meaning and her desire to communicate. You can help this process by adjusting the way you talk to children at different stages of development.

A. Children learning language: Cracking the code

When children begin to talk, it may seem as if they are simply learning words, but they aren't. What they are learning is a *code*.

Language is a code with a system of rules that children learn in a predictable sequence. (This sequence is reflected in the stages of language development described in Chapter 2.) Children learn which sounds are used, how these sounds are combined to form words, and how words are combined into sentences according to the rules of grammar. There are a set number of rules to the code. Once a child learns these rules, she can apply them to any number of sentences; this makes spoken language much more powerful and flexible than nonverbal communication.

No one ever sits down and teaches an infant that, for example, "my" goes before "bottle" or that "me" is what she says when she refers to herself. However, as an active learner, she identifies patterns in the language she hears and uses these patterns to figure out the rules. She tests these rules by using them when speaking to others. If they work, she uses them in other situations. For example, once she learns that the "my" in "my cookie" indicates that the cookie belongs to her, she uses it in sentences like "my car," "my doggie," and "my Mama."

The rules of English grammar are quite complicated, and there are many exceptions to them. For example, we say "I pulled," or "I pushed," but not "I eated." However, young children *do* say "I eated," because they first apply a general rule to every possible situation, and later figure out the exceptions to each rule. By five years of age, children have changed and expanded their use of rules so that their sentences sound more and more adult-like.

The six stages of communication and language development:

Discoverer

Communicator

First Words User

Combiner

Early Sentence User

Later Sentence User

This child is just beginning to crack the code.

Learning rules is an active process, spurred on by a child's search for meaning and her desire to communicate effectively. Everyday conversations with the important adults in a child's life provide the context within which she extracts the rules of language and learns to talk. This process is far more challenging for children who are language delayed or who are learning English as a second language. It takes them longer to "crack the code" and they may need to be exposed to a language pattern many times before they are able to learn the rules that govern its use.

As a teacher, adjusting the way you talk begins with following the child's lead and keeping the conversation going. Once you've made a connection with her, you have many opportunities to provide language models that are matched both to her topic of interest and her stage of language development.

The more rules of language a child has learned, the more adult-like her sentences sound.

B. Adjust the way you talk: Strategies that help children learn language

Adults use some very specific strategies when talking with children – strategies that have been shown to play an important role in helping children learn language. You may use some of these strategies quite naturally, without thinking about it. Some of them, however, may not come naturally to you and you will need to make a conscious effort to use them.

The following strategies help children learn language:

- Make your language easy to understand
- Match your language to the child's interests
- Interpret the child's sounds, actions, and gestures with simple language
- Engage the child in social routines
- Label things in the child's world
- Imitate what the child says
- Expand on what the child says
- Extend the topic

Make your language easy to understand

The way you talk to children is probably quite different from the way you talk to adults. Research has shown that adults make spontaneous changes to the way they talk to children, especially when talking to infants and children who have not yet developed language or who are in the early stages of language development. A most important part of this kind of speech, which is called "Baby Talk" or "Motherese," involves making your language easy to understand so that children can figure out the rules of language. While many people think of "Motherese" as the way mothers talk to their babies, it isn't restricted to mothers. It applies to how any adult talks to a baby or young child in an effort to connect with her, to express tenderness, and to help her become part of the communicating world.

When using Motherese, parents and other caregivers:

- Say less
- Stress
- Go slow
- Show

Say less

- They shorten their sentences.
- They simplify their messages, using less complex grammar as well as simplified vocabulary, such as "doggie" for "dog."

*Let's put your **hat on**, Michael, ok? Put your **hat on**?*

Stress

- They emphasize important words.
- They vary and exaggerate their tone of voice and use a higher-than-normal pitch.
- They use a great deal of repetition.

When you use Baby Talk, it's natural to say the same thing over and over.

Go slow

- They speak slowly, with longer pauses between words.

Show

- They talk about familiar things in the here and now.
- They hold up objects or point to them as they talk.

Adults' use of "Motherese" changes as children's understanding increases and as their language use becomes more mature.

Boom Boom Boom!

Boom! Boom! You're banging the drum!

Wow, you're a really good drummer! You could be in a band!

Put music in your voice for Discoverers

> **Say Less**
> **Stress**
> **Go slow**
> **Show**

Discoverers have not yet learned to send messages directly to you and they can't understand speech. However, they do listen to the "music" in your voice and they are very interested in your face and facial expressions. They will not understand what you *say*, but they may understand what you *mean* if you stress important words and speak slowly. Because Discoverers don't yet attend to the meanings of specific words, your sentences can be longer and less repetitive than they will be once children start to understand words.

Cheryl varies her tone of voice and speaks slower than usual to keep Sammy's attention.

Say less and say it again for Communicators

> **Say Less**
> **Stress**
> **Go slow**
> **Show**

Communicators are working hard to try to understand language. When interacting with them, you have to pay close attention to the kind of speech you use and to your sentence length.

Alex has no idea what his teacher is saying because her sentences are too long and complicated.

Your sentences should be shorter and more repetitive than the ones you use with Discoverers. As well, since pairing gestures with words makes it easier for them to understand you, gestures should become a natural part of your communication with Communicators. Very often, the gestures you use, like waving for "bye-bye" and blowing for "hot" turn into the child's first attempts at conventional communication. So act it out – and let the child *see* what you're saying.

Short and sweet! Now Alex has a better chance of figuring out what his teacher is saying.

When children have oral motor difficulties that interfere with speech development, it's even more important to pair your words with gestures. Your gestures will help the child figure out the meaning of the word and will also give her a way to communicate without speech. You can also pair your words with pictures or signs. Talk with the child's speech-language pathologist to develop a plan for how to best introduce gestures, signs, or pictures.

**By pairing a gesture with a word,
Pia helps Faisel figure out what she means by "pull."**

Emphasize new words for First Words Users and Combiners

Say Less
Stress
Go slow
Show

Making what you say easy to understand is still important for First Words Users and Combiners. Strategies used in Motherese like "Say less, Stress, Go Slow, and Show" draw a child's attention to new words and encourage her to repeat, remember, and use words and phrases spontaneously in other situations.

As a child's understanding of language increases, the gap widens between what she understands and what she is able to say. Therefore, it becomes more difficult to use a consistent sentence length. For example, First Words Users can understand fairly long sentences, but they can say only one word at a time. Therefore, at this stage, you begin modelling language at two levels – a simpler model for the child to try to imitate and a more complex one to increase her understanding of language.

A gesture paired with a new word helps children figure out the meaning of the word. Gestures also give children with oral motor difficulties another way to communicate.

The teacher is modelling language at two levels: first a two-word phrase for the child to imitate and then a longer sentence, which is at the child's level of understanding.

Adjusting your language can even be more challenging when you interact with a child who has a language delay. Here, the gap between what the child can say and how much she understands may be greater than it is typically in a child without a delay. It is important that a speech-language pathologist adequately assess the child's receptive and expressive language skills. That way, you have the information you need to adjust your language according to the child's levels of understanding and expression.

Match your language to the child's interests

When a child shows you what interests her, either by initiating an interaction on a particular topic or by performing an action, that's the time to provide her with information about that topic – information that is matched to her interests.

Discoverers and Communicators can figure out meanings only if the words you use clearly relate to the object they're focused on. For example, if a seven-month-old Discoverer were playing with her toes and her caregiver said "You're getting so big!" the child would not be able to figure out how those words related to her toes. But if the caregiver said, "Nice **toes!** Are you eating your **toes?**" the word "toes" begins to stand out. With enough repetition, she will eventually associate the word "toes" with the body parts she likes to eat!

You also need to match your language to the child's focus for children with language delays. For example, if a two-year-old Communicator loves to pour water from one cup to another at the water table, she needs to hear the word "pour" at the very moment she is pouring in order to understand the link between her action and the word.

Michael is excited that he finally got the puzzle piece in, but Eileen's comment doesn't match his focus or reflect his excitement.

Now Eileen has matched her comment to Michael's focus and she's captured his excitement.

Interpret the child's sounds, actions, and gestures with simple language

Interpreting (also described in Chapter 3, pages 79–81) is a powerful way of letting a child know that she has been understood. When you interpret, you provide her with language models, which give her the words that she herself cannot yet use.

A Discoverer has not yet developed the ability to send messages directly to you, so you need to interpret her behaviour as if it were purposeful and intentional.

Jessie's teacher interprets her behaviour as if it were intentional and provides her with a clear language model.

Communicators are moving toward cracking the code and using their first words. You can help a Communicator learn to say words by interpreting her nonverbal message and "saying it as she would if she could." Keep your language simple so she hears a language model that she can learn from and eventually use.

Sometimes interpreting the child's message takes the form of a question, but the child still hears the words she needs to learn.

Interpreting is useful for any child who uses nonverbal communication, whether her language is developing typically or she has an oral motor difficulty. Children with oral motor difficulties still need you to interpret their messages, but you can also pair words with a sign or a picture card. That way, a child with a speech production difficulty not only hears a language model she can learn from but also has an alternative communication system, which she can use to communicate.

Jason's oral motor difficulties make speech hard for him. Lucy shows him another way to communicate by demonstrating a sign for "wash hands" as she verbally interprets his message.

Engage the child in social routines

In Chapter 4, you learned how social routines provide excellent contexts for developing social interaction with Discoverers, Communicators, and First Words Users. Because social routines are so repetitive and predictable, they also provide children with many opportunities to discover the meanings of words. This kind of repetition is especially helpful for a Discoverer or Communicator with a language delay, who may need to hear a language pattern many, many times before she can crack the code. The beauty of a social routine is that a child learns to anticipate the word that comes next and to "fill in the blank" – at first with a prompt, but eventually with no help at all. Many Communicators "crack the code" and use their first words within a social routine.

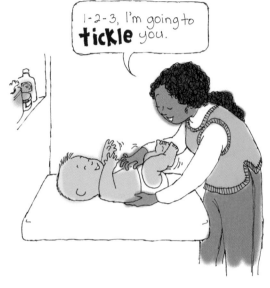

1. Moira repeats Jamie's favourite game many times, each time stressing the word "tickle."

2. After a while, Moira pauses after the phrase, "I'm going to," and waits to see if Jamie will try to say "tickle." Moira is pleasantly surprised when Jamie says "ti-ti" for "tickle." Her repetition of the word "tickle" in a predictable, repetitive social routine has paid off!

3. Moira interprets Jamie's sounds as "tickle" and continues the game.

Label things in the child's world

Your labels and descriptions of everyday events are important for language learners at all stages. When you talk about what you do ("I'm washing my hands") or what others are doing ("Carrie's cleaning the table"), children gain important information. Similarly, if you provide a Discoverer or Communicator with the label "bib" every time you put on her bib, it won't take her too long to connect the word with the object.

That's my necklace!

When Ben is interested in something, Tina labels the object for him, using as few words as possible.

Remember these few guidelines about how to label:
- Use labels to let children know what's going to happen
- Use specific names of objects
- Use "fun" words when possible
- Highlight the label for the child
- Use a variety of different labels

- **Use labels to let children know what's going to happen.** Don't move in without warning – tell the child what's going to happen.

I'm going to clean your nose!

Susan lets Mohammad know what she is going to do before she does it.

◆ **Use specific names of objects** – don't use words like "it," "that," "this," or "them."

Christina knows what a ball is and how to use it, but she doesn't know how to say "ball."
To help Christina learn to say the word, Myra should use the word "ball" again and again.

Myra should say, "Come and give me the **ball!**"

Myra still hasn't said the word "ball." She should say, "Good girl, you rolled the **ball!**"

Christina still hasn't heard the word "ball." Myra should say, "Get ready! Here comes the **ball!**"

- Use **"fun" words when possible** with Communicators and First Words Users. "Fun" words are wonderful labels for things that fascinate children. "Uh oh" is a label for "something has gone wrong," and "wheee" describes going down a slide fast. These labels capture action and change, both of which fascinate children, and motivate them to try to say the word.

Squish! Squish!

"Squish" is a "fun" word that captures Andrew's attention. Once he's heard it a number of times, he'll say "ish" when he squeezes playdough!

- **Highlight the label for the child.** Make the word stand out – say it louder than the other words in the sentence, repeat it, and point to what it means, if you can. Repetition of words is especially important for children who are language delayed or second-language learners. These children may need to hear words repeated many, many times before they learn them.

Nathan is a Communicator with a language delay. Mona repeats the word "juice" three times as she pours the juice. This repetition will help Nathan to understand and eventually use the word "juice."

Umm, **juice**. We're having apple **juice** today. I love apple **juice**.

- **Use a variety of different labels.** Think of a label as much more than the name of an object. Labels include **action words** (e.g., "run," "drink," "stop"), **describing words** (e.g., "hot," "big," "yummy," "more"), and **location words** (e.g., "up," "down," "in," "out"). Using a variety of labels increases a child's understanding, builds her vocabulary, and enables her to create many different kinds of sentences. For example, with a variety of labels, "ball" can become "throw ball," "my ball," or "ball gone."

There is lots you can tell a children about a drink of juice

Tell them when the juice is finished:
"**No more** juice!" "Juice is **gone.**"

Tell them what you do with juice:
"You **drink** juice." "Let's **pour** the juice." "I **spilled** the juice."

Tell them the name:
"**Juice.**"

Tell them how juice looks and feels:
"It's **cold** juice."

Tell them who the juice belongs to:
"It's **your** juice." "It's **Tammy's** juice." "It's **my** juice."

Tell them how you do things with juice:
"Let's pour the juice **slowly.**" "Drink **quickly.** We've got to go outside!"

Imitate what the child says

Children enjoy it when you imitate them – it confirms that you're really listening to them. Imitating what she says is a helpful way to provide information to a Communicator or First Words User who may have difficulty pronouncing words correctly. When you imitate a child, you repeat what she has said, but **you say it correctly.** This confirms the child's message and maintains the flow of conversation while providing a correct model.

Expand on what the child says

When a child says something to you, you have a perfect opportunity to expand on what she has said. You *always* use her words, but you also add some words of your own, showing her more mature ways of expressing herself on that topic. Expanding is one of the most important strategies for First Words Users, Combiners, and Early/Later Sentence Users. It has been shown to significantly increase children's vocabularies and ability to speak in sentences.

You can expand on what the child says in one of two ways:
- Use the child's words and add one or two words of your own to make the phrase or sentence more complete
- Use the child's words and add some new ideas

Use the child's words and add one or two words of your own

Use the child's words and add one or two words of your own to make the phrase or sentence more complete.

When a child says . . .	You say
"Hands."	"Wash hands."
"Wash hands."	"You're washing your hands."
"Wash hands soap."	"Yes, you are washing your hands with soap."

Use the child's words and add some new ideas

Give the child some new information and ideas when you expand. Take her words and add information that she may not know.

Natasha confirms Tony's message by imitating him and providing a correct model. She then expands on what Tony said, adding the words "goes woof, woof!" to the sentence.

Caitlyn's teacher expands on Caitlyn's words by adding a new idea.

You can also expand for children who communicate with pictures or signs by adding another picture or sign to the picture or sign they have used.

When Melanie points to the picture of "juice,"...

... Melanie's teacher expands on Melanie's picture request by adding pictures of an apple and an orange. She shows Melanie how to point to two pictures in a row to indicate "apple juice" or "orange juice."

Extend the topic

The purpose of extending the topic is to give the child new information that increases her understanding of the world. While the information you add should build on the child's interests, it does not need to be in response to what she has said, nor does it need to include her words.

Although a child may not understand everything you say the first time you say it, with time and repetition, the meaning will begin to make sense to her. (See Chapter 8 for further discussion of extending the topic.)

Sara first expands on what Khalid said. Then she extends the topic by building on his interest in the blue paint and adding a fun idea.

Oddly enough, a prime opportunity for extending the topic occurs when things go wrong. When something doesn't go according to plan, you have the chance to offer an explanation. Sometimes, however, teachers may not remember to give the children an explanation, as in the following example when the children's pizza disappears.

A prime time for extending the topic occurs when things go wrong. However, these teachers discussed what was wrong with the pizza with each other, but didn't discuss it with the children.

A simple explanation clears up the confusion.

If we are to encourage children's curiosity and questions, it's important to provide them with simple explanations for things that interest them but which they don't (yet) understand.

Jamie wants to know why Sean is crying, so Valerie gives him a simple explanation.

Combine strategies when you talk to children

When you interact with a child, you often use more than one "adjust your language" strategy at a time:

Tracy

- **imitates** Alberto to provide a correct model ("Sore"), then
- **expands** by adding words to Alberto 's message ("Your finger is sore."), and then
- **extends** by adding the new idea that Alberto 's finger will get better ("It will get better. It's just a little sore.").

Karin

- **expands** on Juan's message with a more complete phrase: "More music?" and then
- **extends** the topic by telling him what she's going to do.

C. Adjust your language for children with language delays

Children with language delays at the Combiner and Early Sentence User stages often speak in short, ungrammatical sentences. These children find it difficult to learn the hundreds of rules of language, especially grammatical rules. Correcting their errors doesn't help at all. For example, if a child says "Him's sitting in my chair," you may try to correct her by saying, "It's not 'Him's sitting in my chair,' it's 'He's sitting in my chair.'" A minute later, however, she will make the same error – even if she has correctly repeated the sentence after you. This is because she has not yet learned the grammatical rule for the use of pronouns. Until she has, her errors will continue.

In addition to grammatical errors, you may have noticed that children with language delays confuse word meanings. For example, a child may say "Stand down" when she means "Sit down."

Think, for a moment, of how confusing it must be for these children to figure out the rules of language, especially when they hear so many words and different types of language usage every day. Obviously, the adjustments we make for typically developing children aren't enough to help children who have language delays.

You can help children with language delays learn both vocabulary and grammatical rules during everyday conversations if you:
- Provide intensive repetition of the same rule
- Time your response to the child's immediate focus of attention
- Slow down
- Use contrasts to highlight the rule
- Use real-life situations in which the child has a real interest

---

Provide intensive repetition of the same rule

Make it easier for a child to figure out a grammatical rule by repeating sentences that illustrate the rule again and again within a short period of time. Don't correct the child; just provide the model.

Child: (pointing to a child who is not wearing mitts) *Him got no mitts.*
Teacher: He *has no mitts? You're right. Jay has no mitts.* **He** *has no mitts.*
(Points to another child) *Ricky has mitts. See?* **He** *has mitts* (points to Ricky),
but Jay has no mitts. **He** *has no mitts. Maybe* **he** *left them at home.*

This teacher provided the child with five examples of "he" in less than a minute. If this kind of repetition is provided throughout the day in natural conversations, the child has a better chance of extracting the principle behind the rule. To avoid confusion, don't provide intensive repetition for every rule a child has difficulty with. Choose one or two and stick with those until she learns them.

Time your response to the child's immediate focus

Timing is critical! At the early stages of language development, children learn best when the information they hear relates exactly to what they are experiencing at that moment in time. Therefore, time your responses so that they correspond with a child's focus of attention.

For example, when a cup falls off the table, a child may say, "Fall down." If the teacher *immediately* says "The cup *fell* down. Look at that! The cup *fell* down," her input is well timed and the child is able to compare her words with the teacher's. This is the first step in learning the correct grammatical rule for the past tense. If, however, the teacher picks up the cup and then says, several seconds later, "Oh dear, the cup fell down," she has missed the boat. The child's focus has moved on to something else, making it less likely that she will learn from the model provided.

Slow down

A child with a language delay will find it easier to process and learn language when you talk at a slower-than-normal rate. Slower speech will enable her to pay closer attention to the way your sentence is phrased, and can help her figure out grammatical rules.

Position the word or words the child needs to hear at the beginning or end of your sentence (not in the middle) and exaggerate them. If, for example, you are stressing the rule that we add "-ing" to verbs to indicate ongoing action (e.g., "I am eating"), consider how clearly the "-ing" can be heard and processed by the child in the following two examples:

Example 1

> **Teacher:** *Look, Adam is play**ing*** (pause),
> *and Jessica is play**ing*** (pause),
> *and Samara is play**ing*** (pause),
> *and Nathan is watch**ing.***

Example 2

> *Teacher: Look, Adam is play**ing** in the playground*
> *and Jessica is play**ing** with him*
> *and Samara is play**ing** with him*
> *and Nathan is watch**ing** them.*

It's easier for children to pay attention to words at the beginning or end of a sentence (as in Example 1). Words in the middle of the sentence (Example 2) may get lost.

Use contrasts to highlight the rule

Children often confuse words or phrases that are closely related. For example, they may say, "Stand down" when they mean "Sit down." If you contrast the two phrases, a child can more easily figure out the rule and the distinction between the words or phrases. Let's look at how a teacher contrasts the phrases for Tammy, who has a language delay.

Teacher: *Look Tammy, we're all going to **sit down**. Jonathon, you **sit down*** (pause while Jonathon sits down), *and Dan, you **sit down*** (pause while Dan sits down), *and Bella, you **sit down*** (pause while Bella sits down). *But I'm not going to **sit down** – I'm going to **stand up**.* (Teacher stands up while the others are sitting down.)

The use of contrast makes the rule much clearer to Tammy. This technique also helps children figure out confusing grammatical rules, like the use of the pronoun "he" for males and "she" for females.

Use real-life situations in which the child has a real interest

Because children use grammatical rules to send real messages, the best way to learn the rules isn't through flashcards or rote repetition. Rather, children must learn the rules in purposeful, real-life situations where they see the effects of their own and others' communication. For example, if a child doesn't use "Where" questions, she is likely to learn to use them from playing Hide-and-Seek or from hearing you ask other children "Where are your mitts?" – both real-life and purposeful situations.

D. Second-language learning: A complex process

In this global village, teachers in early childhood settings meet many children from other countries who are learning English as a second language. These children need you to adjust your language to help them learn to speak English.

All children have a first language, which is any language learned before age three. A language learned after age three is considered to be a second language. When a child younger than three years of age learns two (and sometimes more) languages at the same time, this process is referred to as simultaneous bilingualism. A child who learns a second language after the age of three is involved in a different learning process, called sequential bilingualism.

Simultaneous bilingualism

When infants are exposed to two languages, there are two patterns of exposure: they either experience a "one-person, one-language" situation, where one parent speaks one language and the other parent another, or they experience a situation where both parents speak both languages. Alternatively, some children experience a situation where both parents speak the same language to the child and the teachers and the children in the child-care centre or pre-school speak another. The "one-person, one-language" approach has been found to help children separate and learn the two languages.

> **Three stages of language learning can be identified in children who learn two first languages in infancy:**
> - Stage 1: Child mixes languages
> - Stage 2: Child separates languages
> - Stage 3: Child uses mainly one language

Stage 1: Child mixes languages

Infants who are exposed to two languages "mix" the two into one system. For example, an infant learning Spanish and English may call a "kitty cat" a "kitty-gato" or may use words from both languages in a short sentence. This is called code mixing. The amount of contact with each language determines the number of words learned from each.

Stage 2: Child separates languages

Around age two-and-a-half, the child starts to separate the words belonging to each language and begins to recognize the people to whom each language should be spoken.

While learning the two languages, the child often uses whole phrases or sentences – such as "I wanna" and "Gimme dat" – which she imitates and memorizes. (Unilingual children, in contrast, typically begin imitating single words.) In addition, she engages in "copy-catting," which involves imitating another person's speech and actions. Both these strategies give her language to interact with others and help her eventually learn the rules of each language.

Stage 3: Child uses mainly one language

When one language is used more than the other (as is often the case), that language becomes dominant. By seven years of age, the child can cope with the two language systems without difficulty, using both vocabulary and grammar appropriately for her age.

Sequential bilingualism

When a child learns a second language after the age of three, she has already figured out the basic rules of her first language, and therefore has a head start when it comes to learning the second language. She already knows how to have conversations and is cognitively more mature than the infant learning two languages simultaneously. We often think that younger children learn a second language more quickly, but this is only because they have fewer complexities of the language to master. In fact, a child's ability to learn a second language increases as age and cognitive ability increase.

The process of adding a second language can take years. When a child over the age of three enters an environment where a second language is spoken, it takes approximately three months for her to begin to understand the second language, about two years to be able to carry on a conversation, and five to seven years to be able to think in the second language.

There are five stages of second-language learning in sequential bilingualism
- Stage 1: Home Language Use
- Stage 2: Nonverbal Period
- Stage 3: Telegraphic Speech
- Stage 4: Productive Language Use
- Stage 5: Competent Language Use

These stages are not discrete – a child may add skills from the next level but still maintain those from the previous stage.

Stage 1: Home Language use

Initially, the child either continues to use her home language or stops talking. Some children persist longer than others in their use of their home language, continuing to speak their own language as if their peers and teachers can understand them. This strategy works in some play situations that do not rely heavily on language. Most of the time, however, the child just gets blank looks from the other children.

Stage 2: Nonverbal period

When the child sees that her own language does not enable her to communicate with others, she may stop using that language. Children who speak one language and are learning a second one may say very little for up to seven months! Younger children stay at this stage for longer periods than older children. It seems that children need this "silent period" to build up their knowledge of the new language before they try to use it.

Even though the child may stop talking, she does not stop communicating. Use of nonverbal communication to get attention, make requests, and protest is very common at this stage. The child may also communicate nonverbally by doing funny things that others find amusing (e.g., taking turns with another child at spying on each other through a window). Joking games like these let children play together without using any language.

Stage 3: Telegraphic speech

The child now becomes involved in social interactions with speakers of the second language. During this stage, the child relies on whole, memorized phrases and sentences, like "What's that?" "Know what?" "All right, you guys," "Hey, look it!" or "I don't know." She continues to use nonverbal communication, like pointing, and a number of key words that are useful in social situations (e.g., "please," "Hi"). In general, she tries to act as if she knows what's going on and guesses a lot at what people mean.

Stage 4: Productive language use

The child now communicates with second-language speakers in the second language. The principle at this stage seems to be "start talking." The child begins to create her own sentences, which may include memorized phrases and some new vocabulary. She communicates as best she can, even if her language use is not always correct. Until she figures out the rules of the language, she may make many grammatical errors. She may also show code mixing (using words from both languages in one sentence). Children who are risk-takers learn the language more quickly than those who don't talk much for fear of making a mistake. Outgoing, sociable children will also progress more quickly since they seek out other children and are motivated to make every effort to communicate.

Stage 5: Competent language use

In this final stage, the child attempts to speak correctly, using correct vocabulary, grammar, and pronunciation. She looks for patterns in sentences, just as she did when learning her first language, and then works out the rules.

"Should I be concerned?": Normal patterns of language use in second-language learners

Many children who are second-language learners are thought to be language delayed when, in fact, they are demonstrating normal second-language characteristics. Second-language learners may be mistaken for children with language delays when they:

- ◆ are at the nonverbal stage
- ◆ demonstrate code mixing (using words from both languages in one sentence), or
- ◆ produce many grammatical errors.

Sometimes, if a child has learned a first language but doesn't use it much, she will lose her skills in that language. This means that while she learns English, her ability in both languages will be below age level. Again, this child may be mistakenly labelled as delayed because of her loss of skills in her first language – even though this is a normal process for second-language learners.

Carmen is going through a typical stage for second-language learners – using words from both languages in one setting.

E. Support second-language learners

Children who come to your child-care centre or preschool speaking little or no English must experience feelings of isolation, confusion, and frustration. Fortunately, as their teacher, you are able to support their efforts to learn a second language and to become what we would all like to become – fully bilingual.

> **You can support a second-language learner if you:**
> - Promote the use of the child's first language at home and in preschool
> - Make them feel comfortable in their strange new surroundings
> - Make your input easy to understand

Promote the use of the child's first language at home

It was once thought that the best way to help children learn their second language was to expose them only to that language. Today, the experts tell us that this assumption was incorrect: the better developed the child's first language, the easier it is for her to learn a second language. In light of what we now know, it has become clear that the best way to foster second-language learning is to support the child's first language.

Children under the age of five who are learning one language at home and another at their child-care centre or preschool should be exposed to their first language as much as possible. When parents aren't sure which language to speak to their child, you can safely encourage them to speak their first language. This advice will be a relief to them: interactions suffer when parents try to speak to their children in a language they themselves don't speak fluently. In fact, when parents speak to their children in an unfamiliar second language, they may interact less with their children and have less to say when they do.

By speaking to their child in her first language, parents are laying a solid foundation for the second language. Without this foundation, both first- and second-language learning can be delayed and/or disrupted.

By five years of age, the child has a fairly well-established first language, and the skills for acquiring a second one. While she can certainly still benefit from being exposed to her first language, she will not be at risk for language problems if she is not. By contrast, a younger child with a poorly developed first language can have serious difficulty learning a second language if she doesn't have a strong foundation in her first language.

If more than one language is used in the home with a child under age three, the policy "one person, one language" is best. If children hear both caregivers speak two languages, they become confused. "One person, one language" reduces such confusion.

Suggestions in Chapter 6 on how to support peer interaction will be helpful with second-language learners. The following three factors are critical to successful second-language learning:

- motivation to learn
- feelings of self-confidence, and
- a low level of anxiety.

Let's picture Tanya, three years old, who is newly arrived from Russia. She speaks no English, and is in a preschool classroom with 15 other children, none of whom speaks Russian. Tanya keeps to herself and seldom initiates interactions with teachers or peers. One of her teachers, Novea, makes a point of establishing a close relationship with her, giving her a great deal of support and affection, and spending some time playing with her every day. When Tanya attempts to communicate with Novea in Russian, Novea responds as best she can and never demands that Tanya try to say anything in English. Novea also encourages peer interaction by inviting other children to join their play and then fading herself out.

As a result of all this positive interaction, Tanya has:

- *a great deal of motivation to communicate with her teachers and peers*
- *the self-confidence to seek out others in her new environment, and*
- *a low level of anxiety.*

Within six months, Tanya is using some common single words. She has also learned some phrases like "Know what?" and "You wanna play?" She is on her way to mastering her second language.

Make your input easy to understand

Children will learn a new language only if they can make sense of what they hear. This explains why watching TV programs in a second language or overhearing conversations between two second-language speakers doesn't help people learn the language. If you can't understand it, you can't learn from it. It's that simple!

Your task is to make it as easy as possible for the child to understand you. Once you have that goal in mind, you automatically make all sorts of adjustments and adaptations to the way you communicate (as described in the first part of this chapter). In fact, the way you talk will sound an awful lot like the way you talk to children learning their first language! You make yourself interesting to listen to and provide information that the child can understand and learn from.

Promote the child's first language in the preschool

If you and the child are fortunate enough to speak the same first language, speak to her in that language. If other children in the classroom speak the same first language, encourage them to talk to each other. Consider enlisting the help of volunteers who will play and interact with the child in her first language.

It's wonderful when the teacher can comfort a child in that child's first language.

Te has col piato?
Tu estaras bien.

Even if you do not speak the child's first language, you can ask the parents to provide you with a few important words (e.g., "come and sit," "bathroom," "lunchtime") in the home language. You will then be able to communicate with the child at a basic level in the first few weeks and deliver the message that you value her home language.

Make second-language learners feel comfortable

Children who come to preschool or child care speaking another language, but no English, need to feel accepted and liked – and they need to like you! Their feelings about you and the environment they are in will have an enormous impact on how successfully they learn their new language.

Children also need to feel accepted and liked by the other children. The more they interact with others, the more opportunities they will have to learn English. Second-language learners are frequently socially isolated due to their poor knowledge of English.

Kinue's teacher uses simple language and stresses the important word.

Even though Kinue doesn't understand English, she has a good idea of what her teacher is saying. Kinue's teacher helps her understand what he is saying because he remembers to:

Say less

- ◆ He uses grammatically simple sentences.
- ◆ He uses simple, everyday vocabulary about what is happening in the here-and-now.

Stress

- ◆ He exaggerates important words.
- ◆ He repeats what he has said.

Go slow

- ◆ He speaks slowly.

Show

- ◆ He uses gestures and actions.

As Kinue begins to speak English, her teacher promotes her expressive language by imitating her and providing correct models, expanding on what she says by adding more words, and by extending the topic.

Use music to help the child learn a second language

Because second-language learners imitate whole phrases and sentences and use them to communicate, music can help them learn new phrases and sentences. For example:

Tommy Thumb, Tommy Thumb
Where are you?
Here I am, here I am
And how do you do?

The sentences "Where are you?" and "Here I am" can be modelled for the child in interactive situations so she understands what they mean and can use them herself, when appropriate.

Not only is music a wonderful way of making contact with children – it also helps them learn language!

Summary

The quality and quantity of language that children are exposed to during everyday interactions with their caregivers significantly affects their language development. When learning both first and second languages, children have to make sense of what they hear and figure out the rules of the language. Parents, teachers, and other caregivers help children do this when they adjust the way they talk, making language easy to understand at the early stages of language development and adding more information as a child's ability progresses. Teachers can make this process easier for children with language delays by providing intensive repetition, slowing down their speech, and highlighting the important words. Second-language learners are supported by teachers who make them feel comfortable in their new surroundings and promote their first language both at home and, when possible, at the child-care centre or preschool.

References

Barnes, S., Gutfreund, M., Satterly, D. & Wells, G. (1983). Characteristics of adult speech which predict children's language development. *Journal of Child Language, 10,* 65–84.

Bloom, L. & Lahey, M. (1978). *Language development and language disorders.* New York: John Wiley & Sons.

Bozinou-Doukas, E. (1983). Learning disability: The case of the bilingual child. In D.R. Omark & J. G. Erickson (Eds.), *The bilingual exceptional child* (pp. 213–232). San Diego: College Hill Press.

Chud, G. & Fahlman, R. (1985). *Early childhood education for a multicultural society.* University of British Columbia: Western Education Development Group.

Craig, H. K. (1983). Applications of pragmatic language models for intervention. In T. M. Gallagher & C. A. Prutting (Eds.), *Pragmatic Assessment and Intervention Issues in Language* (pp. 101–127). San Diego: College Hill Press.

Cross, T.G. (1978). Mothers' speech and its association with rate of linguistic development in young children. In N. Waterson & C. Snow (Eds.), *The development of communication* (pp. 199–216). New York: John Wiley & Sons.

Cummins, J. (1981). *Bilingualism and minority-language children.* Toronto: OISE Press.

Dumtschin, J.U. (1988). Recognize language development and delay in early childhood. *Young Children, March,* 16–24.

Esling, J.H. (Ed.), (1989). *Multicultural education and policy: ESL in the 1990s.* Toronto: OISE Press.

Farran, D.C. (1982). Mother-child interaction, language development and the school performance of poverty children. In L. Feagans and D.C. Farran (Eds.), *The language of children reared in poverty* (pp. 19–48). New York: Academic Press.

Ferguson, C.A. (1977). Baby talk as a simplified register. In C.E. Snow & C.A. Ferguson (Eds.), *Talking to children: Language input and acquisition* (pp. 219–235). London: Cambridge University Press.

Houston, M.W. (1990). Teaching English as a second language through daily programming. In Kenise Murphy Kilbride (Ed.). *Multicultural early childhood education: A discovery approach for teachers* (pp. 64–68), School of Early Childhood Education, Ryerson Polytechnical Institute, Toronto.

Kessler, C. (1984). Language acquisition in bilingual children. In N. Miller, (Ed.) *Bilingualism and language disability: Assessment and remediation* (pp. 26–54). San Diego: College Hill Press.

Krashen, S. (1982). *Principles and practice in second language acquisition.* New York: Pergamon Press.

Lasky, E.Z. & Klopp, K. (1982). Parent-child interactions in normal and language-disordered children. *Journal of Speech and Hearing Disorders, 47*(1), 7–18.

McLaughlin, B. (1984). *Second-language acquisition in childhood: Volume 1. Preschool children.* Hillsdale, N.J.: Lawrence Erlbaum Associates.

Newport, E., Gleitman, H. & Gleitman, L. (1977). Mother, I'd rather do it myself: Some effects and non-effects of maternal speech style. In C. E. Snow & C.A. Ferguson (Eds.), *Talking to children* (pp. 109–149). London: Cambridge University Press.

Owens, R.E. (1984). *Language development: An introduction.* Columbus, Ohio: Charles E. Merrill.

Roseberry-McKibbin, C., Eicholtz, G. & McCaffrey, P. (1990). *Second language acquisition: Differentiating language differences from language disorders.* Miniseminar at American Speech-Hearing Association Annual Convention, Seattle, Washington.

Snow, C.E. (1984). Parent-child interaction and the development of communicative ability. In R.L. Schiefelbusch & J. Pickar (Eds.), *The acquisition of communicative competence* (pp. 69–107). Baltimore: University Park Press.

Snow, C., Midkiff-Borunda, S., Small, A. & Proctor, A. (1984). Therapy as social interaction: Analyzing the contexts for language remediation. *Topics in Language Disorders, 4*(4), 72–85.

Tabors, P.O. (1997). *One child, two languages: A guide for preschool educators of children learning English as a second language.* Baltimore: Paul H. Brookes Publishing Co.

Weismer, S.E. (1991). Theory and Practice: A principled approach to treatment of young children with specific language disorders. *National Student Speech Language Hearing Association Journal, 18,* 76–86.

Wells, J.L. (1980). *Children's language and learning.* Englewood Cliffs, NJ: Prentice Hall.

Learning Language and Loving It

Chapter 8

Create an Environment for Talking and Learning

> The paper clip sticks to the magnet but not the block. That's because the block isn't made of metal.

Children start out by using language to satisfy their social needs. In time, language becomes a tool for thinking, problem-solving, and learning.

A. Learning to talk and talking to learn

Learning to talk is part of becoming a social being. It's a way of making oneself heard, of becoming part of a group, part of a community, and part of a culture.

When a child begins to talk, he talks mainly to satisfy his physical and social needs. He uses language to get and keep an interaction going and to talk about things in the here-and-now.

As his caregiver confirms, models, expands, and extends the topic of the conversation during these early conversations, she becomes, in the child's eyes, more than a social partner: she becomes a resource, someone from whom he can gain information.

As the child becomes a more skilled conversation partner, his conversations with his caregivers change in quantity and quality. They occur more often and last longer. More information is exchanged, and the child asks more questions. He doesn't talk only about the here-and-now but about what happened yesterday, what will happen tomorrow, and what might happen if . . .

At this point, the child is no longer simply learning to talk. He is *talking to learn*.

With support from their teacher, these children are encouraged to go beyond the here-and-now to use language to problem-solve.

B. Talking to learn: Using language to think and learn about the world

Listen to children over age three having a conversation and you'll hear them use language to:

- go beyond the here-and-now
- go beyond their own personal experience, and
- go beyond the real world into the imagined world.

Children go beyond the here-and-now

Children talk about the past (what happened yesterday, last week, and last year) and the future (what will happen or what might happen).

Children go beyond their own personal experience

Children use language to project themselves into situations they have not experienced, and consider how they or others would feel or react to those situations (e.g., what it would be like to go to the moon; to be as strong as . . .; as big as . . .; as famous as . . .; as tall as . . .). They also think about possible explanations for things that they don't quite understand.

Children go beyond the real world into the imagined world

With language, children can bring their imagined ideas to life. They can pretend to be whomever they want to be and can act out imaginary situations in any way they can think of.

The four-year-olds at Greenfield Child Care Centre are playing outdoors. The ground is muddy after a night of rain. Matty, who has been digging in the mud for the last few minutes, suddenly sees an earthworm wriggling under the surface. He gets very excited and picks it up with a stick, yelling to the other children, "Look, I got a worm!" Five other boys run over to see the worm, and soon they are all digging for earthworms.

Matty and Liam are digging together and begin to have a very interesting conversation, as they use language to go beyond the here-and-now ...

Let's listen in on Matty and Liam's conversation.

Matty: *Don't dig so hard. You'll break the worms in half if you do that!* (beyond the here-and-now)

Liam: *Break them in half! Ha! You can't break a worm in half.*

Matty: *Yes you can. But if you break an earthworm in half, he won't die. He'll grow a new head and a new body and there will be two worms* (beyond personal experience)

Liam: *Who said?*

Matty: *My mom read me a book about worms* (beyond the here-and-now).

Liam: *Here's one! I got one!*

Matty: *Look how long yours is! He's longer than mine. He must eat a lot or maybe he's just older* (beyond personal experience).

Liam: *Yeah, maybe he's older.*

Matty: *It's so dark down there. How does he find his food? He probably uses a flashlight! (Laughs)* (beyond the real world)

Liam: *Yeah, a big flashlight! (Laughs)*

What children have to say about worms tells us a lot about how they think and try to understand the world.

Not all preschool children have Matty's ability to use language. Liam can barely keep up with him. Matty is the kind of child who's always asking questions, thinking about what he sees and hears, wondering how things work, and reflecting on his experiences – and he uses language to do these things. He has developed not only excellent language skills, but also a way of using language to analyze and understand the world.

Children can't learn to use language like this without lots of help. Matty has learned his language skills from conversations with the important adults in his life, who model and promote the use of language to problem-solve, plan, predict, reason, and imagine. In so doing they have helped him develop "the language of learning," which he has internalized and now uses quite naturally.

> Children with language delays often have difficulty understanding language that goes beyond the here-and-now. They too need exposure to this kind of talk if they are to learn to use it themselves.

Because the ability to analyze and reflect upon the world is so critical to successful learning, all children need to develop "the language of learning." When they begin to talk about things that are beyond the here-and-now (usually when they become Combiners), they are ready to start talking to learn. Children with language delays often have difficulty understanding language that goes beyond the here-and-now. They too need exposure to this kind of talk if they are to learn to use it themselves.

C. Encourage the "language of learning" during conversations

The most important things you can help children learn are: to think and analyze, to problem-solve, to plan, to predict, to reason, and to imagine. You can do this by integrating these uses for language into your programming and your everyday interactions with the children.

You can build the language of learning into everyday conversations if you:
- Clarify word meanings during conversations
- Use children's questions to help them make connections
- Wonder about the world together
- Extend the topic and enrich the children's understanding
- Tell them more of what's happening in the world

Clarify word meanings during conversations

Children will hear many words that they don't understand in the course of everyday conversations. Children who have poor language comprehension, as well as those learning English as a second language, may not understand many of the words you use. As well, children sometimes use words that they don't really understand. A child may say that something is "disgusting," or that he's got "the flu" or ask "why?" without really understanding the meanings of the words.

 David is five years old and is in the kindergarten class at Sunnyview Preschool. Once a week, the class uses the equipment in the gym. When they do, their teacher always says "Everybody remember to use common sense when you're in the gym!"

David came home and told his mother what his teacher had said.

"What's common sense?" his mother asked.

"I don't know," he replied, "but we're supposed to use it every time we go to the gym."

What confusion!

David's mother tried to explain to him what common sense meant, but she knew that even after her explanation, he was still confused. So she made a point of using the term regularly during conversations. When David's older sister wanted to wear a light jacket when the temperature was minus ten, his mother commented: "Your sister is really not using her common sense. That jacket isn't nearly warm enough for such cold weather. She's going to freeze!"

The next day, David said, "I'm using common sense today. I'm wearing my warm jacket to school 'cos it's so cold outside."

"Yes, you are using common sense," said his mother. "That way, you know you'll stay warm. And I'm going to use common sense too. I'm going to fill up the car with gas on the way to school so we don't run out of gas in this freezing cold weather."

And so, after many, many conversations and discussions, David's understanding of the term "common sense" increased. But he won't understand its full meaning and implications until he is in his teens.

Take the time to involve children in conversations to see if they really "get it." By having conversations with children and providing them with the information they need within those conversations, you can help them change or expand their understanding of word meanings. You can explain what words mean, substitute simpler words, and use words in different contexts to help children understand their meanings. That's the beauty of conversations: so much learning goes on without much teaching!

Many words and expressions like "common sense" are confusing to children hearing them for the first time.

Use children's questions to help them make connections

When children ask questions, they create the ideal conditions for learning: they draw you into conversations and obtain valuable information from your responses. And the questions they ask give you a bird's-eye view into the workings of their minds, as in the example illustrated below:

Kevin's teacher can help him understand the other meaning for "foot" by:

- providing a simple, on-the-spot explanation for the meaning of a "foot" as it relates to measurement
- at another time, by showing him a "foot" on a ruler and tape measure and letting him handle them so he becomes familiar with the length of a "foot"
- letting him measure things or people in "feet" with a ruler or tape measure, or
- using the word "foot" meaningfully in future conversations to refer to measurement.

Kevin's question makes it obvious that his concept of "feet"
doesn't include "feet" used in measurement.

If children seldom ask questions, they miss critical opportunities to talk things through with other people and gain a better understanding of the world.

We have to wonder whether children who don't ask questions are reluctant to interact or haven't yet learned to use language to reflect on the world with interest and curiosity. A child with a language delay may not even know how to put words together to form a question. Whatever the reason, a child's intellectual development is likely to suffer if he doesn't ask questions. He needs your help to discover the wonders of the world.

If children seldom ask questions, they miss critical opportunities to talk things through with other people and gain a better understanding of the world.

Wonder about the world together

Most young children think that adults know everything. Although they'll eventually find out on their own that this isn't true, there is good reason to disillusion them early on. We want children to think that learning is a wonderful, never-ending process – and that adults don't know everything! We want children to realize that adults also wonder about how things work, what things mean, and why things happen. The best way to encourage this attitude is to model being an active, curious learner. You can encourage an attitude of learning and discovering by:

- **admitting to not knowing things** when children ask you questions and suggesting that you find out the answer together
- **searching for answers to questions with the child** through experiments, looking in books, or asking someone who knows
- **wondering aloud about things that interest or puzzle you** and getting excited about the small wonders of the world, like a spider's web or a bird in a tree, or
- **stressing the many possible solutions and answers to questions** and downplaying the idea of "right" and "wrong" answers.

When you and a child question and search for answers together, discuss ideas, consider possibilities, and share the small wonders of the world, then you have created an ideal environment for talking and learning.

This approach can be hard for teachers because it means not correcting children's mistakes right away, not asking too many "fact" questions (see Chapter 4, page 139), and not giving all the answers. But just because you're not teaching, it doesn't mean that the children aren't learning. They are. Look at some of the ideas Barbara and Phillip came up with when they wonder about the goldfish together....

Extend the topic and enrich the children's understanding

In Chapter 7, we introduced the idea of extending the topic. Extending the topic is an important strategy to use with children at more advanced stages of language development, since it plays a major role in helping them talk to learn.

When you extend the topic, you provide additional information that increases a child's understanding. You go beyond the here-and-now, and beyond concepts such as colours, shapes, sizes, and textures, which do not really expand children's understanding of how the world works.

Extending the topic involves responding to children's initiations or building on their interests by using language to talk about the past and future, think about reasons and explanations, project into others' experiences, and imagine and pretend.

There's a lot more to a rabbit
Than his colour, shape, and size.
You could talk about his twitchy nose
And about his big, sad eyes.
You could imagine how it feels
To be stuck inside a cage,
And what it's like to have no mother
At such an early age.
You could compare him to a hamster,
To a dog, a mouse, a cat.
You could talk about the importance
Of a very gentle pat.
You could wonder what would happen
If he ever ran away.
There's so much to interest children,
So much they'd have to say!

Extending the topic should be part of a balanced conversation with a child, where both you and he take turns talking. As discussed in Chapter 1, interaction must come before information. In other words, extending the topic will be effective only if the child has as many opportunities as you do to take a turn and say what he thinks. Pause after you make a comment or ask a question to give the child a chance to share his ideas. His ideas then give you a chance to add more information – and the conversation will go on and on. If, however, you find that you are doing all the talking, then the child's opportunities for active involvement and learning will be limited.

Six ways to extend the topic

When you have a conversation with a child, you have lots of options for extending the topic.

Inform	example
◆ Give information about past or present. ◆ Relate present experience to past experience. ◆ Provide details. ◆ Compare/contrast two things.	◆ "Yesterday, I saw a man with three big dogs." ◆ "We are making animals just like the ones we saw at the farm last week." ◆ "That rock is very shiny and hard and is found in South America." ◆ "The orange juice is much sweeter than the grapefruit juice."

Explain	example
◆ Give reasons for what is happening. ◆ Explain outcomes. ◆ Justify opinions or preferences.	◆ "We can't play outside **because** it is raining." "We are using purple paint today **because** we used up all the red paint yesterday." ◆ "He forgot to tie up his shoelace **so** he tripped on it and fell." ◆ "I don't like loud noise **because** it hurts my ears." "I really like grapes **because** they are so sweet."

Talk about feelings and opinions	example
◆ Talk about how feelings express sadness, anger, fear, frustration, excitement, happiness, friendliness, or delight. ◆ Talk about opinions and impressions.	◆ "I am **sad** because my Mom is in the hospital." "I am **excited** because I am going to the ball game tonight." "I **worry** that my dog will run into the street and get hurt." ◆ "I think that it is a good idea to brush your teeth every morning and every night."

Project	example
◆ Project into other people's (or into animal's) lives, experiences, and feelings to help children think about others and understand that their experiences, lives, needs, and points of view are different than their own. ◆ Project into situations never experienced.	◆ "Think about this boy in this story, who lives in a house on stilts, so high up off the ground. He probably loves to watch all the birds in the trees right beside his house" [*projecting into others' experiences*]. "The boy in this story must be very frightened because he is lost" [*projecting into others' feelingsp*]. ◆ "If I could fly to the moon, I'd look down at the Earth and it would look so small."

Talk about the future	*example*
◆ Talk about/predict what will happen.	◆ "After you finish your pictures, we **will** have story time." "It's **going** to rain today."
◆ Speculate about what might or could happen.	◆ "Carolyn **might** come back to school tomorrow **if** her doctor says she's all better." "**If** I put these plants in the sun, **I think** they **will** grow quicker."
◆ Anticipate possible problems and possible solutions.	◆ "The water is spilling out of the bucket **because** there's a hole in it. **If** I put some playdough in the hole, **maybe** it won't spill out any more."
◆ Put potential problems into words and plan ahead to avoid them.	◆ "**If** you don't put away all the blocks, **then** someone might trip over them and get hurt. Let's all help to put all the blocks in the bin **so that** no one gets hurt."
◆ Consider alternative ways of handling a situation. Help children learn to describe problems, think them through, and come up with solutions.	◆ "Both of you want to play with this truck. You can **either** play with it together **or** one of you will have to wait until the other one is finished."

Pretend	*example*
◆ Talk about imaginary things.	◆ "I have a crocodile under my bed."
◆ Play a pretend role.	◆ "I'm the doctor and I'm going to give you some medicine to make you better."
◆ Create an imaginary "story" (based on real life or fantasy).	◆ "The little boy saw a bear in the woods. The bear wanted the boy's food. So he gave the bear his peanut butter sandwich and then he ran home."

Sometimes you can combine several ways of extending the topic (e.g., "We'd better stir the cake batter slowly so it won't spill [*explain*] and when we're finished mixing it, we'll put it in the oven to bake" [*talk about the future*]. "If you grab Josh's car [*talk about the future*], he will be very sad" [*talk about the future, talk about feelings* and *projecting*].).

Consider the child's stage of language development when you extend the topic: the information you provide to Combiners will be less complex than the information you provide to Early or Later Sentence Users. Later Sentence Users, however, can benefit from hearing the most abstract uses of language, such as explaining, projecting, predicting, and imagining.

Respond to the child's "Sssshhh! She's sleeping" and extend the topic by:

Informing
"Your baby is sleeping in her bed just like you sleep on your cot." (comparing)

Talking about feelings
"You'll be mad at me if I wake your baby."

Explaining
"I'll be quiet because I don't want to wake the baby."

Projecting
"If I were that baby, I'd like you to sing me a song while I went to sleep."

Pretending
"I'm tired too. I'm going to sleep right next to the baby." (Lie down and pretend to sleep)

Talking about the future
"When that baby wakes up, she won't be tired any more!"

Tell them more of what's happening in the world

Often, adults don't think of pointing out or explaining to children the many "little things" that make up their world. Children are extremely sensitive to changes in their environments or routines and are fascinated by things that don't work. When things go wrong, then, don't immediately set them right. Take the time to describe and explain what happened. These unexpected incidents are built-in opportunities for language learning. This applies equally to children who are language delayed or who have reluctant conversational styles. These children may be interested in what is happening around them but may not always make their interest obvious to you.

Things you could point out to children include:

- a new arrangement of furniture
- a new supply teacher
- a new toy
- a change in the weather
- a bird outside, or
- mud after the rain.

Children are always interested in the misfortunes of others – like a teacher's sore finger.

Things you could explain include:

- why you were absent from the preschool
- why you got new furniture
- why the playdough is cold or hard
- why a toy doesn't work, or
- why the rabbit gets so little food to eat.

D. Helping children become better story-tellers

Those of you who work with young children are exposed to story-telling every day – not yours, but theirs. Narrative, or story-telling, is a very important skill, and it takes time to develop. While adults' stories can be extremely long and complicated, a child's first stories may consist of just one word! From these brief, immature accounts of events grows the ability to tell detailed, complex stories – stories that describe personal experiences or the experiences of others.

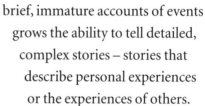

The beginning of story-telling: what she's trying to say is, "Gaby grabbed the book from me and broke it."

To tell a good story effectively, children must be able to:

- ◆ use specific vocabulary
- ◆ select the relevant information
- ◆ provide necessary background information for the listener
- ◆ describe events and situations, using appropriate detail
- ◆ explain relationships between people and events, using conjunctions like "because," "but," and "when" and relative pronouns like "who," "that," and "which"
- ◆ describe the events in a logical sequence, and
- ◆ make the story interesting!

The story-teller has to be aware of his listener's needs and background knowledge and has to adjust his use of language to accommodate these factors. If communication breaks down and the listener becomes confused, the story-teller has to judge what information he must provide to clear up the misunderstanding. Children with language delays may be particularly poor at story-telling due to difficulties with vocabulary and grammar and with describing events in a logical sequence. They may also have great difficulty filling in the information the listener needs to understand the story.

Good story-telling and descriptive skills are critical in both social and academic situations. Children need to be able to tell stories in order to participate fully in conversations and dramatic play situations, where stories are acted out. When children reach school age, their ability to recount experiences and tell stories will help them write, read, and understand stories.

Use questions and comments to keep stories on track

Questions and comments (described in Chapter 4 as useful ways to continue the conversation) are excellent tools for supporting a child's story-telling. They help him keep the story going and clear up any confusion. Questions in particular let the child know what information you as a listener need in order to follow the story.

Ask questions that:

- clear up confusion
- help the child continue the story, and
- request specific information.

Make comments that:

- acknowledge what the child has said
- show him that you're listening, and
- provide new information he can build on.

Sometimes you can use a comment to acknowledge what the child has said and follow up with a question to help him continue his story. (See Chapter 4, pages 133–140, for a description of how comments and questions help a child take another turn in a conversation.)

Listen to how this teacher supports Dwayne, aged four, in telling a story about his visit to the zoo:

Dwayne: *My Dad took me to the zoo and then he went home, and I stayed there all day.*

Teacher: *What do you mean your Dad went home? Didn't he go with you to the zoo?* (question to clear up confusion)

Dwayne: *Well he drove me and my big cousin there, and then he left us there, and my cousin took me to see the animals.* (The teacher's question makes Dwayne realize that he needs to clarify his statement that his father "took" him to the zoo. He realizes that he needs to mention his cousin.)

Teacher: *Oh, I see. So you went to the zoo with your big cousin. And what did you see there?* (question to help the child continue the story)

Dwayne: *We saw them spraying themselves with muddy water – they got so dirty and muddy!*

Teacher: *Who was spraying themselves with muddy water?* (question to request specific information)

Dwayne: *The elephants – they were covered with mud. They really liked getting dirty.* (The teacher's question with the emphasis on "who" makes Dwayne realize that he hadn't mentioned which animal he was talking about.)

Teacher: *Wow! You were lucky to see that! Elephants do that to keep their skins cool. They don't like the heat.* (comment child can build on)

After similar conversations, Dwayne will develop the ability to tell a story without needing as much support and guidance.

Plan to encourage story-telling

As a teacher of young children, you have probably listened to many wild and wonderful stories. To become more aware of your role as a promoter of story-telling, ask yourself the following questions:

1. Do all the children in my room have opportunities to tell me stories in relaxed, informal situations?	◆ Encourage story-telling in unstructured situations (e.g., during free play, sensory-creative activities, outdoor play, and meal and snack time). ◆ Encourage children's story-telling in small groups and in one-to-one interactions, not in a large group activity. Circle or group time is not the best time to have each child tell a story – children will quickly get restless, and you'll lose your audience!
2. Do I make it possible for the quieter or less verbal children to tell me stories?	◆ Invite all children to tell stories. If one child in a group has just told a story, you could ask a quiet or less verbal child, "Has anything like that ever happened to you?" or "What happened when you . . .?" (See Chapter 5 on "SSCAN" for more ideas on how to involve quieter or less verbal children.) ◆ Make leading statements that invite children to tell a story (e.g., "I'll bet you did something special during your holiday."). ◆ Use questions and comments to help the children continue their stories (see chapter 4).
3. Do I listen well and give children time to finish their stories?	◆ Listen carefully to stories. Your facial expressions will show your interest – and will encourage the child to continue! ◆ Make comments that relate to the child's story. You can encourage children to continue their story with comments like, "That must have been so scary, getting lost in the supermarket!" ◆ Stay on the child's topic. Don't interrupt or change the topic. Adults hate being interrupted – and so do children! ◆ Don't turn the story into a "lesson" or "test." If a child is telling you about his grandmother's new cat, *don't* ask, "What do cats say?" or use his story as an opportunity to teach the child about cats.
4. Do I model story-telling by telling children stories about my own experiences?	◆ Remember to tell your own stories!

There's more than one way to respond to a story-teller. This teacher could respond with a comment, "Oh no, so you had no food to eat," a question, "So then what did your Mom do?" or both.

Summary

Children learn to talk and talk to learn during the conversations they have with their caregivers. Talking to learn involves using language to think and analyze, problem-solve, plan, predict, reason, and imagine, all of which provide children with a solid foundation for all kinds of learning. Teachers can promote the "language of learning" by going beyond the here-and-now during their conversations with children, and by modelling the more abstract uses of language. They can also encourage and support children's story-telling, which demands the specific, logically sequenced, well-organized, and descriptive use of language. By asking appropriate questions, making relevant comments, and creating opportunities for all children to tell stories, teachers can promote this important skill.

References

Blank, M. (1973). *Teaching learning in the preschool: A dialogue approach.* Columbus, OH: Charles E. Merrill.

Blank, M. (1982). Language and school failure: Some speculations about the relationship between oral and written language. In L. Feagans and D.C. Farran (Eds.), *The language of children reared in poverty* (pp. 75–92). New York: Academic Press.

Crais, E.R. (1990). World knowledge to word knowledge. *Topics in Language Disorders, 10*(3), 45–62.

Farran, D.C. (1982). Mother-child interaction, language development and the school performance of poverty children. In L. Feagans and D.C. Farran (Eds.), *The language of children reared in poverty* (pp. 19–48). New York: Academic Press.

Graves, M. (1985). *A word is a word ... or is it?* Richmond Hill, Ontario: Scholastic.

Heath, S.B. (1983). *Ways with words.* Cambridge, England: Cambridge University Press.

Heath, S.B. (1985). Separating "Things of the imagination" from life: Learning to read and write. In W.H. Teale & E. Sulzby (Eds.), (1985). *Emergent literacy: Writing and reading.* (pp. 156–172). Norwood, NJ: Ablex.

Hohmann, M., Banet, B. & Weikart, D. (1979). *Young children in action.* Ypsilanti, MI: The High/Scope Press.

Lucariello, J. (1990). Freeing talk from the here-and-now: The role of event knowledge and maternal scaffolds. *Topics in Language Disorders, 10* (3), 14–29.

Shafer, R.E., Staab, C. & Smith, K. (1983). *Language functions and school success.* Glenview, IL: Scott, Foresman.

Snow, C.E., Dubber, C. & de Blauw, A. (1982). Routines in mother-child interaction. In L. Feagans and D.C. Farran (Eds.), *The language of children reared in poverty* (pp. 53–71). New York: Academic Press.

Tough, J. (1983). Children's use of language and learning to read. In L. Feagans and D.C. Farran (Eds.), *The language of children reared in poverty* (pp. 3–17). New York: Academic Press.

Tough, J. (1985). *Talking and learning.* London: Ward Lock Educational.

Umiker-Seboek, D.J. (1979). Preschool children's intraconversational narratives. *Journal of Child Language, 6,* 91–109.

Van Manen, M.(1986). *The tone of teaching.* Richmond Hill, Ontario: Scholastic.

Vygotsky, L. (1962). *Thought and language.* Cambridge: MIT Press.

Wallach, G.P. (1987). *Learning disabilities as a language problem: What to look for and what to do?* Presentation for the Toronto Association for Children with Learning Disabilities.

Warr-Leeper, G. (1992). *General suggestions for improving language.* Presentation at Clinical Symposium on "Current Approaches to the Management of Child Language Disorders," University of Western Ontario, London, Ontario.

Wells, G. (1986). *The meaning makers: Children learning language and using language to learn.* Portsmouth, New Hampshire: Heinemann.

Wells, J.L. (1980). *Children's language and learning.* Englewood Cliffs, NJ: Prentice Hall.

Wertsch, J.V. & Addison Stone, C. (1986). The concept of internalization in Vygotsky's account of the genesis of higher mental functions. In J. V. Wertsch (Ed.), *Culture, communication and cognition: Vygotskian perspectives* (pp.162–179). New York: Cambridge University Press.

Westby, C.E. (1985). Learning to talk – talking to learn: Oral-literate language differences. In C. Simon (Ed.), *Communication skills and classroom success* (pp. 181–218). San Diego: College Hill Press.

Yardley, A. (1988). *Discovering the physical world.* Toronto, Canada: Rubicon.

Chapter 9

Promote Pretend Play: Imagine the Fun, Imagine the Learning

Teachers can encourage children to pretend and use their imaginations in many ways.

A. Pretend play and language development: A dramatic connection

What separates humans from animals is our ability to use symbols. Your dog may be clever, but he can't talk, read, or write! Humans use words as symbols, which makes it possible to represent the here-and-now, the past, the future, and flights of fantasy. Your dog, however, has no way of letting you know that he enjoyed those cookies you left on the counter last night!

Pretend play, like language, involves the use of symbols, which is why it is also called symbolic play. During pretend play, children use pretend objects to represent absent objects. In time, children's ability to use symbols becomes so advanced that they no longer need objects at all – they can "act out" or use language to create make-believe.

Many experts believe that symbolic play is critical to a child's cognitive development in that it fosters abstract thought, problem-solving, self-control, and creativity. A child's ability to use her imagination freely and creatively helps her in almost every aspect of life. As Albert Einstein said: "Imagination is more important than knowledge." And he knew!

> Many experts believe that symbolic play is critical to a child's cognitive development in that it fosters abstract thought, problem-solving, self-control, and creativity.

Because pretend play and language reflect the same underlying cognitive capacity – that is, the ability to represent things symbolically – children whose ability to use symbols is impaired (e.g., children with developmental delays) will have delays both in language and pretend play. Children with language delays may also have immature pretend-play skills if their comprehension of language is impaired. However, some children with language delays may have excellent pretend-play skills since only their ability to express themselves is delayed, not their ability to understand language and to think using symbols.

Because of its connection with language, pretend play provides a rich context for using and learning language in social situations (see Chapter 6 for information on the relationship between peer interaction and pretend play). Children who have strong symbolic play skills but poor language skills can be helped to develop their language through pretend play, while children whose language skills are more advanced than their symbolic play skills can be helped to use their language to pretend in more advanced ways.

Research has shown that if pretend play is not modelled and encouraged by caregivers, its development suffers. Therefore, it is important to encourage children to pretend and to use their imaginations in many ways. Some children won't need much encouragement to pretend and imagine, but those whose symbolic abilities are delayed or lacking will need lots of playful guidance.

Sociodramatic play: A theatrical context for developing the language of learning

When children begin to develop pretend play, they don't need to be able to talk very much. However, as pretend play progresses, it becomes more and more dependent on children's language skills: they use language to interact with others, create imaginary situations, and act out roles within those situations, with little need for objects.

The most sophisticated use of language in pretend play takes place during sociodramatic play. In sociodramatic play, a group of children collaborate to develop a theme (like "house," "doctor's office," or "school"). Within this theme, they assume and play pretend roles (like "mother," "doctor," or "teacher"). Sociodramatic play depends highly on children's ability to understand and use abstract language. In any sociodramatic play scenario, children use the language of learning (see Chapter 8, pages 269–271), going beyond the here-and-now, beyond their own personal experiences, and beyond the real world. What may appear to be a creative pretend game is actually a tool that helps them develop the most advanced forms of language. Within the play scenario, children learn to use language to plan, predict, explain, problem-solve, negotiate, analyze, and understand concepts they have never been exposed to. This is the kind of language children need to succeed in school.

In sociodramatic play, a group of children collaborate to develop a theme and assume pretend roles.

Children use language for three reasons during sociodramatic play:
- ◆ To imitate people
- ◆ To establish and broaden the make-believe setting
- ◆ To coordinate and manage the play

Use of language to imitate people

When children engage in sociodramatic play, they are actually engaging in imitation: each child imitates a real person (like a parent or a teacher) or a person with whom she identifies (like a queen) and tries to act, talk, and look like that person. Through play, children try to recreate a typical situation in the life of the person whom they are imitating.

In order to imitate the person they are pretending to be, children have to use language so that they can say the kinds of things that person is likely to say. For example, a child pretending to be a doctor might say, "Open wide" as she looks inside another child's mouth.

Use of language to establish and broaden the make-believe setting

During sociodramatic play, children can reproduce a real-life situation only by creating it with words. They describe the make-believe setting to each other, interpret their own actions so the other children understand what they are doing and why, and elaborate on the play theme using language.

I'll yell "**FIRE!**" and then you come and say, "**WHERE'S THE FIRE?**" and put it out.

Children need good language skills to plan their sociodramatic play.

Use of language to coordinate and manage the play

There is no shortage of disagreements when children engage in sociodramatic play! They have to use language to discuss their problems, explain their points of view, negotiate, and come up with creative solutions, as in the following example:

Brian: *I wanna be the father.*

Audrick: *You can't be the father because I'm the father.*

Brian: *How 'bout we both be fathers?*

Audrick: *You can't have two fathers. Nobody has two fathers.*

Brian: *Well, my cousin does. One lives with him and his mom, and the other one lives in a different house. He calls the one at his house "Frank" and the other one "Daddy."*

Audrick: *Okay then, but I want to be the one that's called Daddy.*

Brian: *Okay, I'll be Frank.*

Through sociodramatic play, children learn to follow the rules of conversation (described in Chapter 4) and to see things from other children's points of view. Perhaps, as they assume the identity of another person, they are forced to consider what it must be like to be that person in order to play the role; role-playing, therefore, helps them appreciate the other person's perspective.

Children also learn to use clear, specific language during sociodramatic play. If they don't, confusion results. Research has also shown that children who engage frequently in sociodramatic play understand stories better than those who don't.

Because so much can be gained from engaging in sociodramatic play, all Later Sentence Users need to be encouraged and supported so they can participate in it regularly.

B. The development of children's pretend and dramatic play

Chapter 6 describes the types of play children engage in, including functional play, constructive play, dramatic play, and games with rules. In this chapter, we will take a closer look at the development of pretend and dramatic play.

Children's pretend play develops in a predictable sequence of stages from about age one until seven years of age, when it starts to fade. Children who have developmental delays and some children who have language delays take longer to reach these stages and may not demonstrate the imagination seen in their typically developing peers at each of the stages.

As children's pretend play develops and becomes more and more sophisticated, it tends to progress through the following five steps:

- Self-pretend play
- Simple pretend play
- Sequence pretend of familiar events and the beginnings of role play
- Sequence pretend of less familiar events with substitution of dissimilar objects
- Sociodramatic play – planned pretend themes

Self-pretend play

Self-pretend play can be seen in typically developing First Words Users between 12 and 18 months. In this sort of play, the child plays at being herself (e.g., pretending to sleep when she's not tired) and performs pretend actions on herself, using real-life objects or realistic-looking toys (e.g., she may pretend to drink from a cup or eat with a spoon).

Are you pretending to sleep, Brian?

Self-pretend play – the child pretends to go to sleep when he's not tired.

Simple pretend play

Simple pretend play is seen in typically developing Combiners between 18 months and two years. In this sort of play, the child performs single actions (e.g., brushing a doll's hair or offering an adult a toy phone) on people or toys, or the same action on two different people, dolls, or toys (e.g., feeding herself and then her doll with a spoon). She will substitute a toy object for the real thing as long as the toy looks similar enough to the real object. She will also pretend to do things she sees adults do, like covering a sleeping doll with a piece of paper or picking up a magazine and pretending to read it.

Sequence pretend of familiar events and the beginnings of role play

This kind of play is seen in typically developing Early Sentence Users between the ages of two and two-and-a-half years. Now, a child will perform, in the appropriate order, a sequence of several pretend actions from a familiar event (e.g., eating dinner, getting ready for bed, and going to sleep). She will begin to play the role of another person she knows well (e.g., her mother), an indication of her developing awareness of others. At this stage, a child can substitute one object for another as long as they are similar in shape (e.g. a stacking ring may represent a doughnut, but not a block). She may give her toys more active roles in her play: for example, she may make a stuffed bear hold a cup and drink from it.

Little children often play the role of "mother" or "father."

Sequence pretend of less familiar events with substitution of dissimilar objects

This play stage is seen in typically developing Early Sentence Users between two-and-a-half and three years. Now, a child begins to act out less familiar events (e.g., pretending to go on a trip to the doctor's office or be a hairdresser). She may talk while she plays, but talking is not essential. The child creates imaginary objects to support her play, using mime, gestures ("empty-handed miming"), and/or words to show what she is pretending to do. At this stage, she can pretend with objects that don't look like the objects for which they stand (e.g., a stacking ring can be a block). This development – the ability to separate a symbol from the object itself – is necessary for thinking, creating, and problem-solving.

By three years of age, the child's ability to create mental symbols enables him to use imaginary objects in his play.

Sociodramatic play – planned pretend themes

This stage is seen in typically developing Later Sentence Users between three and five years. It has four elements:

1. Children develop imaginary themes and take on make-believe roles

Children may act out themes as kings, queens, and monsters.

2. Two or more children interact and cooperate together in a play episode for an extended period (at least 10 minutes)

3. Children use make-believe instead of realistic objects

Children create imaginary objects for their play by using gestures or mime and/or by stating what the imaginary object is. For example, a child may open and close two fingers to pretend to cut something. When she uses objects to pretend, they may look nothing like the real-life objects they represent.

4. Children use language to create make-believe

At this stage, children imitate people and play roles of characters who come together to solve a problem or to produce some result. For example, a child pretending to be the doctor might say, "First I'm going to look in your mouth, then in your ears, and then I'll give you some medicine to make you better."

Children coordinate and manage the play, discussing problems, explaining points of view, negotiating, and problem-solving. For example, one child may say, "You have to lie down if you are sick." Another child may argue, "No you don't – only if you are very sick."

> **Children establish and broaden the make-believe setting to:**
> - **assign roles** ("I'm the Mommy, you're the Daddy, and she can be the baby.")
> - **establish the identity of objects** (saying "This is my ice cream" while pretending to hold an ice cream cone)
> - **substitute for actions that are verbalized but not performed** ("Let's pretend that I already fed the baby and put her to bed."), and
> - **develop a "story" with a plot, a sequence of events, and an outcome** ("Let's pretend that I'm the doctor and you've come to my hospital because your arm is broken.").

Use Observation Guide 4 (at the end of this chapter) to determine the level at which children in your classroom engage in pretend play.

C. Set the stage for pretend and dramatic play

> **To set the stage for pretend play and, in particular, for sociodramatic play, you need to provide five things:**
>
> - Materials
> - Time
> - Space
> - Models of playful pretend play
> - Stimulating experiences

Materials

Children's dramatic play is heavily influenced by the play materials available to them. It's important, therefore, for teachers to pay a great deal of attention to these materials. Chapter 6 (pages 200–204) provides information on how to plan materials so that children are encouraged to interact with each other. For children to be able to participate fully in dramatic play activities, materials should match their cognitive, motor, language, and social skills.

Interesting new props from the teacher help enrich the play and keep it going!

Children at the early stages of pretend-play development prefer realistic materials and props. For them, a house centre with miniature toy dishes, pots, pans, and recognizable toy food will stimulate pretend play. They will not, however, use open-ended materials like boxes and blocks to represent anything other than boxes and blocks.

Children whose dramatic play skills are more advanced will benefit from playing with open-ended objects. Blocks, boxes, milk cartons, and paper-towel rolls present them with endless possibilities for using their imaginations. As they play with these open-ended materials, children develop the ability to create symbols in their minds without depending on what the objects look like.

In a classroom with children at various stages of pretend-play development, a mixture of realistic and open-ended props will accommodate children's varied levels of make-believe – and will provide something for everybody. Remember to include props that will stimulate collaboration and cooperative play.

Keep in mind that it's also important to provide new materials that will change the theme in the dramatic play area. Materials that represent a store, an airplane, a doctor's office, or a restaurant are just a few examples of themes that children enjoy.

Time

Children need indoor free-play periods that are long enough to let them get really involved in their play. They require at least 30 to 50 minutes of uninterrupted time for this kind of play. Whenever possible, teachers should provide even longer periods.

Space

Every early childhood classroom – even those for toddlers – needs a well-defined dramatic play area. A block area, which also encourages pretend play, should be provided as well.

Models of playful pretend play

If children see that you value pretend play and are a playful pretender yourself, they will follow suit. They will be stimulated to create many imaginative ideas of their own.

Seeing their teacher on all fours pretending to be the "Big Bad Wolf" encourages the children to become the "Three Little Pigs."

Stimulating experiences

When children are familiar with the events about which they are pretending, their dramatic play is at its richest and can last for extended periods. Playing "House," for example, can last for half an hour, whereas playing "Astronauts" may last only five minutes because the children don't know enough about astronauts to keep the play going.

As we discussed in Chapter 6 (pages 205–206), successful pretend play depends on children having a "shared understanding" of the concepts and themes used in the play. This understanding, in turn, depends on children's exposure to and involvement in similar life experiences, with an adult there to explain and interpret the experience. Children who have been exposed to stores, museums, and various workplaces, and who have been taken on outings to a variety of stimulating places, have developed a store of "raw material" to use in dramatic play. The content of their dramatic play will be far richer than that of children who haven't had these experiences.

You can provide children with experiences that enrich their world knowledge. When you combine field trips and special visitors to the child-care centre with discussion and enrichment through books and educational films, children gain a broader understanding of the adult world. Soon after, they will try out these ideas in their pretend play.

D. Model pretend play for the non-pretender

Children who should be able to pretend but don't – even when you "set the stage" – need you to model and actively encourage pretend play.

You can encourage pretend play for non-pretenders in three ways:

- ◆ model pretend play

- ◆ encourage imitation of pretend actions, and

- ◆ interpret the child's actions as meaningful pretending.

Sherri, aged two and a half, is a First Words User who appears to understand far more than she can say. She sits on the floor, pushing the buttons on the toy phone but not pretending with it. Jan, her teacher, has been observing her for over a week and has noted that she engages in functional play [see page 186], but never in pretend play.

*Jan observes that Sherri engages only in functional play – so she decides to **model pretend play** for her.*

> Hello Sherri. How are you today?

*Jan pretends to talk to Sherri on the phone and offers her the other receiver to **encourage Sherri to imitate her actions.***

> Should we call your Mommy at work and say, "Hi, Mommy! Hi! It's Sherri calling!"

*Sherri imitates Jan's actions, saying nothing but showing an obvious interest in this game – which is a good beginning. Jan responds as if Sherri is actually pretending to talk on the phone, **interpreting her action as meaningful pretending.***

Jan models pretend play for Sherri, encourages her to imitate pretend actions, and, when Sherri holds the phone to her ear, treats her action as if it were a pretend action. By showing Sherri how a toy object can symbolize a real-life one, and by using language to clarify the meaning of her action, Jan exposes Sherri to a model of pretend play that she should, in time, be able to follow.

Jan will continue to model the use of pretend objects for Sherri in many situations. For example, she will invite Sherri to play in the house centre and will pretend to drink from a cup or to eat some pretend food. If Sherri looks confused or looks for the water in the cup, for example, Jan will say, "I'm pretending! See? I'm not really drinking. I'm just pretending." Jan will show Sherri the empty cup and "drink" again.

E. Facilitate sociodramatic play

If some children in your classroom are Later Sentence Users who can pretend but can't use one or more of the elements of sociodramatic play, they need your help in order to learn to use these missing elements.

You can help children acquire the following four elements of sociodramatic play:

1. Development of imaginary themes and taking on make-believe roles
2. Interaction and cooperation with at least one other child for an extended period
3. Use of make-believe instead of realistic objects
4. Use of language to create make-believe situations

(See Observation Guide 4 at the end of this chapter for a detailed list of language use during sociodramatic play.)

Guide sociodramatic play from inside or outside the group

In Chapter 6, you read about how you can help children interact with their peers either by setting up interactions from inside the group while taking on a pretend role, or setting up interactions from outside the group by making suggestions but not actually becoming part of the group.

The same principle applies to helping children participate in and use all the elements of sociodramatic play. You have to decide whether you will take part in the play or provide support from outside the group. Ultimately, your goal is for children to play successfully without your support. Until, however, they are able to integrate all the elements of socio-dramatic play into their interactions with their peers, they will continue to need your guidance.

In order to help children participate in and use all the elements of sociodramatic play, you can either:

- Guide from outside the group – without taking part in the play
- Guide from inside the group – while you participate in the play

---

Guide sociodramatic play from outside the group

You can promote a child's participation in sociodramatic play by making comments and suggestions, but without joining the group.

When you provide guidance from outside the group, you:

- act as a coach, without taking on a pretend role

- talk to the children as if you were talking to the characters they are role-playing (so as not to disrupt the make-believe atmosphere), and

- make suggestions that encourage the children to use sociodramatic play behaviours and interact with other children.

Guiding sociodramatic play from outside the group: an example

Donna, who has a reluctant conversational style and engages only in solitary-dramatic play, needs help to get involved in the sociodramatic play in the "Super-market."

Joanne, her teacher, makes a suggestion designed to encourage Donna to:

- *join in the "supermarket" theme and take on a make-believe role (Element 1)*
- *join in the play and interact with another child (Element 2)*
- *use her doll as a make-believe child (Element 3), and*
- *use language to act out her role and broaden the make-believe (Element 4).*

Joanne has succeeded in encouraging Donna to:

- take on a role in the play **(Element 1)**, and
- approach another child (the first step to **Element 2**).

However, she realizes that Donna needs additional guidance. Donna is not actually interacting with the other children **(Element 2)**, nor does she seem to know how to use language to act out her role or to broaden the make-believe **(Element 4)**.

Joanne gives Donna a clear instruction to let her know how to participate in the play – she models the language Donna needs to interact with the other children and helps broaden the make-believe **(Element 4)**.

Guide sociodramatic play from inside the group

Guiding sociodramatic play from inside the group gives you the advantage of being able to model sociodramatic play behaviours that children are not using while assuming a pretend role in the play. You can then support a number of children at the same time – as long as you know which element of play you need to emphasize with each child. Children may respond slowly to your efforts to introduce them to the elements of sociodramatic play. However, as soon as they demonstrate all the elements, you can withdraw and let them gain confidence in their ability to play independently. Or you can stay – but make sure you follow their lead.

You may need to play the director role in order to establish the theme and guide the play. However, it is important to direct in a gentle, playful manner that encourages the children to participate.

When you guide from inside the group, you:

- establish a theme
- take on a pretend role
- invite the children to participate
- assign roles if necessary
- help establish and broaden the make-believe
- model language to imitate real-life characters, establish the make-believe situation, and manage the play, and
- make suggestions that encourage the children to interact with each other.

Linda takes on a pretend role and models language to imitate a real-life character.

Guiding sociodramatic play from inside the group: an example

Gill is going to play with Petra, Craig and Nicki.

Petra *still depends on realistic objects for her play. Therefore, Gill needs to model the use of make-believe instead of realistic objects (**Element 3**).*

Craig *uses all the elements of sociodramatic play, so he is a good model for the other two children.*

Nicki *engages in action-based pretend play, but not in any kind of dramatic play. Gill needs to:*

- *model dramatic role-play for her (**Element 1**), and*
- *show her how language can be used to role-play a character and to create a make-believe situation (**Element 4**).*

Who wants to give me a haircut? I really need a haircut.

I will!

Me, too!

Gill starts the "hairdresser" theme off with an invitation that no one can refuse. Thus, she:

- *establishes a theme*
- *demonstrates how language can be used to create a make-believe situation, and*
- *encourages the children to participate.*

Gill invites Petra to wash her hair by spraying make-believe water onto her head. Thus, she models:

- *taking on make-believe roles (**Element 1**), and*
- *using language to create make-believe (**Element 4**).*

*Craig offers a cup as the shampoo bottle, modelling the use of make-believe instead of realistic objects (**Element 3**).*

Now Nicki is really interested in the dramatic play!

Petra, will you be the hairwasher and spray water on my hair and wash it like this?

Here's some shampoo.

I also wanna wash your hair.

Gill asks Nicki to hold the "towel" (really a blanket) so she can dry Gill's wet hair. She's using a make-believe, rather than real, object **(Element 3)**. When Petra rejects the use of a blanket as a towel, Gill clarifies the make-believe by showing her how to transform any object by making a statement about what you want it to be. Thus, she uses language to establish the identity of objects **(Element 4)**.

> Could you hold this towel ready so you can dry my hair when Petra is finished?

> That's not a towel. That's a dolly blanket.

> Let's pretend that it **is** a towel.

> I've got my scissors and I'm ready to cut your hair.

> My hair's nearly dry. Nicki's just drying it a little more.

Nicki, who is now actively contributing to the play, is being exposed to the use of language to create and extend the make-believe **(Element 4)**.

> Let me look in my mirror. Wow, my hair looks great! And it feels so clean!

After one last look in Gill's imaginary mirror (modelling use of make-believe instead of realistic objects – **Element 3**), she and the children are delighted with the results!

F. Join in and add to the children's sociodramatic play

Children with well-developed sociodramatic play skills don't need you to direct their play, but they will enjoy it when you join in from time to time, assume a make-believe role, and follow their lead.

Too much direction usually means less interaction.

When you join in and play, the interaction takes off.

When you join in and add to children's sociodramatic play, you have many opportunities to:

- model play behaviours that expand and extend the interaction
- encourage more conversation within pretend roles, and
- add ideas that will enrich the children's understanding of the play theme (e.g., offer new props or introduce a problem to solve or possibility to debate).

Let's see how Leslie adds to the play when she visits the children's "Restaurant."

Leslie joins in by pretending to be a customer. She models play behaviours that expand the play.

Leslie is invited to join the group, and she does. Since the children are role-playing adults in a real-life restaurant, Leslie models real-life adult conversation and requests a menu, expanding the play further.

Leslie's true-to-life imitation of a customer in a restaurant adds ideas and helps the children enrich their play.

Leslie models the kind of language adults really use in restaurants, thereby encouraging more mature language use and more play-related conversation.

G. Encourage pretend play during sensory-creative activities

Because sensory-creative activities are so open-ended, they have great potential for fostering pretend and dramatic play. Children often let you know they are ready to pretend. Respond to their cues – and watch the play take off!

Manny is ready to pretend, but his teacher is stuck in the here-and-now.

Look at how much fun they have when the teacher follows Manny's lead and expands on the make-believe.

Summary

Pretend play is an important part of children's lives. It fosters cognitive development and provides an excellent context for language development. Sociodramatic play, which involves the collaborative role-play of themes by a group of children, is the most advanced form of pretend play. It is crucial to the development of children's social and language skills. In early childhood settings, teachers need to set the stage for pretend play by providing space, materials, adequate time to play, stimulating experiences, and a playful model. Teachers can encourage the development of pretend play by modelling it for children who seem unable to pretend and by guiding participation in sociodramatic play with comments, suggestions, models of the missing elements, and creative ideas for expanding the play's theme.

Observation Guide 4: The development of pretend play

Before you can promote more mature forms of pretend play or use pretend play as a context for enhancing a child's language skills, you must be familiar with her stage of pretend play.

To determine a child's stage of pretend play, check off the items in the following chart that describe how the child plays.

Stage	Description	Teacher's Observations of Child's Behaviour
Self-pretend Play In typically developing First Words Users between 12 and 18 months	❑ Child plays at being herself ❑ Child performs pretend actions on herself, using real-life objects or realistic-looking toys	
Simple Pretend Play In typically developing Combiners between 18 months and two years	❑ Child performs: • single actions on people or toys; or • the same action on two different people, dolls, or toys ❑ Child substitutes toy object for the real thing as long as the toy looks similar to the real object ❑ Child pretends to do things she sees adults do	
Sequence Pretend of Familiar Events and the Beginnings of Role Play In typically developing Early Sentence Users between two and two-and-a-half years	❑ Child performs a sequence of several pretend actions (of a familiar event) in the appropriate order ❑ Child begins to play the role of another person she knows well ❑ Child can now substitute one object for another as long as it is similar in shape ❑ Child can give a toy a more active role in the play so that it performs actions for itself	

Stage	Description	Teacher's Observations of Child's Behaviour
Sequence Pretend of Less Familiar Events with Substitution of Dissimilar Objects In typically developing Early Sentence Users between two-and-a-half and three years	❏ Child begins to act out less familiar events ❏ Child may talk while she plays but talking is not an essential part of the pretense ❏ Child pretends with objects that don't look like the objects for which they stand ❏ Child creates imaginary objects to support her play. She may use mime or gesture ("empty-handed miming") and/or words to show what she is pretending to do.	
Sociodramatic Play: Planned Pretend Themes In typically developing Later Sentence Users between three and five years	Child joins one or more peers to: ❏ develop imaginary themes and take on make-believe roles ❏ interact and cooperate together in a play episode for an extended period (at least 10 minutes) ❏ use make-believe instead of realistic objects ❏ imitate what people say and do and play roles of characters who come together to solve a problem or to produce some result ❏ coordinate and manage the play: discuss problems, explain points of view, negotiate, problem-solve ❏ use language to establish the identity of objects and substitute for actions verbalized but not performed ❏ develop a "story" with a plot, a sequence of events, and an outcome	

References

Bretherton, I. (1984). Representing the social world in symbolic play: Reality and fantasy. In I. Bretherton (Ed.), *Symbolic Play: The development of social understanding* (pp. 3–41). New York: Academic Press.

Bretherton, I. (1986). Representing the social world in symbolic play: Reality and fantasy. In A.W. Gottfried and C. Caldwell Brown (Eds.), *Play interactions: The contribution of play materials and parental involvement to children's development.* Proceedings of the eleventh Johnson and Johnson Pediatric Round Table (pp.119–148). Lexington, Mass: Lexington Books.

Christie, J.F. & Wardle, F. (1992). How much time is needed for play? *Young Children, 47*(3), 28–31.

Copple, C., Sigel, I.E. & Saunders, R. (1984). *Educating the young thinker: Classroom strategies for cognitive growth.* Hillsdale, NJ: Lawrence Erlbaum Associates.

Fenson, L. (1986). The developmental progression of play. In A.W. Gottfried and C. Caldwell Brown (Eds.), *Play interactions: The contribution of play materials and parental involvement to children's development.* Proceedings of the eleventh Johnson and Johnson Pediatric Round Table (pp.53–65). Lexington, Mass: Lexington Books.

Garvey, C. (1990). *Play.* Cambridge, Mass: Harvard University Press.

Johnson, J.E., Christie, J.F. & Yawkey, T.D. (1987). *Play and early childhood development.* Glenview, IL: Scott, Foresman.

McCune, L. (1986). Play-language relationships: Implications for a theory of symbolic development. In A.W. Gottfried and C. Caldwell Brown (Eds.), *Play interactions: The contribution of play materials and parental involvement to children's development.* Proceedings of the eleventh Johnson and Johnson Pediatric Round Table (pp. 67–79). Lexington, MA: Lexington Books.

McCune-Nicolich, L. (1981). Towards symbolic functioning: Structure of early pretend games and potential parallels with language. *Child Development, 52,* 785–797.

Nelson, K. & Seidman, S. (1984). Playing with scripts. In I. Bretherton (Ed.), *Symbolic Play: The development of social understanding* (pp. 3–41). New York: Academic Press.

Paley, V. (1990). *The boy who would be a helicopter.* Cambridge, Mass: Harvard University Press.

Pellegrini, A.D. (1985). Relations between preschool children's symbolic play and literate behavior. In L. Galda and A.D. Pellegrini (Eds.), *Play, language and stories: The development of children's literate behavior* (pp. 79–97). Norwood, NJ: Ablex.

Pellegrini, A.D. & Galda, L. (1990). Children's play, language and early literacy. *Topics in Language Disorders, 10*(3), 76–88.

Segal, M. & Adcock, D. (1981). *Just pretending: Ways to help children grow through imaginative play.* Englewood Cliffs, NJ: Prentice Hall.

Smilansky, S. & Shefatya, L. (1990). *Facilitating play: A medium for promoting cognitive, socio-emotional and academic development in young children.* Gaithersburg, MD: Psychosocial and Educational Publications.

Weininger, O. (1988). "What if" and "As if': Imagination and pretend play in early childhood. In K. Egan and D. Nadaner (Eds.), *Imagination and Education* (pp.141–149). New York: Teachers College Press.

Westby, C. (1980). Language abilities through play. *Language, Speech, and Hearing in the Schools, 11,* 154–168.

Wetherby, A. (1991a). *Profiling communication and symbolic abilities: Assessment and intervention guidelines.* Presentation at Toronto Children's Centre, Toronto, Ontario.

Wetherby, A. (1991b). Profiling pragmatic abilities in the emerging language of young children. In T, M. Gallagher, (Ed.), *Pragmatics of language: Clinical practice issues* (pp. 249–281). San Diego, CA: Singular.

Part 4

Let Language Lead the Way to Literacy

Children learn about literacy from birth, and they learn about it much the same way as they learn about spoken language.

In natural, day-to-day interactions, children see their caregivers use print in meaningful ways – and they discover that those marks on paper actually mean something. Once they discover that print communicates, they want to know how.

As a teacher, you play a critical role in helping children develop the attitudes, skills, and knowledge that lead to literacy.

Children must be helped to discover that:

- What I do or see or hear or touch, I can talk about
- What I talk about, I can write about, or someone can write for me
- What is written down, I can read or someone can read for me

In this approach to literacy, children develop reading and writing skills as they participate in and communicate about real-life, meaningful literacy events. This approach, which is based on the strong connection between language and literacy development, can benefit all children, including children with language delays.

Chapter 10, "Pave the Way for Young Readers and Writers," provides in-depth information on how teachers can lay the foundations of literacy by making reading and writing a natural, meaningful part of every day. Since the development of literacy skills is strongly linked to the development of language, this chapter will refer back to many of the conversational strategies described in earlier chapters, which also become an integral part of sharing books.

In Chapter 11, "Circle Time: An Interactive Language-Learning Experience," you will read about stimulating and interactive circle and group times that build the language skills children need in order to become literate.

Learning Language and Loving It

Pave the Way for Young Readers and Writers

As a teacher, you play an important role in helping children develop the attitudes, skills, and knowledge that lead to literacy.

A. Laying the foundations of literacy

Preparing children for literacy involves immersing them in an environment where interactions with reading and writing are a natural part of each day. There was a time when early literacy began with teaching children the alphabet. Not any more. Children have many more important things to learn about spoken language, reading, and writing before they are ready to understand the purpose of the alphabet.

You can prepare all children for success at school by helping them learn and develop the following skills. Children must:

- develop positive attitudes toward the use of print
- build their general knowledge and language skills
- develop an awareness, through "playing" with words, that language is made up of many parts
- develop an awareness of print, and
- be exposed to books and become familiar with the special "language" of books.

You don't need to teach these skills directly. Children will learn them by being exposed to print, books, and language in ways that show them how wonderfully useful, meaningful, and enjoyable print really is.

Helping children develop positive attitudes toward the use of print

The attitudes that children develop toward reading and writing – and that they bring to the task of developing literacy – are incredibly important. In order to become competent readers and writers, children must *want* to read and write.

Positive attitudes toward reading and writing are passed on to children from their parents and caregivers. Children of actors, singers, and tennis players often want to be actors, singers, and tennis players. In the same way, children whose parents frequently read and write also want to be readers and writers.

As a teacher, you send strong messages to children (even to infants and toddlers) about how important reading and writing are to you. That means it's important to let the children in your classroom see your positive attitude toward reading and writing.

To let children see your positive attitude toward reading and writing, you can:

- get really excited about books
- talk about the books you read
- show the children the books that were your childhood favourites
- bring in interesting pictures or articles from newspapers and magazines, and
- let children see that writing is a natural part of your day.

We'll discuss more of these ideas later in this chapter.

When you get excited about books, so do all the children.

This was my favourite book when I was little!

The importance of general knowledge and language skills to reading

For a child to become a successful reader, he needs good language skills and a well-developed store of general knowledge. While knowledge of letter-sound relationships (phonics) is also important, phonics alone are not enough to help children understand what they are reading. Successful readers rely on their language abilities to make sense of what they read. They are able to predict which words will come next in a sentence, based on their "feel" for language and their knowledge of grammar and phonics.

To develop the kind of language skills that will make them successful readers, children must:

- have a wide vocabulary
- grasp the rules of grammar so that they can read sentences that contain grammar more complex than their own
- be familiar with the language of books, which is more complex and formal than spoken language, and
- use the language of learning to explain, predict, project, and imagine. They must constantly analyze what they read, decide what it means, imagine the scene in their minds, and correct their predictions or assumptions when they are proved incorrect.

Read the story below and see how you use your language skills and background knowledge to fill in what's missing.

Miranda's Miserable Day

Miranda's alarm clock didn't go off and now she was late for an important meeting. She couldn't afford to lose her (i)_____ and she knew that if she missed this meeting, there was a good chance that she (ii)_____. She locked (iii)_____ door of her apartment and rushed outside. She tried to hail a (iv)_____, but her efforts were entirely unsuccessful. Finally, she decided to take the (v) b_____, which resulted in her arriving at her office 20 minutes late. She (vi) draimed up the stairs and into the meeting room, where she was met by a stony-faced Mr. Crimp, who said, (vii) "_____ _____!"

Let's look at how your language skills and knowledge of the topic enabled you to:
- Reach conclusions
- Anticipate words that come next in sentences
- Figure out words using your knowledge of:
  - grammatical rules
  - phonics and spelling, and
  - the context
- Figure out phrases that are part of the language of books
- Predict what would happen next and
- Imagine a scene in your head

Reach conclusions

You probably figured out what the story was about from the title – "Miranda's Miserable Day" – and from the first sentence: "Miranda was late for an important meeting."

The title and the words "late" and "meeting" made you assume that the story was about Miranda's problems at work. You were able to reach this conclusion fairly easily because you are familiar with this theme from reading novels, watching movies, and, perhaps, personal experience. Your ability to use language enabled you to make this assumption and reach your conclusion.

Children, too, must learn to make assumptions and reach conclusions about what they read. Their ability to use language to think, problem-solve, and reason enables them to understand things not specifically mentioned in the story. For example, if a child with good language skills read the sentence, "Michael ran into his room, reached for the switch, and immediately began searching for the ring," he would immediately make a number of inferences: it is nighttime (because Michael reached for the switch), Michael switched on the light (so he could look for the ring), and the ring was lost (because Michael was searching for it).

Because authors never include every detail in their stories, children have to reach many conclusions on their own. If they are unable to use language to draw these conclusions, they are likely to miss the meaning of the story and become frustrated. Therefore, the ability to problem-solve and look for connections and possible explanations – an important part of the language of learning – is critical to becoming an effective reader.

Having a broad general knowledge helps children make the assumptions and draw conclusions so they can understand printed stories. If they are read to regularly, children develop this knowledge, and they draw upon it when they listen to and read stories. In the same way that your exposure to the topic "problems at work" helped you figure out what Miranda's story was about, children with some background knowledge about detectives, jungle animals, dinosaurs, or birds of prey will find it easier to understand books on these topics.

Anticipate words that come next in sentences

You knew that the missing word for number (i) ("She couldn't afford to lose her _____") was "job" and that the missing word for number (iv) ("She tried to hail a _____") was "cab" or "taxi." Your knowledge of language helped you decide what would make sense in these sentences. Within the theme "problems at work," you would expect "lose her . . ." to be followed by "job," as opposed to "umbrella" or "set of keys." The phrase "hail a . . ." is usually followed by "cab" or "taxi." With your background knowledge of the context of "trying to get somewhere fast," it wasn't difficult for you to reach this conclusion.

Children with well-developed language skills also use their "feel" for language to help them anticipate what word comes next in a sentence. They learn vocabulary and common expressions during conversations with adults (see Chapter 4) as well as from regular exposure to books.

Figure out words using your knowledge of grammatical rules

Your knowledge of English grammar told you that the missing word for number (ii) (". . . and she knew that if she missed this meeting, there was a good chance that she _____.") was "would" and that the missing word for number (iii) ("She locked _____ door of her apartment and rushed outside.") was "the."

If English is your first language, your instinctive knowledge of the rules of English grammar makes these answers obvious. This task is more difficult for people who speak English as a second language and have not learned all the rules of English grammar.

When children learn to read, their instinctive knowledge of grammatical rules helps them figure out unknown words in the same way that your instinctive knowledge of rules helped you in the examples above. Children gain important clues from the position of words in sentences and from the words that come before and after an unknown word. For example, if a child couldn't read the word "flung" in the sentence "He flung the bag into the air," he would, without realizing it, still know a lot about the word. For example, he would know that the word "flung" was a verb because it came after the subject of the sentence (even if he didn't know the exact definitions of "verb" and "subject" yet). Because the subject of the sentence was a person and not an object, he would know that the verb probably involved an action of some sort, performed on the bag. All this knowledge would make it easier for him to figure out the meaning of the word.

Children with immature or delayed language – and second-language learners – often have trouble learning to read, partly because books contain grammatical rules that they haven't yet grasped. For example, if a child isn't able to use the passive tense, as in the sentence "The dog was bitten by the bird," he is unlikely to understand such a sentence. Therefore, he will incorrectly interpret the sentence as "The dog bit the bird" – which destroys the meaning of the story. These children need help to learn grammatical rules (see Chapter 7) and need a great deal of exposure to books that they can enjoy and understand.

> Children with immature or delayed language – and second-language learners – often have trouble learning to read, partly because books contain grammatical rules that they haven't yet grasped.

Figure out words based on your knowledge of phonics and spelling

Your knowledge of phonics and spelling made it obvious that number (v) ("Finally, she decided to take the b_____, which resulted in her arriving at her office 20 minutes late.") had to be "bus." If the letter "b" hadn't been there, the word could have been "train," "streetcar," or "subway," but the "b" made the choice obvious. In this way, you used your knowledge of phonics to work out what would make sense.

As children learn letter-sound relationships (phonics), they use this knowledge to help them narrow down the possibilities when reading an unknown word. However, knowledge of phonics is not enough to help them understand what they are reading (see below for a discussion of the meaning of "draimed").

Figure out words based on what makes sense in a context

You have a good idea of what "draimed" means in the sentence "She draimed up the stairs and into the meeting room," even though you've never seen the word before.

There is no such word as "draimed"! But you knew what would make sense in the context and concluded that "draimed" meant something like "rushed," "charged," or "dashed." Because we constantly search for meaning in what we read, we do this kind of "educated guessing" frequently. And we become quite good at it.

Because children come across many, many words that they don't know when they learn to read, they must be encouraged to make educated guesses at them. "Sounding out" the word doesn't always help; words that are easy to "sound out" may still mean nothing to a child. For example, words like "mist," "snub" and "tot" aren't hard words to read, but they aren't part of most children's vocabulary. And while sounding out words can be useful, if that's the only strategy children use, they often lose the meaning of what they read. Children who are encouraged to work out what would "make sense" in a particular context become readers who always try to understand what they read – and after all, that's what reading is about.

Figure out phrases that are part of the language of books

Exposure to "the language of books" helped you understand the phrase "but her efforts were entirely unsuccessful." Even though most of us don't talk like this, we have read enough books for these kinds of expressions to be part of our receptive vocabularies.

Children who have been read to frequently become familiar with the language of books, which helps them comprehend more complex language.

Predict what will happen next to help you understand the story

You probably guessed that the stony-faced Mr. Crimp said "You're fired!" or "You're late!" for number (vii). Your sense of story, gained from reading many stories and from watching movies and television, enabled you to predict what Mr. Crimp was likely to say.

Predicting is a critical skill for readers to develop. It gives them expectations about what will happen next, which is part of their ongoing efforts to interact with and understand the story. Predicting what will happen next makes reading more meaningful and more interesting (especially if your prediction isn't right, which is why many people love good mysteries).

Children who have had many stories read to them and who are encouraged to predict during story reading become good predictors.

Imagine a scene in your head

As you read the story, you were able to use the words to help you create an image of this scene in your mind. You could picture Miranda in her desperation and the miserable Mr. Crimp. Your ability to understand language and to use it to go beyond the real world enabled you to imagine something you had never experienced.

Children with excellent language skills and vivid imaginations find it easier to interpret what they read; their ability to use symbols helps them transform verbal descriptions into mental images. (See Chapters 8 and 9 for how to develop children's ability to imagine through extending the topic and encouraging pretend play.)

As you can see from this exercise, a child's language skills – his knowledge of grammar, his ability to use the language of learning, and his familiarity with the language of books – are what enable him to become a successful reader.

> Children with excellent language skills and vivid imaginations find it easier to interpret what they read; their ability to use symbols helps them transform verbal descriptions into mental images.

> **To help children build their general knowledge and language skills to become successful readers:**
>
> - encourage and model the language of learning during your everyday conversations with them (see Chapter 8)
> - expose them to many, many books so they learn to go beyond the here-and-now, gain exposure to the language of books, and develop a broad general knowledge
> - encourage them to figure out what words mean based on the context
> - encourage them to think about a story – to predict, imagine, and project, and
> - encourage them to make sense of the book by relating it to what they already know.

These suggestions will be discussed in more detail later in this chapter.

Encouraging children to "play" with words

Children need to learn that language is made up of many different parts, that sentences can be broken up into words, and that words can be broken up into syllables and sounds. They must also become aware of the rules (including grammatical rules, described in Chapter 7) that dictate how all the parts of language go together.

The process of thinking about language starts early in life. Even infants show signs of thinking about language when they "repair" a breakdown in communication by changing the way they send their messages. When a three-year-old says "pumpernickel" 20 times, giggling uncontrollably because the word has such a funny sound, he's actually thinking about language – and better still, he's playing with it!

Listen to three- and four-year-olds as they:

- **change the words of rhymes and songs:** "Nathan the red-nosed reindeer, had a very shiny nose . . ." (Nathan, aged four, was not impressed)
- **make up funny-sounding words:** "Your name will be Mr. Boodleboodle!" (hysterical laughter)
- **change the sounds in words:** "I'm eating a nabana." (banana)
- **make up rhyming words:** "You're Jake the snake, and you're Matt the bat."
- **play with word meanings:** "In winter, a somersault should be called a wintersault." (amazing for a four-year-old)
- **say phrases or lists of words that sound alike:** "Big baby boy, big baby boy . . . those all sound the same."
- **recognize pronunciation errors:** "He says 'top' instead of 'stop.'"

These children are already aware of how words and sentences can be broken up and put back together again. Children who can "play" with language like this will find it easier to learn reading, writing, and spelling.

Teachers who prepare young children for reading by teaching them "'C'-is-for-cat" kinds of phonic skills are way ahead of schedule. Young children need to "play" with language in the ways described above before they are ready to learn how words can be broken down into individual sounds. This is especially important for children with language delays whose ability to "play with words" is often below age level.

You can encourage children to play with words by:

- following their lead when they play with words! Add your own ideas, too.
- playing with words yourself: "See ya later alligator!" "In the house, little mouse; on a chair, big brown _____."
- making up new songs to old tunes
- singing songs whose verses can be changed to make many different rhymes: "There was Shane, Shane / Dancing in the rain / In the store, In the store . . . / There was Mark, Mark / Sleeping in the dark / In the store, In the store . . ."
- Point out interesting things about words or names: "Hey! Ryan and Rob both have names that start with 'rrrr'!" (Make the sound "r" rather than tell them the name of the letter.) "My name is so loooong. Listen to how many parts it has – Chris-ti-na. Three parts!" (Tap once for each syllable.)

Remember: be playful and informal – that's why it's called playing with words!

Helping children develop an awareness of print

From an early age, children become aware of the print they see, and they try to figure out what it means. This marks the beginning of reading.

By three years of age, many children can read signs in the environment, like "EXIT," "STOP," or "McDonalds" (of course!). From being read to, they have learned where a book begins, in which direction to turn the pages, that the print tells the story and the pictures illustrate what is in the text. They know that the story continues from page to page, and they use words like "read," "story," and "page" appropriately.

Children know that writing involves making marks on paper, and their earliest attempts at writing involve scribbling. Scribbling is an important part of learning to write and shows a definite progression: from random to controlled scribbles to naming of scribbles.

In time, children come to realize that writing is organized in lines, and they develop a sense of what letters should look like. As a result, their scribbles become repetitive and go across the page, and they enjoy "reading" what they have "written." Before too long, they start to write mock letters and words. Finally, they progress to writing real letters and words (especially their names). They experiment, writing what they know again and again in many ways, copying words in the environment, and eventually learning to write from left to right.

Developing an awareness of print is a process of discovery, and you can encourage this process in a very natural way.

Scribbling and experimenting with "letter-like" forms are important parts of learning to write.

What you can do to encourage an awareness of print

- Point out print in the environment and in books: first words in a story, strange-looking words, long words, short words, unusual print (e.g., "BOOM!"), labels on boxes, signs, etc.

- Provide many opportunities for drawing and scribbling with crayons, markers, pencils, fingerpaint, etc.

- Encourage children to write in their own way for many different purposes (e.g., to label their pictures; to write to their friends, parents, etc.)

- Don't worry about correct spelling or perfect letter formation; writing, like talking, is a developmental process and improves with exposure and experience. Correcting spelling and letter formation too early distracts children from the purpose of writing, which is to communicate.

- Provide help with printing, spelling, or writing stories only when asked.

- Let the children know that you consider their writing to have meaning. Respond to what they want their writing to "say."

We will discuss how to encourage an awareness of print in more detail later in this chapter.

B. Book-reading: A time for sharing and learning

Books connect children with the world – their own world and new worlds. The illustrations and stories transport them into situations that expand their knowledge, experience, and imagination. Their fascination with books will bring them back to their favourites again and again.

In the same way that good language skills support the development of literacy skills, much language learning takes place through reading and listening to books (especially reading the same book again and again). By listening to stories, and by discussing them with an interested adult, children develop a store of knowledge about the world and come to understand words and concepts that they could not learn as easily from casual conversation. Research has also shown that children who are read to frequently before they start school have better oral language skills when they get to school than those who are not read to. In fact, familiarity with books from a very young age is an important predictor of later reading success.

It's never too early to enjoy books.

Because of the strong connection between exposure to books and language development, it is vitally important to read to children who have language delays. Books have an advantage over conversation: the language in books doesn't "disappear" as the language of conversation does – it comes back each time the book is read. For this reason, book reading is an excellent context in which children can increase their language skills. As children hear the stories in a book again and again, they understand more about the book, and its language becomes familiar. It becomes so predictable, in fact, that eventually the child takes over and "reads" the book to himself. This is one of the best ways to encourage children to read independently: when they know the book well, they feel as if they can read it. And, eventually, they will.

When you hear a child talk about a Tyrannosaurus Rex or use a phrase like "to the very top" or "once and for all," which he heard in a book, you can be sure that he has begun that all-important journey into the language of books.

The keys to successful book reading

- Don't just read the book – give it all you've got!
- Choose books that match children's interests and stage of development
- Make book reading a time for interaction and conversation

Don't just read the book – give it all you've got!

Reading aloud to children isn't just an activity – it's a performance! Your task as the reader is to draw your listeners into the story by creating the right mood and by being aware of your audience's reaction and adapting accordingly. Whether you are reading informally to one or two children or to a larger group of children at circle time, the interaction between you and your listeners is the key to success.

So give it all you've got – be dramatic and animated and look excited. Add different voices for different characters and use sound effects for noises in the book. Get the children involved and keep them involved!

And he ran away from his mother saying, "You can't catch me."

This teacher is just reading . . .

*And he **ran** away from his mother, saying, "You can't catch me!!!" Oh! Oh! Now there's going to be trouble! What would your Mom do if you ran away from her?!!!*

. . . but this teacher is animated and expressive, and she's captured the children's attention.

Choose books that match children's interests and stage of development

All children's books are not created equal. Some are excellent, some are mediocre, and some are dreadful! If children become restless during book reading, consider whether the fault lies with the book: it may be too simple, or simply too boring!

In deciding which books to read to children, there is really only one important guideline: children should be exposed only to the best books!

Reading to children is important in laying the foundation for them to become readers, but it's not enough to turn them into enthusiastic readers. Books that enchant, amuse, move, and delight children will inspire them to become readers. Therefore, choose books carefully, keeping in mind children's interests and stage of language development. (Remember that their ability to appreciate a book depends on what they can understand, not on what they can say.) Because the children "read" the illustrations while you read the book, the book's illustrations should be interesting, attractive, clear, and quite large, and they should correspond to the book's content.

> Reading to children is important in laying the foundation for them to become readers, but it's not enough to turn them into enthusiastic readers. Books that enchant, amuse, move, and delight children will inspire them to become readers.

If the children aren't paying attention, you may be reading the wrong book.

Make book reading a time for interaction and conversation

Book reading should involve a great deal more than simply reading aloud to children. It is a wonderful time for interaction, conversation, and learning. Watch during reading time for how children interact with both you and the book – they point to illustrations, ask questions, and make comments as they try to make sense of the book and relate it to what they already know (using many of the strategies you used when you read "Miranda's Miserable Day"). This is how much of the learning takes place.

Since book reading is such an ideal time for learning, you can't simply read the book while the children listen passively.

During book reading, your role is to:

- actively engage children in conversation to help them make sense of the book
- read slowly and, at key points in the book, stop and wait expectantly to encourage children to make comments and ask questions
- model the language of learning and use comments and questions to encourage the children to use it too, and
- make comments and ask questions so children can relate the book to their own experiences. If you and the children become engaged in an interesting discussion about the book, feel free to abandon reading the text for a while since these discussions are just as important as reading the text.

C. Exposing Discoverers and Communicators to books

The first thing that babies do with books is eat them. Before children understand that pictures in books represent real objects and people, they tend to enjoy chewing on them. Trying to "read" the book to a child at these early stages of language development usually results in his pulling the book away from you and putting it straight back in his mouth!

The first thing that babies do with books is eat them.

Let's read the book, Kelly. Can I have the book?

Choosing the right books for Discoverers and Communicators

Cardboard books with good, clear illustrations and books containing collections of nursery rhymes are best for very young infants or older Discoverers and Communicators with language delays.

Guidelines for reading with Discoverers and Communicators

- **Observe, wait, and listen (see Chapter 3):** Observing, waiting, and listening will tell you what about the book interests the child. Let him look at one book for a long time if that's what he wants to do.
- **Be face-to-face (see Chapter 3):** If you are face-to-face with the child, he will be able to pay attention to you as well as to the book.
- **Follow the child's lead (see Chapter 3):** Imitate the child's sounds; interpret his eye gaze, sounds, and actions as if they were meaningful; and comment on what seems to interest him in the book.
- **Take turns (see Chapter 4):** Encourage turn-taking by waiting expectantly after

you take your turn to give the child a chance to make another sound or to look at or touch a picture. Share books mainly with individual children or perhaps two children at a time.

- ◆ **Make your language easy to understand (see Chapter 7):** Exaggerate the intonation and rhythm in your voice.

Penny observes, waits, and listens so that Talia can let her know what interests her in the book. Then Penny interprets Talia's action by making an interesting comment.

D. Building on First Words Users' fascination with books

First Words Users have started to use words (the beginning of symbol use), and they realize that pictures in books represent real people and objects (pictures are symbols too). As a result, they become fascinated with books.

Choosing the best books for First Words Users

Some of the best books for First Words Users are:
- Mother Goose collections
- board books with pictures that encourage the labelling and pointing that is typical of children at this stage of language development
- books with illustrated songs
- family photograph albums, and
- interaction books (e.g., *Pat the Bunny* by D. Kunhardt).

Books should:
- appeal to the children's interests and level of understanding
- have clear, colourful, and appealing illustrations
- have only a small amount of print on each page
- be short, and
- be easy to manipulate.

Guidelines for reading with First Words Users

- **Observe, wait, and listen (see Chapter 3):** Much of the learning that takes place during book-reading occurs as the children interact with you and communicate about the book. Observe the children and notice how they communicate with you – at this stage, they may use words, eye gaze, pointing, sounds, gestures, or a combination of these. Don't rush the reading. Pace yourself according to the children's interests and give them time to look at each page (often they will be fascinated by one page in particular). When you wait, you will encourage children to initiate. If you listen closely, you may find that a very quiet child has a lot to say (even if the sounds aren't real words).

- **Be face to face (see Chapter 3):** If possible, seat children so you can see their faces and notice their initiations. Because most young children love to sit on your lap when being read to (often two at a time), try seating them at a slight angle so you can see whether they are staring intently at an illustration or pointing at something.

- **Follow the child's lead and take turns (see Chapter 3 and 4):** Respond to the children's initiations by labelling, interpreting, and commenting. Children at this stage often point to pictures and want you to label them. And they enjoy it when you ask them to label the pictures whose names they know. Have little conversations as you label pictures or imitate sounds together. Fill-in-the-blank sentences can also be a useful way to cue a First Words User to take a turn (e.g., "The cow says _____."). From these interactions, children learn that books are fun to talk about.

- **Adjust your language (see Chapter 7):** There's a lot of language that First Words Users can't understand, so you have to help them make sense of the book. This means that you can't always read the book exactly as it's written! In the same way that you adjust your language when you talk to children to help them understand you, so you need to adjust the way you read books to them.

  - **Say less:** Use clear, simple language to describe pictures to the child. (The text in the book may give too much information or not enough.)

  - **Stress:** Repeat and exaggerate key words. Use "fun" words, like "Boom!"

  - **Go slow:** Read slowly enough that the child can process what he's hearing.

  - **Show:** Use gestures or pantomime. Show props or real objects that are similar to the pictures in the book.

A simple, clear sentence helps the child understand what's in the book.

She's saying, "Hullo Sarah!"

Pantomime helps children understand what the words in the book mean.

Use props to reinforce what you have shown the child in the book.

Here's our phone! Does Sarah want to talk to Mommy on our phone?

- **Extend the topic (see Chapter 7):** Help the children to make sense of the text and begin to introduce the language of learning. Compare or contrast the information in the book with something in the immediate environment. For example, when reading a book about a child getting dressed to play in the snow, ask the children what they wear when they go out in the playground. You can also provide simple explanations (e.g., "We have to wear mittens outside so our hands don't get cold.").

E. Using books to stimulate and satisfy Combiners' curiosity

Combiners are incredibly curious, and books provide them with a wonderful source of stimulation – a source they can return to at any time. Now that their receptive language has increased, they can enjoy a wider variety of books.

Choosing the best books for Combiners

Some of the best books for children at the Combiner stage are:

- books with collections of pictures (e.g., Richard Scarry books)
- books with a repetitive theme and "fun-sounding" words (e.g., *Hand, Hand, Fingers, Thumb* by Al Perkins)
- theme books on topics like zoo animals, babies, toys, "things I can do myself," etc.
- short stories with a very simple plot and story line (e.g., *Just for You* and *Just a Mess* by Mercer Mayer)
- classics (e.g., *Goodnight Moon* by Margaret Wise Brown)
- stories that are repetitive and predictable (e.g., *The Gingerbread Man*)
- collections of poems and nursery rhymes, and
- participatory books (e.g., *Pat the Bunny* by D. Kunhardt and *Where's Spot?* by Eric Hill).

Guidelines for reading with Combiners

- **Observe, wait, and listen and follow the children's lead (see Chapter 3):** Remember to go slowly and pause frequently during the story to give children a chance to make comments and share their thoughts on a book. Build on the children's interests and respond to their initiations by confirming and expanding on them.

Children's initiations during book-reading give you lots of opportunities to expand on their message.

- **Take turns (see Chapter 4):** Let the children join in! No child can resist the appeal of "Who's been sleeping in my bed?" or "Run, run, as fast as you can, you can't catch me, I'm the Gingerbread Man!" These stories are fun to listen to, and they have children anxiously waiting to chime in! As children wait for the opportunity to yell out the word or words that complete the sentence, they are learning to predict what comes next. And, as we discussed in "Miranda's Miserable Day," predicting is an important reading skill.

Once the children are familiar with a predictable story, give them a chance to chime in by stopping and waiting expectantly at the appropriate spot.

- **Rephrase the text:** Rephrase the text when necessary. Some books have wonderful illustrations but poor text. Consider whether the text relates to the illustration in a way the children can understand. If not, you'll need to rephrase it.

There's no mention of the word "shoe"; you'll need to rephrase the text.

- **Extend the topic (see Chapter 8):** Model and encourage children to use language to relate the content of the book to what they already know, to explain what has happened, to predict what will happen next, and to talk about the characters' feelings. When you relate the content of the book to something the children already know and when you provide opportunities for them to interact with the story, you bring the book to life. There are many opportunities to encourage pretending and imagining. For example, if you read *The Gingerbread Man* to a group of children, you can bring in real gingerbread men for them to eat. Once they are familiar with the story, you can give each child a cardboard gingerbread man and have them "act out" the story as you read it.

F. Encourage the "language of learning" with Early and Later Sentence Users

Language has opened up the world to Early and Later Sentence Users (typically between the ages of three and five). They can go beyond the here-and-now, beyond their own personal experiences, and beyond the real world into the world of make-believe – and books enable them to do just that. They have developed the "language of learning" (see Chapter 8), which they use to think about and understand books in the same way you did when you read "Miranda's Miserable Day."

Children at this stage can understand and appreciate both fiction and non-fiction. However, they still have a very wide range of abilities and interests, and you must carefully choose the books you read to them in order to reflect those abilities and interests.

Choosing the best books for Early and Later Sentence Users

- **The book's topic or story line should appeal to the children's interests, imaginations, and level of understanding:** As children develop more advanced receptive language skills, they enjoy and understand stories with more complex plots and imaginary themes. Four- and five-year-olds, who engage in imaginative dramatic and sociodramatic play, are well able to appreciate books about fantasy, such as *Where the Wild Things Are* by Maurice Sendak and *Miss Nelson is Missing* by Harry Allard. Children who can recognize their own feelings and fears will love books like *There's a Nightmare in My Closet* by Mercer Mayer and *I Have to Go* by Robert Munsch.
- **Provide books with excellent language:** Descriptions like " . . . and he sailed off through night and day and in and out of weeks . . ." (from Maurice Sendak's *Where the Wild Things Are*) cannot help but enchant children, while exposing them to imaginative ways of using language. Let the children hear language that has a more sophisticated style, grammatical structure, and vocabulary than everyday speech. The beauty of the words "The wild things roared their terrible roars and gnashed their terrible teeth . . ." combines a wonderful use of repetition and rhythm with new vocabulary, which children respond to and remember.
- **Read more detailed and complex stories:** Children develop story structure or a "sense of story" from having many stories read to them. Story structure (illustrated below by the fairy tale "The Three Little Pigs") consists of the following basic parts:
  - an introduction to the setting and the main character(s) (the three little pigs and the big bad wolf)
  - an event or problem that leads the reader into the story (the wolf huffs and puffs and blows down two pigs' houses)

- a response from the main characters or an attempt to deal with the problem (the third pig builds a strong house, saves his brothers, and puts a kettle of boiling water at the bottom of the chimney)
- the outcome of the response or attempt (the wolf falls into the boiling water and dies), and
- a reaction from the main characters (the three pigs live happily ever after).

Fairy tales have a well-defined story structure that helps children develop a sense of story, making it easier for them to follow the plot and predict what will happen next.

After much experience with story reading, children can appreciate stories that are more detailed and complex. In time, they will enjoy stories that have more complicated problems, more than one attempt to solve the problem (including some failed attempts), and less obvious outcomes.

- **Provide a mixture of non-fiction and fiction:** Satisfy the children's all-encompassing curiosity about the world by reading them books on topics like dinosaurs, animals and their young, and the solar system. They aren't too young for this – as long as the books have excellent illustrations and the language is clear and appropriate to their language level. By exposing children to the language style of non-fiction books, you are preparing them for the kinds of books they will read at school.

Guidelines for reading books with Early and Later Sentence Users

Before reading the book
- Preview the book
- Read the book's title, show the children the cover, and encourage them to predict what the book is about
- Introduce the author and illustrator
- Create a purpose for reading the book

While reading the book:
- Observe, wait, and listen and follow the children's lead
- Take some time to respond to questions and comments
- Take turns and involve the children in conversation
- "SSCAN" the group to encourage all the children to participate in the conversation
- Encourage the language of learning by:
  - explaining things children don't understand
  - using children's questions to help them make connections

- wondering about what might happen next, and
- extending the topic.

After reading the book

- Encourage the children's spontaneous comments
- Help the children make connections between this and other books
- Offer some interesting follow-up activities
- Encourage the children to "read" the book themselves

Before reading the book

Preview the book

Read the book beforehand to make sure it's appropriate. When you're familiar with its content and vocabulary, you will be better able to respond to the children's questions and comments.

Read the book's title, show the children the cover, and encourage them to predict what the book is about

Encourage the children to guess what the book is about from looking at the illustration on the cover and listening to the title. In so doing, you model the search for meaning that readers engage in before they even begin to read a book.

Introduce the author and illustrator

Tell the children the names of the people who wrote and illustrated the book and, if provided, show them the author's and illustrator's photographs. Remind them of other books written by the same author. Let them see that books are written and illustrated by ordinary people. If the children in the group have written and illustrated their own stories, let them know that they too are authors and illustrators.

Create a purpose for reading the book

Start off by creating a purpose for reading the book. For example, if you are about to read *A Promise is a Promise* by Robert Munsch, you might ask, "Have any of you ever made a promise, or have your parents ever made a promise to you?" After some discussion on this topic, encourage the children to find out how the promise they are going to hear about in the book is similar to or different from a promise that they made or someone made to them. Such an introduction motivates the children to approach the book with a sense of purpose, encouraging them to engage in that ongoing search for meaning.

While reading the book

Make the most of opportunities to actively engage Early and Later Sentence Users in conversation during book reading. Use the "language of learning" to help them make sense of the book and to relate it to what they already know. Remember to:

Observe, wait, and listen and follow the children's lead (see Chapter 3)

Use a slow pace and wait expectantly to give children opportunities to point to illustrations, ask questions, and make comments – and then follow their leads. This is the way children try to make sense of books and relate them to what they already know.

Take turns (see Chapter 4)

Use a variety of comments and questions and wait expectantly to actively engage the children in conversation about the book. Talk about what they think is going to happen in the book and how the book relates to their own experiences, and get their reactions to the story. Instead of asking "testing" questions, which ask for simple facts, ask interesting questions that encourage the children to think and use their imaginations to continue the conversation. (See Chapter 4, pages 133–140: "Use questions to continue, not control the conversation.")

"Fact" questions don't stimulate children to think about the story.

It would feel so strange to be as big and heavy as an elephant. How would you like to be this big and this heavy?

I'd like it because then I'd be the strongest animal in the world!

I wouldn't. I'd be so heavy I couldn't run fast.

I'd like it cos I could reach the leaves on the highest trees with my trunk.

This question encourages children to use language to imagine, making them go beyond the book and think about the story in a new way.

SSCAN (see Chapter 5)

Early and Later Sentence Users are frequently exposed to books at group or circle time. However, discussion in large groups can be difficult. It is therefore important to read books at times other than circle time, when you can interact more readily with individual children.

During these interactions, watch the quieter children. They may be initiating in their own way or they may need some encouragement to participate. A gentle comment or question may be all that's needed for a reluctant communicator to join in.

If you look closely, you'll see that each child is initiating, and you can then respond to each one.

Me ball!

Encourage the "language of learning" (see Chapter 8)

- Explain things the children don't understand
- Use children's questions to help them make connections
- Wonder about what might happen next
- Extend the topic
- Get children thinking about the book

- **Explain things the children don't understand:** You need not stop every time an unfamiliar word comes up. Children learn to figure out what things mean from the context (as you did with the word "draimed" in "Miranda's Miserable Day"). However, from time to time, children ask what a word means or you feel that an explanation is needed.

  For example, Janet and Allan Ahlberg repeat the phrase "I spy" many times in their book *Each Peach Pear Plum*. Young children likely won't understand the word "spy." In this case, you could provide a brief explanation for the word "spy" or you could use the word in a context that makes its meaning obvious (e.g., "Who can spy Tom Thumb? There he is! We all spy Tom Thumb with our eyes!"). As the word is repeated in this and other contexts, chances are the children will figure out its meaning before the story is over.

  To help children understand the meaning of illustrations, you can point out movement lines and facial expressions that a young child may not understand.

Explain to the children what the movement lines and crumpled sheets mean.

- **Use children's questions to help them make connections:** Although it's not desirable to interrupt the reading of the story too often, there are ways to maintain continuity and still encourage children to be curious and interactive. Sometimes all it takes is a quick confirmation of a child's comment (e.g., "Yes, he *is* big, isn't he?") or a brief answer to a question (e.g., "He doesn't want to go to sleep, that's why.") to help children make connections.

    While you'll need to answer some questions right away in order to help children understand the story, sometimes the book itself will provide the answer. By saying, "Let's wait and see. The book will tell us!" you can usually satisfy a child. When questions or comments are better left for discussion after you have finished reading the book, you could say, "That's an interesting question. Let's talk about that at the end of the story" – and make sure that you do!

- **Wonder aloud about what might happen next:** Keep the search for meaning going. Making comments like, "I wonder what he'll do when he finds the treasure" shows the children you're trying to predict and will encourage them to do the same.

- **Extend the topic:** Draw children into a conversation about the book using the "language of learning" to go beyond the book and to think about the story in many different ways.

- **Get the children thinking about the book** by encouraging them to:
    - predict what will happen next
    - draw upon their own knowledge and experiences and relate these to the book (e.g., "Has anyone here ever been lost like the boy in this book?")
    - talk about how the characters might be feeling
    - project themselves into the story and describe how they would feel or behave in that situation
    - explain why something happened or why one of the characters said or did something, and
    - pretend/imagine (e.g., imagine a different ending or imagine what happened beyond the ending of the story).

You can't do all these things at once. Favourite books, however, should be read and reread so they turn into old friends – and you will be able to get the children thinking about the book in different ways over the course of repeated readings. After several readings, children reach conclusions, predict, project, and imagine far more easily than they can at the first reading.

After reading the book

Encourage the children's spontaneous comments

Don't end the interaction as soon as you have finished reading the book. Give the children time to react to it. To make the story more meaningful, help them relate its theme or topic to what they know and have experienced.

Help the children make connections between the book they just read and other books

Ask the children if this book reminds them of other books they have read. Draw upon what they have learned from other books and help them see the connections. Let them know which books this particular book reminds you of and in what way. (You can also make connections to other books while you read the book.)

Ask interesting questions (e.g., "Does Viola Swamp in *Miss Nelson is Missing* remind you of the wolf in *Little Red Riding Hood?* How are they the same and how are they different?" "Thomas in *Thomas's Snowsuit* and Alexander in *Where the Wild Things Are* both had trouble with adults. What kind of trouble did each one have? What would your Mum or Dad do if you said or did what Thomas and Alexander did? What would you do if you were Thomas/Alexander?"). Discussions like these help children go beyond the book, which is what thinking readers do.

Offer some interesting follow-up activities

What about everyone getting down on all fours and pretending to be "wild things" after reading *Where the Wild Things Are?* Or perhaps doing a fingerplay about caterpillars and butterflies after reading *The Very Hungry Caterpillar?* You could all pretend to be dinosaurs after reading about dinosaurs, or have the children act out the story as you read it with each child playing a small part.

Using their bodies as well as their minds as they interact with the story brings the book to life for children and lets them imagine and interpret the book in different ways. Pretending to be a dinosaur gives the child more of an idea about what it might have been like to be a fierce Tyrannosaurus Rex.

You can also provide materials that encourage the children to create something related to the book they have read. Children might like to make a mask of ugly Viola Swamp after reading *Miss Nelson is Missing* or make thumbprint caterpillars with holes punched in them after reading *The Very Hungry Caterpillar*. Or they might enjoy re-enacting a story in the puppet centre, with flannel board characters or props they create themselves.

*Pretending to be "wild things" brings the book **Where the Wild Things Are** to life.*

Encourage the children to "read" the book themselves

After you read a book to the children, leave it out for them, saying "The book is here if anyone would like to read it." (More than one copy of the book is desirable.) Many children will take the book and "read" it. Of course, they aren't really reading, but they are practising telling stories, using the language of books, and getting a feel for reading, all of which are important steps in becoming a reader.

G. The book centre

The book centre is frequently a neglected area of the classroom. Too often, the centre faces out onto the free play area, is not enclosed, doesn't have comfortable seating, and has a limited selection of books.

Most people like to read in a cozy, quiet place that has comfortable seating. Try to create such a place for the children; a cozy place will encourage them to go and read.

Fill your classroom with books: big books, small books, giant books, story books, fun books, easy books, hard books – lots of books! Provide quality, quantity, and variety.

Some suggestions for books:

- story books (including those you have read to the group)
- predictable or patterned books, which are so predictable that the children sit down and "read" them
- non-fiction books about dinosaurs, animals, insects, machines, etc.
- wordless books (which encourage children to read by themselves)
- very large books, which are usually very repetitive and predictable
- interaction books, in which the child has to perform some action on the book (e.g., *Pat the Bunny*)
- store catalogues (especially those with toys)
- bulletin boards placed at children's eye levelpoetry and nursery rhyme books
- children's magazines (e.g., *Sesame Street Magazine, Big Backyard*)
- books made together by teachers and children
- taped books (tape yourself reading the book and provide a tape recorder with earphones)
- travel brochures
- novelty books (e.g., pop-up books)
- poetry and nursery rhyme books.

Aaaaah! This is the life!

H. The writing centre

Every preschool and kindergarten classroom needs a writing centre. While book centres encourage reading, writing centres encourage writing.

Writing and reading develop at the same time, and build upon each other. As children learn to read, their awareness of print helps them write, and their ability to write, in turn, improves their reading. Writing centres encourage children to experiment with drawing and writing and to share what they write with others.

Set up your writing centre in a relatively quiet area, perhaps alongside the book centre, and have available a variety of writing materials that children won't be able to resist, like:

- a chalkboard with coloured chalk
- magnetic letters
- unlined and lined paper of different colours, sizes, shapes, and textures
- stapled paper books for story writing
- a typewriter or computer
- cards, postcards, and notepaper of various shapes and sizes
- markers, pencils, crayons, and pens
- stamps and envelopes, and
- an ink stamp, tape, a stapler, glue, and scissors.

The materials in the writing centre should be so interesting and so varied that children see endless possibilities for their use.

Keep records of children's writing over the year. The changes in the way they write will be quite amazing.

I. Make print talk in your classroom

Because preschool and child care offer so many good reasons to use print and so many people to share it with, they are wonderful places for children to learn about the printed word. When children's interactions with their caregivers involve the printed word – and when caregivers demonstrate the use of print during these interactions – children become interested in print. They try to figure out what words mean and start experimenting with both reading and writing.

If the print in your classroom is not at the children's eye level, they can't benefit from it. If you want children to try to read print, don't put it where *you* can read it – put it where *they* can read it!

To get children interested in print, you have to show them that print, in fact, "talks." So don't make signs and lists when the children are asleep or at home! They need to know why and how print is used and what it says. When you make print talk, let the children see you in action so that they can watch, ask questions, make comments, and see print's purpose. And remember: if the print in your classroom is not at the children's eye level, they can't benefit from it. If you want children to try to read print, don't put it where *you* can read it – put it where *they* can read it!

Print will talk in your classroom if you provide:

- an environment rich in the printed word (not only the alphabet but also print that has meaning)
- many demonstrations of how print is used
- interactions around the use of print, and
- opportunities for children to use and experiment with print.

Make print talk in your classroom . . .
- During daily routines and activities
- For pleasure and social interaction
- To communicate with others
- To record information
- To gain information and knowledge

Note: The following sections contain suggested activities and strategies that are appropriate for Early and Later Sentence Users (typically over three years of age). However, those of you who work with children at lower stages will find that many of these activities and strategies can be used with these children as well.

Use print during daily routines and activities

Adults use print as part of their everyday lives, and so should children.

Signs and labels

Use signs to communicate rules and instructions and to provide labels. Just as there are "No Parking" and "Entrance" signs in the real world, put up signs that relate to your daily routines and activities at the children's eye level! Some ideas for signs include:

- labels for cubbies, toy containers, activity centres, cupboards, and supply containers
- signs about the number of children allowed in an activity centre
- instructions for the care of pets and plants
- signs that provide necessary information (e.g., "Fish has been fed" / "Fish has not been fed")
- signs that post rules that teachers have discussed and developed with children (e.g. "Tidy up the blocks")
- large sheets of paper with recipes written on them (e.g., for fingerpaint or play-dough), which the children watch you write, and
- signs that children make for their own purposes (e.g., "Do Not Touch" or "Keep Out").

Important information is worth reading.

Sign-up sheets

Sign-up sheets give children the opportunity to write or attempt to write their names. They can be used to assign "jobs" in the classroom, for activity centres, for checking materials or books in or out, etc. They can also be used for surveys, with children signing their names to indicate their responses to a question.

What do you like to eat on your crackers?	
Peanut Butter	Cheese

Labelling artwork

Encourage children to write their names on their artwork and respond to their attempts to write their "names," even when you can't read them.

Respond to the meaning of the child's writing, even if you can't read it.

Attendance

You can take attendance in a number of ways that children enjoy. When children arrive in the morning, for example, they can:

- put their name cards on a large chart
- write their names on a large sheet of paper, or
- check their names off a large list.

When attendance sheets are visible, children can see who is absent by looking at the list. This encourages reading.

Coupons

Let the children help you find coupons for the groceries and supplies you buy for the centre. Show them the items you need and give them supermarket flyers to leaf through. This is lots of fun – and a good lesson in budget planning!

Lists

Lists have an important purpose in life (if you can find them when you need them), and children should be exposed to them early on. Show children how you use lists to remind you which groceries to buy or which supplies to replace. Write in large print and keep your lists in visible places. Let the children help you make the lists, even if it means drawing the articles you need to buy. You can then write the word next to the picture.

Completing forms

Children love to imitate adults' "work." With this in mind, the teachers at one child-care centre decided to let the children do the teacher's "job" of filling in their daily records. They drew up forms, which included pictures and print, for the children to complete. On the form, each child checked off whether he had a lot or a little to eat at lunch, whether he had a long or short nap, and what he did outside, etc. What a wonderful, purposeful use for print!

When filling in their own daily records, children experience a real purpose for using print – and they love doing it!

Use print for pleasure and social interaction

Help children experience the pleasure that comes from using print and the opportunities it provides for social interaction.

Making books

"Centre-made" books are great fun to make and read together, especially when the children are the topic of the book and when their photographs are used as illustrations. So get out your camera and take pictures of the children on a field trip, during Halloween, at the annual holiday party, or engaging in their activities on a regular day. Then, together with the children, make a book, letting them tell you what to write. Place the finished product in the book centre and watch how often they "read" their book.

Make the book together . . .

. . . and watch the children read it again and again!

Children should also be encouraged to make up their own stories. Provide blank books in the writing centre and let the children know that you are available if they want to dictate a story to you. You can help them develop their story-telling skills by writing down the stories they dictate, and then reading their stories back to them. In addition to making comments on the interesting content of their stories, ask scaffolding questions (see Chapter 8) to let them know what information they need to include or clarify. Make time for the children to act out the stories they write – let them assign roles and direct the "production" themselves. This is a wonderful way for them to develop their story-telling abilities and to see their words transformed into a real-life play.

> Make time for the children to act out the stories they write – let them assign roles and direct the "production" themselves. This is a wonderful way for them to develop their story-telling abilities and to see their words transformed into a real-life play.

Encourage children to try writing their stories themselves. Reassure them that their writing doesn't have to look like an adult's, and encourage them to use invented spellings, which involves spelling words the way they hear them. Spelling, like language, develops according to a predictable sequence. In the same way that children look for grammatical patterns when learning to talk (see Chapter 7), they look for patterns in letter sequences that can be used for spelling words. We expect children's early sentences to be short and ungrammatical, and we should likewise expect their early attempts at spelling to be limited. For example, look at the changes in one child's spelling of the word "train" at different ages:

- HN (5 years, 6 months)
- HAN (5 years, 9 months)
- CHRAN (5 years, 11 months)
- TRANE (6 years, 3 months)
- TRAIN (6 years, 9 months)

At first, children may start off writing only one letter per word (and it may not even be the right letter), but with practice and exposure, their spelling will change and develop. If children ask you how to spell a word, ask them what sounds they can hear in the word and encourage them to write these down (they tend to ignore the vowels, and this is normal). If you do spell a word for them, write it on a piece of paper while you spell it out loud. Seeing the whole word is probably easier for a young child than listening to the letters being spelled one at a time.

Encourage children to illustrate their books, and then put the books in the book centre – after all, these books are written by budding young authors.

Rules and instructions

Let children see how reading is necessary for some pleasurable activities, like playing games with rules or computer games, or for assembling a toy. Let them see you read the instructions, and point to the print as you read them.

Dramatic play

Children will incorporate the use of print into their dramatic play – if you provide the necessary materials. Every dramatic play area should have pads of paper and pencils available. Whether the dramatic play area is a store, a bank, or a post office, the children will enjoy labelling objects, writing prices on groceries, making bank deposit slips, or addressing letters.

Dramatic and sociodramatic play are full of opportunities for reading and writing.

Use print to communicate with others

It's exciting to write a letter or a card and to have someone read and appreciate it. It's also exciting to receive mail from someone else. Both of these experiences can be a regular feature of your classroom.

Letters and greeting cards to friends and family

Although you should always make materials available to the children who enjoy writing letters and cards, card-making can be a special activity around Valentine's Day, seasonal holidays, Mother's and Father's Day, and friends' birthdays.

If you make writing materials available at all times, you may even get a birthday card yourself.

Letters of thanks and invitation

Letters of invitation to special guests or letters of thanks are good ways of getting children involved in using print to communicate with others. Let each child contribute to a letter written on a large sheet of paper. They can either dictate their messages to you or write them themselves.

Have a mailbox in the classroom

Create a mailbox where children can mail their letters to you or to their friends. The mail can then be delivered to the children's labelled cubbies. Make sure that you write letters to the children at regular intervals too. Let them know that you saw how they enjoyed playing in the block centre or that you're glad they're back from vacation.

Penpal program

Consider setting up a penpal correspondence program with a neighbouring preschool. In these programs, each child is matched with another child of the same age in the other centre, and letters are exchanged every few weeks. The children write or draw something for their penpal, put the letter in an envelope, and are helped to address it. When they get their mail, a "letter carrier" is appointed to deliver the mail to the children's labelled cubbies – it's really an exciting event.

Children are always excited to receive letters from their penpals at a nearby child-care centre – and they learn a lot about print at the same time.

Send letters home

From time to time, write personal letters to parents, telling them something that happened to their child that day (e.g., he made an interesting construction with Lego or enjoyed a new book). Discuss with the child why you are writing the letter and let him help you compose it. Make him feel important in his role as "letter carrier."

Badges

Together with the children, make cardboard badges that express feelings or send personal messages (e.g., "I am happy that my friend Cindy is back" or "Ask me why I'm looking forward to tomorrow"). Badges like these, pinned to the children's chests, are sure to get a great deal of attention from both adults and children.

Use print to record information

Show children how print enables us to record and remember information. Record things on charts at the children's eye level.

Birthdays

Put up a list of the children's names and birthdays so they can point to them and compare dates and years. You can make a "birthday chart" with the children in your classroom, letting them tell you their birth dates and if they can, letting them write their names. Remember: this kind of chart is useful only when it is at children's eye level.

Weather

It is interesting for children in kindergarten to record weather patterns and temperature values so they can see how these change over the seasons. This activity also helps the development of number concepts and encourages the recognition of printed words like "snow," "sunny," "hot," and "cold." If you have cards with these words on them, the children can select the appropriate word and place it on the weather chart. This is best done informally and quickly (and not as part of every circle time) so children's interest remains high.

Observations

Recordings needn't be confined to weather. You can record attendance, number of books taken from the library, favourite snacks, favourite books, number of siblings, languages spoken, etc.

Announcements

Watch children rush in and try to read your announcement, especially if their name is on it! Announcements are exciting and interesting – use them often!

Songs and poems

> *Happy birthday to you,*
> *Happy birthday to you,*
> *Happy birthday dear Cindy,*
> *Happy birthday to you.*

Write the words to a well-known song, like "Happy Birthday," on a large piece of paper. Seeing the words as they sing encourages children to point to and "read" them. Introduce written songs or poems at group or circle time and let the children read along with you. Then paste them on the wall at the children's eye level. By "reading" songs and poems to themselves, children begin to figure out where words begin and end, and which letters make which sounds. Soon they will start to recognize some words.

Open-ended bulletin boards and suggestion boards

Your bulletin boards can be left blank – let the children fill them in with their own artwork, letters, stories, and signs.

Have a suggestion board where children can write or draw any ideas they have for activities, outings, rules, menu items, etc. When possible, try to act on their suggestions.

You can also create bulletin boards or charts related to a theme, or to a story you have read with the children. For example, if you have read *The Very Hungry Caterpillar,* you could have a bulletin board that says "The Very Hungry Children in Kindergarten: Look at what they ate through!" Each child could draw or write in some of the things she or he ate; if necessary, you could write the word underneath. Interactive bulletin boards are a lot of fun, but they are only valuable when you talk about them with the children and when they see you write down their ideas.

> **Interactive bulletin boards are a lot of fun, but they are only valuable when you talk about them with the children and when they see you write down their ideas.**

Classroom Stories

The children can make up a story as a group, and then dictate it to you. You write it on a large piece of paper as they dictate, reading aloud as you write. For this activity to be effective, read the story as a group once it's written. As you read, point to the words, moving your finger smoothly across the lines. The children will feel as if they are reading, because they are so familiar with the story (after all, they made it up!). When this activity is over, hang the story on a board or wall, and the children will read and reread it to themselves.

Use print to gain information and knowledge

Children need a good deal of experience in using print to learn about new and interesting things.

Newspapers, magazines, and flyers

Bring in newspaper articles with large, interesting pictures and read them to the children. Make sure the topic is interesting and adapt the language to the children's level. Make available children's magazines and advertisements that might interest them.

Maps

Maps are fascinating for children, especially if they identify places of personal interest, such as where the children now live and where they or others used to live. Place a map of the world permanently at the children's eye level and refer to it to find places mentioned in books, where people go on vacation, in the news, etc.

Children can discover many interesting things from reading maps.

Non-fiction books

Books are the greatest source of information, and children should often see you demonstrate how to use them as a reference. Show how you use a book to gain information: let the children see the table of contents and the index.

Books shouldn't be placed only in the book centre; they should also be placed at the science table and anywhere else they can provide children with information. For example, teachers in a child-care centre that had an earthworm composter put many books about worms near the composter. The children who were interested in the composter really enjoyed reading these books.

Summary

Child care and preschool are ideal environments for learning about literacy because they contain so many real purposes for using reading and writing. In order to help all children become readers and writers, children should be exposed to books from birth. As children's language development progresses, teachers must encourage the "language of learning" during conversations and book reading, and should expose children to a variety of excellent books. Book reading should be interactive, with children being encouraged to talk and think about the book in many different ways. Classrooms should have a book centre and a writing centre, and children should have many opportunities to use print as part of their daily activities: for pleasure, for communicating with others, and for recording and gaining information. From participating in meaningful, purposeful print-related activities, children will begin to use reading and writing for their own purposes and will be well on their way to becoming readers and writers.

References

Ahlberg. A. & Ahlberg, J. (1978). *Each peach pear plum*. London: Penguin Books.

Allard, H. (1977). *Miss Nelson is missing*. Boston: Scholastic.

Applebee, A.N. (1978). *The child's concept of story*. Chicago: University of Chicago Press.

Blake, J. (2001). How early should parents start reading books with their infants? *IMPrint, Newsletter of the Infant Mental Health Promotion Project, 30,* 5–6.

Booth, D., Swartz, L. & Zola, M. (1987). *Choosing children's books*. Markham, Ontario: Pembroke.

Brown, M. W. (1947). *Goodnight moon*. New York: Harper and Row.

Butler, D. (1980). *Babies need books*. New York: Atheneum.

Cambourne, B. (1988). *The whole story: Natural learning and the acquisition of literacy in the classroom*. Auckland, New Zealand: Ashton Scholastic.

Carle, E. (1987). *The very hungry caterpillar*. New York: Scholastic.

Chafel, J.A. (1982). Making early literacy a natural happening. *Childhood Education,* May/June Issue, 300–304.

Church, E.B. (1991). Reading aloud to children. *Scholastic Pre-K Today,* January Issue, 38–40.

Cochrane-Smith, M. (1984). *The making of a reader*. Norwood, NJ: Ablex.

Forester, A.D. & Reinhard, M. (1989). *The learners way*. Winnipeg: Peguis.

Dickinson, D.K. & Tabors, P.O. (2001). Beginning literacy with language. Baltimore: Paul H. Brookes Publishing Co.

Dickinson, D.K. & Tabors, P.O. (2002). Fostering language and literacy in classrooms and homes. *Journal of the National Association for the Education of Young Children, March 2002,* 10–18.

Gillet, J.W. & Temple, C. (1986). *Understanding reading problems*. Boston: Little, Brown.

Goodman, K. & Goodman, Y. (1983). Reading and writing relationships: Pragmatic functions. *Language Arts, 60* (5), 590–599.

Goodman, K. (1986a). Reading: A psycholinguistic guessing game. *Journal of the Reading Specialist, 6,* 126–135.

Goodman, K. (1986b). *What's whole in whole language?* Richmond Hill, Ontario: Scholastic.

Goodman, Y. (1984). The development of initial literacy. In H. Goelman, A. Oberg & F. Smith, (Eds.), *Awakening to Literacy* (pp. 102–109). Exeter, NH: Heinemann.

Graves, D. & Stuart, V. (1986). *Write from the start: Tapping your child's natural writing ability*. New York: Plume.

Hill, E. (1980). *Where's Spot?* Toronto: General Publishing.

Holdaway, D. (1979). *The foundations of literacy*. Sydney, Australia: Ashton Scholastic.

Jewell, M.G. & Zintz, M.V. (1986). *Learning to read naturally*. Dubuque: Kendall Hunt.

Kimmel, M.M. & Segel, E. (1983). *For reading out loud*. New York: Delacorte Press.

Kunhardt, D. (1962). *Pat the Bunny*. Racine, Wisconsin: Western.

Lamme, L.L. (1984). *Growing up writing*. Washington, DC: Acropolis Books.

Loughlin, C.E. & Martin, M.D. (1987). *Supporting literacy: Developing effective learning environments*. New York: Teachers College Press.

Mayer, M. (1968). *There's a nightmare in my closet*. New York: Dial Books.

Mayer, M. (1975). *Just for you*. Racine, Wisconsin: Western.

Mayer, M. (1987). *Just a mess*. Racine, Wisconsin: Western .

Miller, S.A. (1991). Whole language: It's an experience! *Scholastic Pre-K Today,* January Issue, 44–72.

Munsch, R. (1985). *Thomas' snowsuit*. Toronto: Annick Press.

Munsch, R. (1987). *I have to go.* Toronto: Annick Press.

Munsch, R. (1988). *A promise is a promise.* Toronto: Annick Press.

Neuman, S.B., Copple, C. & Bredekamp, S. (2000). *Learning to read and write: Developmentally appropriate practices for young children.* Washington, DC: National Association for the Education of Young Children.

Perkins, A. (1969). *Hand, hand, fingers, thumb.* New York: Random House.

Sendak, M. (1983). *Where the wild things are.* New York: Scholastic.

Strickland, D. & Morrow, L.M. (Eds). (1989). *Emerging literacy: Young children learning to read and write.* Newark, DE: International Reading Association.

Taylor, D. (1983). *Family literacy: Young children learning to read and write.* Exeter, NH: Heinemann.

Teale, W.H. & Sulzby, E. (Eds.), (1985). *Emergent literacy: Writing and reading.* Norwood, NJ: Ablex .

Temple, C.A., Nathan, R.G. & Burris, N.A. (1982). *The beginnings of writing.* Boston, Mass: Allyn and Bacon.

van Kleeck, A. (1982). *Metalinguistics and language disorders in children: Does meta matter?* Miniseminar presented at the American Speech-Language Hearing Association Annual Convention, Toronto, Canada.

van Kleeck, A. (1990). Emergent Literacy: Learning about print before learning to read. *Topics in Language Disorders, 10* (2), 24–45.

Chapter 11

Circle Time: An Interactive Language-Learning Experience

Circle time is a time for children to have fun and learn.

A. Circle time: Time for fun and language learning

We know that children learn language naturally during their day-to-day interactions with their caregivers. So what does a formal, structured activity like circle time (also known as group time) contribute to language learning and literacy?

Some teachers say that children learn to listen at circle time. Others disagree, saying that children listen better in small, informal groups.

Some teachers say that circle time encourages children to share ideas and experiences. But others disagree, saying that a lot more sharing takes place at the lunch table and in small, informal groups.

Some teachers say that children can learn concepts at circle time. Again, many others disagree, saying that most learning takes place when children are involved in hands-on activities with an interested teacher nearby.

Despite these differences in opinion, many teachers believe that circle time is valuable and are looking for ways to make it as rich and stimulating an experience as possible.

When children aren't interested in the topic and when circle time goes on for too long, its purpose is lost – and so is the children's attention.

Let's assume that the purpose of circle time is for children to have fun and to learn. If activities at circle time are planned with this purpose in mind, then children can:

- expand their ability to use the language of learning
- expand their understanding of familiar topics
- expand their general knowledge to include unfamiliar topics
- be encouraged to use their imaginations
- learn to share information in a group, and
- expand their story-telling abilities.

The suggestions that follow on making circle time as fun and educational as possible are most appropriate for children three and older.

The right questions at circle time encourage children to use the language of learning and expand their imagination.

B. Set the stage for successful circle time

Circle time involves a lot more than getting the children in your classroom together in a group. When you give some thought to the set-up and organization of circle time, you set the stage for success.

Small groups are best

Small groups allow for more interaction, participation, and individual attention. Teachers tend to find it far more productive and manageable to stagger circle time or to have two small groups, each with one teacher.

Choose an appropriate time and place

The best time for circle time is *before* children get tired, restless, and hungry. In many classrooms, circle time is early in the morning, before free play.

Children feel more comfortable during circle time if they can sit in a cozy corner on a soft rug or mat. They will be less likely to be distracted if there are no toys or equipment nearby to tempt them.

Start an interesting activity before all the children have gathered

Rather than waiting for everyone to join the group and getting frustrated with stragglers, begin with an upbeat song or fingerplay. Or, as one imaginative teacher suggested, create a make-believe spaceship and invite children to walk along a make-believe ramp, up some "stairs," and into your spaceship, which is about to leave for an exciting place. In this way, the children who are already sitting in the group get involved quickly and the others hurry to join them because they don't want to miss out.

Be enthusiastic!

Whether you are telling a story, explaining a game, describing something, introducing a theme, or singing a song, your style sets the tone for the group. Your animation and enthusiasm will rub off on the children and will be reflected in their interest and involvement.

Be prepared to change your plans

Things don't always go according to plan. The children may not be interested in the topic you have chosen, or they may be interested in a different aspect of it. They might want to continue with one activity longer than you had planned or have you repeat it. Be flexible and willing to adapt or change your plans – that's the way to encourage children's curiosity and keep them interested.

Short and sweet is best

Remember to quit while you're ahead. Don't drag out circle time, even if one or two children are still attending. Cater to the majority – and that usually means stopping while all the children are still paying attention, involved, and stimulated.

Use large, appealing props

Props attract children's attention and provide additional visual cues. They should be large, clear, appealing, and appropriate to the children's developmental level. If props aren't large enough, the children lose focus as they push others aside to try to see them.

C. The Six "I"s: A guide for planning and conducting circle time

The Six "I"s provide you with practical guidelines for planning and conducting circles that expand children's language, general knowledge, imagination, ability to share information in a group, and story-telling.

> **The Six "I"s**
>
> In circle or group time, the topic should be:
>
> - **I**nteresting
> - **I**nformative
> - **I**ntroduced
> - **I**nterrelated (with other topics and activities)
> - **I**nteractive
> - **I**maginative

Interest the children

Choose a theme or topic appropriate to the children's ages and interests. If your topic is related to the theme of the week (or month), make sure that theme is drawn from the children's interests. Last year's group may have been fascinated by bugs, but this year's may be interested in dinosaurs, outer space, or sea creatures. It's seldom a good idea to repeat the same themes year after year!

When children are interested in the topic, they do more than listen. They search for meaning by analyzing what they hear and drawing conclusions about it. They relate what they hear to what they already know, predict what will happen next, and use their imaginations to visualize what you discuss. In other words, they use the language of learning as they build their general knowledge and understanding of the world around them. (See Chapter 8 for more information on exposing children to the language of learning.)

Inform the children

Too often, teachers choose circle-time themes in order to teach concepts like colours, shapes, or farm animals. Not only are such topics uninformative (most preschoolers already know them) but they are also extremely concrete. Because children as young as three years have vivid imaginations and are very curious, themes at circle time should allow them to think beyond concrete concepts.

This doesn't mean that you have to abandon familiar topics. Themes like "colours" or "pets" *can* provide a base for expanding children's knowledge – if you set up circle time to inform children. For example, while names of colours are familiar to most preschoolers and kindergartners, the colour wheel and primary and secondary colours are not. If you teach children about primary and secondary colours and give them opportunities to mix powder paint to make new colours, they can learn a great deal. Similarly, a theme about pets or farm animals could go beyond names and descriptions of pets to include eating habits, physical characteristics, ancestors, and movement.

> Because children as young as three have vivid imaginations and are very curious, themes at circle time should allow them to think beyond concrete concepts like colours and shapes.

New topics are fascinating to children, especially four- and five-year-olds. When you research these topics, you may discover some fascinating new facts yourself! (One teacher who researched the theme "dangerous sea creatures" was surprised to discover that most sharks are not human-eaters and that the whale shark, the largest shark of all, has allowed divers to ride on its back!)

Be cautious about focusing on festivals or holiday themes, like Easter or Halloween, weeks in advance. Although painting eggs and dressing up for Halloween are fun, these topics mean nothing to children who don't understand the idea of an annual event and who don't remember it from the previous year. Three-year-olds don't understand the significance of a pumpkin early in October. But if you talk about pumpkins just before Halloween and then explore them and other holiday symbols in more detail after Halloween (when the children's experience of the holiday is recent and meaningful), they will be better able to learn more and participate fully.

Introduce the topic

Always introduce the topic to the group. An introduction orients the children and stimulates them to draw upon their background knowledge in order to make sense of what will be discussed.

You need to reintroduce the topic each day you discuss it. Children don't automatically know that today's discussion or story is related to yesterday's. Your introduction helps them make this connection.

Interrelate the topic with other topics and activities throughout the day

Children learn new concepts when those concepts build upon what they already know and are presented as part of an integrated whole (not as isolated pieces of information). That's why teaching through themes helps children learn.

Circle time provides you with opportunities to introduce a new theme or topic, interrelate new and old knowledge, and reinforce and build upon concepts learned. As children gain new knowledge, they reorganize their view of the world and develop a more integrated understanding of it. The more knowledge they have, the more background knowledge they bring with them to the books they read and the stories they write.

> To make learning meaningful, always interrelate new and old knowledge.

Circle time is also an opportunity to prepare children for topics and materials that will be incorporated into other activities, such as the dramatic play.

By using circle time to ensure that all children have a shared understanding of an activity, you increase the likelihood of participation and peer interaction in that activity. (See Chapter 6, page 205–206, and Chapter 9, page 303, for more information about developing shared understanding.)

To help children interrelate and integrate their new knowledge, incorporate themes into a number of learning experiences throughout the day. Give children many opportunities to explore materials and resources on the topic, and plenty of time for theme-related hands-on activities, discussions, observations, and dramatic play.

For example, if your theme is "water," children could be provided with opportunities to:

- play with water, snow, and ice and compare their properties
- experiment with what dissolves and what doesn't dissolve in water
- experiment with objects that sink and float and try to draw conclusions about buoyancy
- make paper boats and sail them at the water table
- read books about water
- look at a globe to see how much of the Earth consists of water
- paint with different colours of water
- play with bubbles in water
- make books about water, or
- play in the dramatic play area, which has been transformed into a ship or a beach.

Notice that most of these activities involve children exploring and experimenting with a focus provided by the activity itself. The less structure and direction you provide, the more children will explore, experiment, and learn. The best role for you to play is that of "resource" – answering children's questions and providing guidance when they need it. Theme-related activities should always be relatively open-ended and should allow for individual children to explore and discover in their own way.

Encourage **I**nteraction

Although *you* carefully plan and direct circle time, children must play an active role! Sitting quietly and listening does not guarantee that they'll learn anything. The more actively involved children are, the more they will learn. Of course, sometimes you will talk and they will listen, but those times should be followed by interactive group activities.

Hands-on experience with a parachute gets the children actively involved in the theme of "Air Transportation."

Plan for a change of pace

The pacing of activities is critical in circle time. Keep the children involved and participating at different levels and in different ways. For example, plan for energetic activities to follow listening times, for child talk to follow teacher talk, for something novel to follow something familiar. You can make circle time more active and interactive through:

- short group discussions
- group games (especially cooperative games)
- story-telling (to which the children contribute)
- fingerplays
- action songs
- drama (acting out something related to the theme or topic)
- creating experience charts
- group read-alouds from a story or chart, or
- children creating, drawing, or writing something in response to a story or theme and sharing it with the group.

Pacing counts: children especially enjoy energetic activity after they've been sitting still for a while.

Encourage interaction through sharing ideas and information

At circle time, many teachers give children opportunities to share information with the group. For example, children may describe an experience (like a visit to the doctor) or talk about an object they have brought for Show and Tell. This kind of "sharing" is different from an exchange of information during informal conversation because it involves addressing a group and presenting information in a clear, organized way (similar to the type of language required for telling good stories).

"Sharing" at circle time can be a valuable experience for children, but it can also be boring. If every child is given a turn at one sitting, or if the teacher ends up doing all the talking or asks question after question, sharing is no fun at all. "Sharing" at circle time can work if:

- not every child "shares" at each circle, but gets a turn during the week
- children do as much of the talking as possible
- children are encouraged to share experiences and ideas and not just show off toys, and
- children are given the opportunity to hold their own sharing times in small groups, with one child acting as "leader" and fielding questions and comments from the others. With some support and specific guidelines, children at the kindergarten level are mature enough to conduct sharing time alone. With practice, it can work.

SSCAN to keep track of attention and participation

You can if you SSCAN	
S mall	groups are best
S et up	an appropriate activity
C arefully	observe each child's level of participation and interaction
A dapt	your response to each child's needs
N ow	keep it going!

In Chapter 5, we discussed the importance of keeping track of each child's involvement and interest in small-group activities. By "SSCAN"-ing a group, you can maximize participation and interaction.

SSCAN-ing also works at circle time. If you keep track of children's attention and participation levels, you can provide each child with the attention and encouragement she needs. While keeping track of children is far more difficult in a large than a small group, it is somewhat easier if you have a partner who co-leads circle time with you, or if you limit yourself to tracking the children whom you know have difficulty with circle-time activities.

When you track children's levels of attention and participation, you will have a good idea of what you can do to help each child become more actively involved in circle-time activities. Watch for children who aren't paying attention, children who pay attention but don't participate, and even for children who both pay attention and participate, but who may be dominating the circle.

Children who aren't paying attention

- If most of the group isn't attending, perhaps the topic is inappropriate or there's too much sitting and listening. In this case, the children need activities that are more active and interactive.
- If only one or two children aren't attending, they may be uninterested or unable to follow the topic. If they are unable to follow the topic, another teacher may need to sit with them and explain the topic.
- If you introduce circle-time topics or activities to certain children (like those with language delays) individually a few days before that circle time takes place, you can ensure that they have some understanding of the topic or activity. Their greater understanding will increase the likelihood of their attending and participating.
- Children who frequently disrupt circle time may be telling you in their own way that they can't understand the discussion and that they haven't developed the ability to pay attention for very long. Making circles more active and interactive helps these children stay involved. However, if they still disrupt the group, consider

allowing them to play quietly somewhere else. In time, as they mature and develop more advanced language skills, they should be able to attend and participate.

- Sometimes, children don't attend because they are too far away from you. Moving them across from you (*not* next to you, where they can't see you, the book, or the prop) may get them more involved. Calling them by name to make them feel included may also help focus them on the activity. Sometimes, saying something personal, like, "You've been to a beach like this one, haven't you, Matthew?" may draw a child into the activity.

Children who are paying attention, but who aren't participating

- You have the child's attention, but perhaps she's reluctant or too shy to join in. Seat the child in the front and centre of the group so you can make easy eye contact with her.
- Children who are reluctant communicators need time to get comfortable. It will also help if you smile at them encouragingly. When they take the risk of joining in, however, don't make too much of a fuss – their reward comes from the pleasure of involvement, not from praise.
- Perhaps children who don't participate don't fully understand what's required of them, although they really want to join in. Make sure that you clarify what the activity or topic is about – possibly on an individual basis before the circle takes place. Often children who speak English as a second language don't have the receptive language skills to participate fully. When their receptive language skills improve, they are likely to participate more actively.

Children who are paying attention and participating fully in the group's activities

These children may be getting all your attention – so watch out! Ensure that individual children do not dominate the interaction by:

- directing your questions and comments to the quieter children in the group
- reserving the spots directly in front of you for the more reluctant children and placing the very sociable children on the sides of the circle
- directing comments and questions from the sociable children back to the group to encourage other children to become involved, and
- reminding children of the "rules" of turn-taking. For example, if a child is drawing your attention away from other children, use gestures or give a verbal cue, like "I'm listening to Sara now," to encourage the child to wait her turn.

Include **I**maginative activities

Children's ability to pretend and imagine plays an important role both in their understanding and appreciation of stories and in the development of literacy (see Chapter 10). Circle time is a prime opportunity to get children to use language to create make-believe and engage in dramatizations.

Using drama in a group, where everyone pretends without realistic props, is fun and helps children develop the ability to use make-believe. For example, you can model the use of language to create make-believe by telling the children that a parachute is going to become a huge popcorn maker. When they hold the parachute and shake it up and down, they pretend to make popcorn. Once all the popcorn has "popped," they pretend to eat it.

> We're going to imagine that we've all taken parachuting lessons and that we're all experienced parachutists. We're going to pretend to go up into the air in a plane and when we're flying high above the clouds we're all going to jump out of the plane and parachute down to the ground!

Language can bring exciting imaginary experiences to life!

Jumping out of an imaginary plane with an imaginary parachute is really exciting.

Circle time is the perfect time for thematic fantasy play (based on a story, like "Little Red Riding Hood," or a rhyme), which encourages children to use language to create make-believe situations. After reading a story, give everyone a role to play and let the children act out the story. This is a lot of fun – and it helps children understand the story better. It also develops their sense of story, which is important for understanding stories in books.

Thematic fantasy play develops imagination and makes stories come alive.

Summary

When circle time is interesting, informative, and interactive, teachers promote the kind of language use that prepares children to become successful readers and writers. Instead of sitting and listening, children become actively involved in group activities like dramatic play, story-telling, action songs, and group games – all of which build upon their background knowledge, expand their general knowledge, and encourage them to use their imaginations. To help every child participate, teachers must "SSCAN" the group to monitor each child's attention and involvement. When necessary, they can provide extra encouragement and attention to children who are not fully involved in the group's activities.

References

Bredenkamp, S (Ed.). (1987). *NAEYC position statement on developmentally appropriate practice in programs for 4- and 5-year-olds.* Washington, DC: National Association for the Education of Young Children.

Hendrick, J. (1990). Total learning: *Developmental curriculum for the young child.* Columbus, OH: Merrill.

McCracken, R.A. & McCracken, M.J. (1987). *Reading is only the tiger's tail: A language arts program.* Winnipeg, Canada: Peguis.

Moyer, J., Egertson, H. & Isenberg, J. (1987). The child-centered kindergarten. *Childhood Education, 63*(4), 235–242.

Nash, C. (1989). *The learning environment: A practical approach to the education of the three-, four- and five-year old.* Don Mills: Collier McMillan Canada.

Siks, G.B. (1983). *Creative drama with children.* New York: Harper and Row.

Wilmes, L. & Wilmes, D. (1983). *Everyday circle times.* Elgin, IL: Building Blocks.

Index

abilities, matching activity to, 156–57

activities *See also* Games; Toys; Play
appropriate materials for group, 158
children's interest in, 160–61
circle time, 376–88
conversation during, 131–32
daily, and size of groups, 173
face to face, 158
for group participation, 156–58
level of involvement, 159–61, 163
matching with abilities, 156–57
observing children during, 159–61
and peer interaction, 200–204
to promote interaction, 200
role of teacher in, 208–16
sensory-creative, 167–71, 315
use of print in everyday, 359–61

Ahlberg, Allan, 352
Ahlberg, Janet, 352
Allard, Harry, 347
animation *See also* Facial expression
cue to turn taking, 121
using with Discoverers, 86, 111
when reading, 336
announcements, 367
Autism Spectrum Disorder, 32

baby talk, 230
behaviours
non-play, 187
appropriate with peers, 185
bilingualism
sequential, 254–56
simultaneous, 253–54
birthdays, 367
body language, as cue to turn taking, 120
book centre, 356, 369

books
choosing appropriate, 337
for Combiners, 344
for Communicators, 339–40
for Discoverers, 339–40
for Early Sentence Users, 347–48, 348–55
for First Words Users, 341
for Later Sentence Users, 347–48, 348–55
for information, 369
for knowledge, 369
making, 362–63
reading for interaction, 338
reading, with children, 335–38
Brown, Margaret Wise, 344
bulletin boards, 368

cheerleader role, 21
childhood experiences, early, importance of, 1
circle time
conducting, 380–88
creating successful, 378–79
and language learning, 376–77
planning, 380–88
classroom
breaking up space in, 196
groupings in, 198–99
noisy areas in, 198
private areas in, 198
quiet areas in, 198
size of play areas, 196–97
use of space in, 195–98
Combiners
as equal partners in conversation, 131–43
becoming Early Sentence Users, 47
choosing books for, 344
cues for turn taking, 133–40
encouraging clarification requests, 140–41

imitation with, 78
keeping on topic, 141–42
and language delays, 46, 250
language development, 38, 234–35
level of understanding, 47
method of communication, 47
method of interaction, 47
purpose of communication, 46
reading guidelines for, 344–46
and simple pretend play, 297
taking turns, 142–43
with language delay, 131
commenting
to allow child to lead, 82–84
during reading, 350
during sensory-creative activities, 170
comments
combining with question, 135
in conversations, 134
as tool in story-telling, 283–84
using with waiting, 133–34
communication skills
in developmentally delayed children, 14
importance of, 12
communication
and information, 10
communication
breakdown in, 66
children's methods, 36–37
Combiner, 38, 46–47
Communicator, 38, 41–43
development of, 9
Discoverer, 38, 39–40
Early Sentence User, 38, 48–49
encouraging child, 68–69
encouraging conversation, 108–109
encouraging in language delay children, 92
First Words User, 38, 44–45

and teacher's thought process, 22–23

timekeeper, 20

too-quiet teacher, 20

routines

changing to maintain interest, 122

creating new, 122–23

daily, and SSCAN, 172–79

dressing for outdoors tips, 179

and equipment, 176

factors affecting 172–78

pacing of, 177

role of teacher in, 178

size of groups, 173

social, and language development, 238

and special needs children, 175, 177

staggering, 174

supporting Communicator's initiative, 123

timing of, 177

rules of conversation, 108, 192

Scarry, Richard, 344

second language, learning, 253–61

second language learners, reading abilities, 330

self-help skill, encouraging, 179

Sendak, Maurice, 347

setting limits, 95–101

"shared understanding", 205–206, 303

sociable child, *15*, 16, 18

social development, 66

social needs, and communication, 33

social routine *See also* Routine

with Communicators, 119–23

cues for turn taking, 114–15

encouraging turn taking, 117

and everyday interactions, 113–17

First Words Users becoming initiators, 126

and games, 114, 115–16, 199

repetitive activities, 114

songs in, 114

social skills

immature, 25

importance of, 1, 12

songs

cues to taking turns, 119–20

as part of social routine, 114

and reading, 368

sounds, as basis for conversation, 110

space, private areas, 198

special needs children

communication skills, importance of, 12

findings about, 11, 12

inclusion of, 11–12

and nonverbal communication, 37

observing, 71

and peers, 11

and physical environment, 175

and routines, 175

social skills, importance of, 12

timekeeper role, 20

speech, lack of functional, 37

speech development *See* Language development

speech patterns, in second language learners, 256

spelling, 330

SSCAN

at circle time, 385

in daily routines, 172–79

definition, 153

in group situations, 165–66

observing children, 159–61

at reading time, 351

and sensory-creative activities, 167–71

in small groups, 154–55

stories, in classroom, 368

story-tellers, children as, 282–86

suggestion boards, 368

taking turns

appropriate behaviour, 142–43

Communicators, 118–25

cues for, 113, 114–15, *116*, 117, 119–21

during busy times, 144

First Words Users, 126–30

and social routines, 117

strategies for encouraging, 109

to allow child to lead, 91

talking, as a method of learning, 268, 269–71, 272–81

tasks, collaborative, 207

teachers, child's interactions with, Observation Guide, 26–27

timekeeper role, 20

toddlers

interaction with peers, 189

type of play, 189

too-quiet teacher role, 20

toys *See also* Activities; Games; Play

for development levels, 202

imitating with, 86–87

number of, 203

providing duplicate, 202

as tools for interaction, 92–93

as topic of conversation, 131–32

using with Communicators, 118

using with Discoverers, 111

turn taking *See* Taking turns

wait-and-see approach, 73

waiting

for child to lead, 72–73, 116

cue to turn taking, 120

during reading, 350

expectant, use of, 133–34

weather, 367

word meanings, clarifying, 272–73

writing centre, 357

writing *See also* Print

becoming aware of print, 333–34

developing positive attitudes, 326–27